I0792973

IMAGES
of America

POLAND

On the Cover: Main Street is shown in Poland on December 2, 1945. The image is from the photograph collection of Janie Jenkins, donated to the Poland Historical Society. (Courtesy of Poland Historical Society.)

IMAGES
of America

POLAND

Robert L. Zorn with the
Poland Historical Society

ARCADIA
PUBLISHING

ISBN 978-0-7385-7812-5

Published by Arcadia Publishing
Charleston, South Carolina

Printed in the United States of America

Library of Congress Control Number: 2009937223

For all general information contact Arcadia Publishing at:
Telephone 843-853-2070
Fax 843-853-0044
E-mail sales@arcadiapublishing.com
For customer service and orders:
Toll-Free 1-888-313-2665

Visit us on the Internet at www.arcadiapublishing.com

Dedicated to all the people of Poland, Ohio: past, present, and future.

Contents

Acknowledgments

Appreciation is extended to acknowledge the following people for their assistance to make this book a reality: my wife, Joan, for her help and research on the photographs and topics; Dave and Pat Grimm and Susan Holloway of the Poland Historical Society for making available the photographs and records of the society; the Poland Board of Education for making the archives and records of the school system available; Debbie Becherer and Pattie Kelley for their help with the photographs; and Barbara Cooper for typing the photograph captions.

Appreciation is also extended to Gene Merdich of TPI Photograph Lab for all the work on pictures and to Alexandra Bennett for all the help on computer technology.

Recognition is also given to the 1966 Poland Centennial Committee whose outstanding hard work produced the treasure *Poland Historical Highlights*, and to the Poland Township Bicentennial Committee for their outstanding work in 1996 producing *Township One, Range One, Our Western Frontier*, and *Poland Township History 1796-1996*.

Thank you to Arcadia Publishing and senior acquisitions editor Melissa Basilone for all her assistance and encouragement.

Sources of the photographs in this book are listed under each picture. If there are no sources cited, they came from my own collection. Hope you enjoy reading this brief pictorial history of Poland as much as I enjoyed putting it together.

Royalties from the sale of this book will be donated by the author to the Poland Historical Society.

Introduction

Poland, Ohio, was the site of several major Iroquois Indian pathways in the early and mid-1700s and, in 1795, became "Town One, Range One" in the Western Reserve, a part of Connecticut's Western lands that went up for sale. As the first town in the sale of Connecticut's 3 million acres in the Western Reserve, Poland became the gateway to the area and an important stagecoach stop on the main highway between Cleveland and Pittsburgh.

Poland's population immediately soared, and by 1810, Poland boasted 837 residents compared to Youngstown's 773 and Cleveland's 547. This all changed by 1840 due to the coming of the railroads north of Poland along the Mahoning River bottomland through Youngstown.

Poland was also home to the Poland Furnace or "Hopewell Furnace" as it was called in 1802 when it was built on the banks of Yellow Creek in what became Poland Township. The Hopewell Furnace was the first blast furnace to come to the area west of the Alleghenies and was the forerunner of the giant steel blast furnaces to come to the area north of Poland along the Mahoning River.

William McGuffey, author of the nationally renowned *McGuffey Readers* in the early 1820s, taught in one of Poland's little one-room schoolhouses before going on to national fame.

Poland became home to the Poland Academy in 1830, and in 1859, graduated its most famous student, William McKinley, who became the 25th president of the United States.

William McKinley was sworn into Civil War military service on the front porch of the local general store, a building still standing and in use today as an antique store on South Main Street. This store, Old Stone Tavern Antiques, is one of the oldest standing large structures in the Western Reserve.

Poland, in 1862, became home to the famous Poland Seminary, one of the first schools in northeast Ohio to admit girls on an equal basis with boys. Seminary at the time meant coed institution.

Ida Tarbell, who became a prominent national journalist, was preceptress of the Poland Seminary in the early 1880s, teaching English and composition. She went on to author a national best seller, *The Early Life of Abraham Lincoln*. She also pioneered investigations in the trust-busting of the nation's big monopolistic businesses with her book, *The Standard Oil Company*.

The Poland Seminary's most notable graduate was William Calhoun, who became an elected representative, senator, and then ambassador to China from 1910–1913.

Poland's College Street was home to eight colleges including the Poland Academy, Poland Seminary, Poland Female College, Poland Law School, and Poland Medical College.

Poland today still maintains a quaint, New England–like atmosphere showing its colonial heritage originating with the settlers who came to the area from Connecticut. Poland still has many historical houses showing their Western Reserve influence.

POLAND HISTORICAL SOCIETY

The Poland Historical Society was founded in 1986 with the mission of preserving the historical heritage and landmarks of the Poland community.

The society's most notable accomplishment to date was the restoration and maintenance of Poland's little red, one-room schoolhouse on what is now State Route 224. Built in 1858, the building operated as a school until the 1914–1915 school year, when it closed. William McKinley, the 25th president of the United States, taught in this school in 1860. Today it is a restored schoolhouse and the home of the Poland Historical Society. It is on the National Register of Historic Places in America.

If you would like to request more information about Poland, become a society member, or make a contribution toward community preservation, please contact the Poland Historical Society.

Poland Historical Society
P.O. Box 5052
Poland, OH 44514

One

Town One, Range One

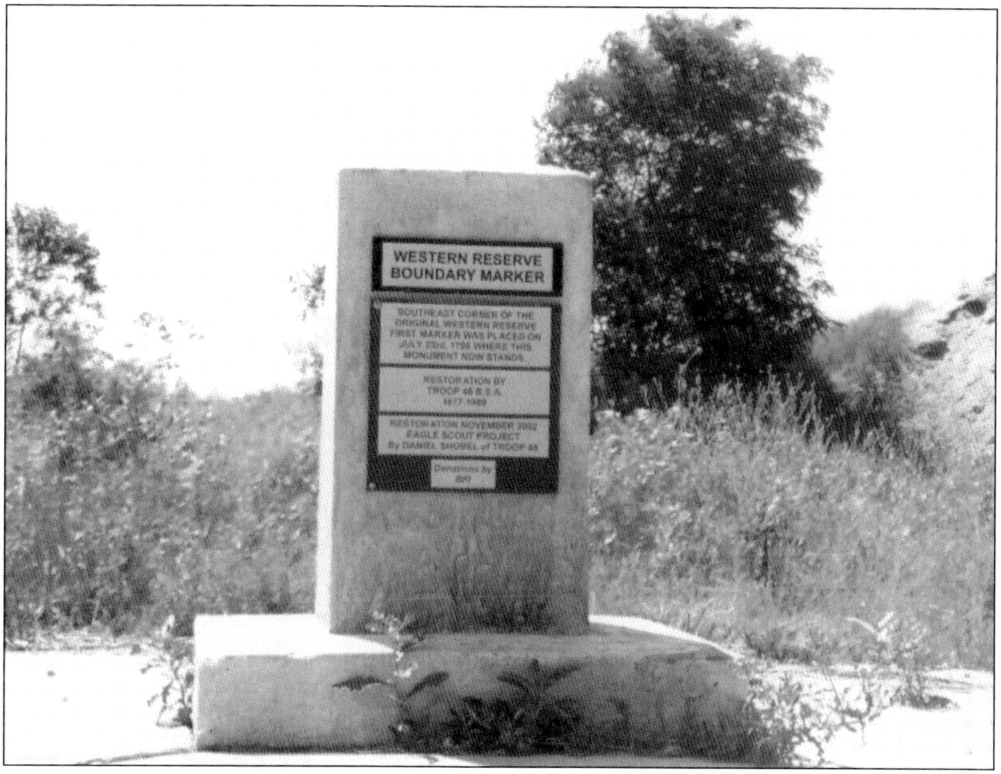

In the 1700s, several major Iroquois Indian pathways crossed through what is now known as Poland, Ohio. In 1795, since Connecticut relinquished its rights to the vast Western claims, the Connecticut assembly decided the 3 million acres should be sold for no less than $1 million or not less than 33¢ per acre. Pictured here is the Western Reserve boundary marker on State Line Road in Poland Township. The marker was set July 1, 1796, by Connecticut land surveyors as the starting point for the township in the Connecticut Western Reserve.

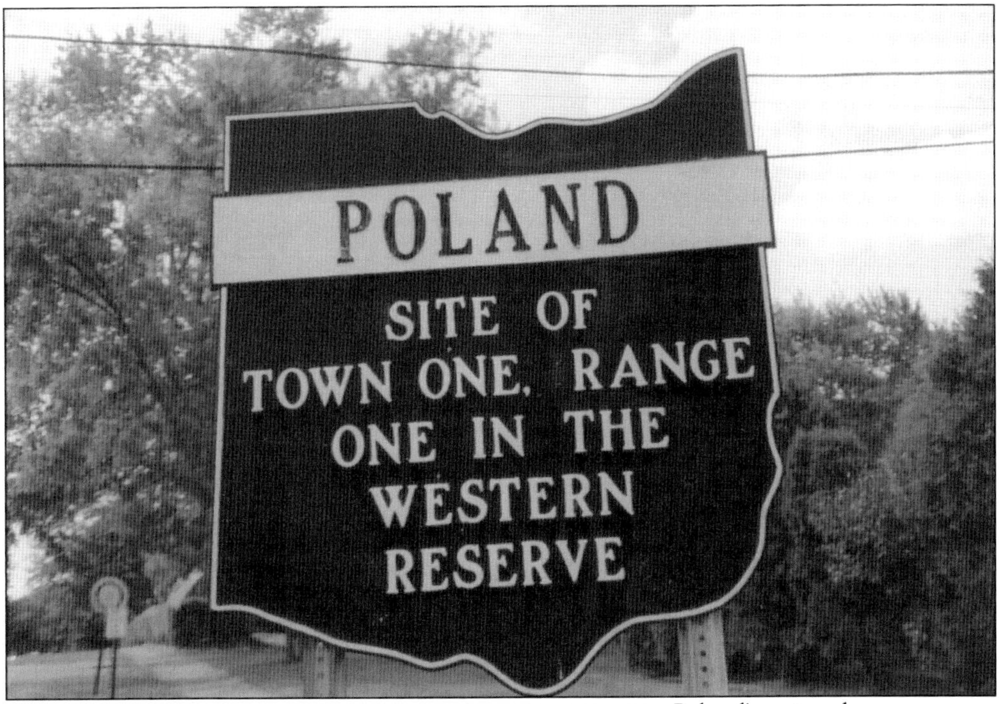

Poland's unique honor as "Town One, Range One" in the Western Reserve means it was the first area to be surveyed and settled west of the Allegheny Mountains in 1796.

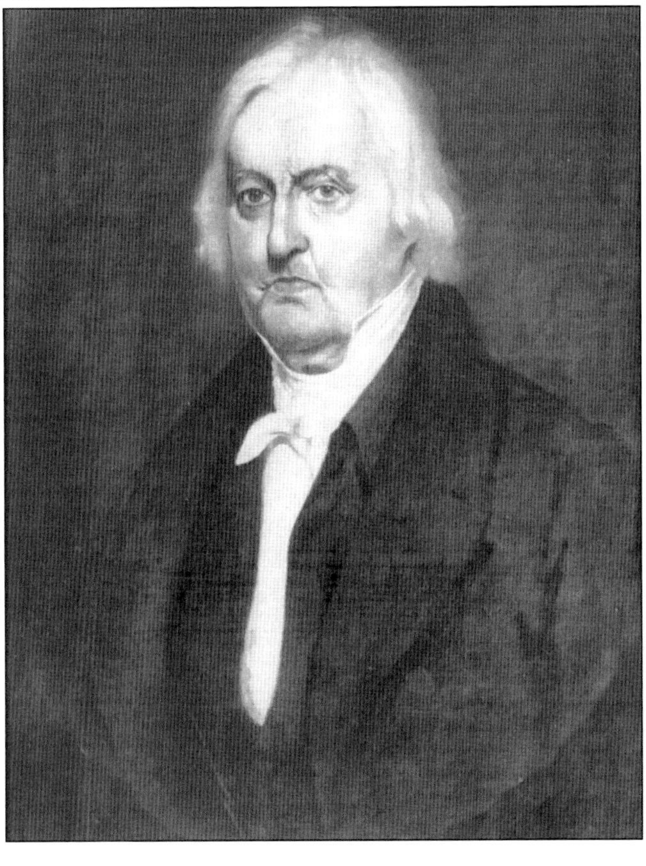

Turhand Kirtland, 1755–1844, was one of Poland's founders, along with Jonathan Fowler. (Courtesy of Poland Historical Society.)

American Mercury Newspaper Article Regarding

Turhand Kirtland and the Connecticut Land Company

Published March 19, 1807

The text can be somewhat hard to read until it is understood that the letter "f" was apparently used in 1807 in place of today's letter "s" (except at the end of a word).

Following is a more readable translation:

The subscriber takes this method to inform those concerned, that he has resided nine years on the *Connecticut Western Reserve* – and has a general knowledge of the lands lying East of the Cayahoga river – that he has personally explored every township on the Western side of said river – has accurate maps of the same, the surveyor's field notes and his own exploring notes – together with a particular description of the face of the country, waters, timber, quality of soil, minerals, and the natural advantages of each township. Any person wishing to purchase or sell any of these lands, or proprietors who want their lands surveyed into Farms, or sold to settlers, may depend upon having their business done on the most reasonable terms, by applying to their humble servant,

TURHAND KIRTLAND

Who will reside at Mj. John Ripley's in Hartford, until after the meeting of the Connecticut Land Company in April; after which he will return to the town of Poland, in Trumbull county, state of Ohio. March 12.

An ad was placed in the *American Mercury Newspaper* on March 19, 1807, by Turhand Kirtland, one of the founders of Poland, to sell land in the Western Reserve area owned by the Connecticut Land Company. This is a photograph of the old ad, donated by Edward Kirtland Jr. in fall 2008 to the Poland Historical Society.

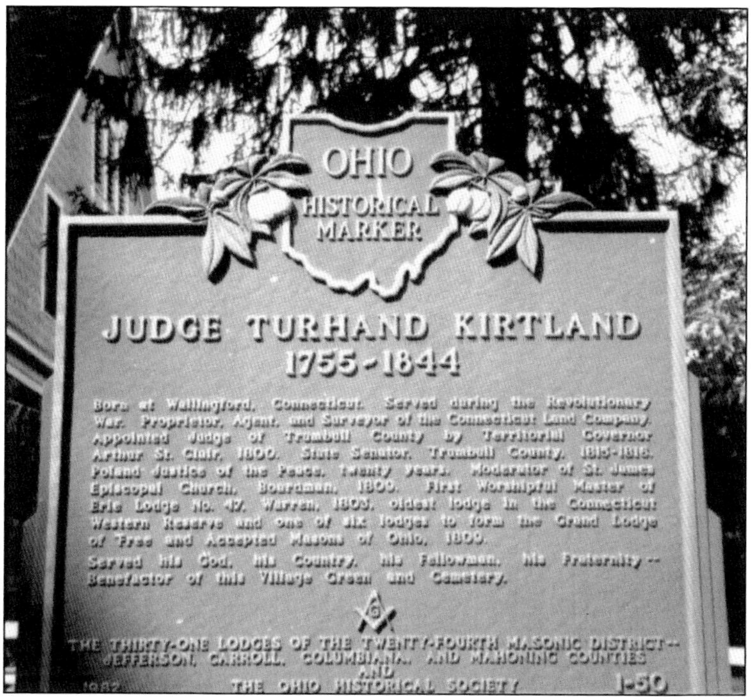

The Ohio historical marker for Turhand Kirtland, near the front of the Poland Presbyterian Church, denoting Kirtland's contributions to the founding of the city is seen here. Kirtland is buried in the cemetery behind the marker in land he gave in 1804 to be used as a cemetery for the community.

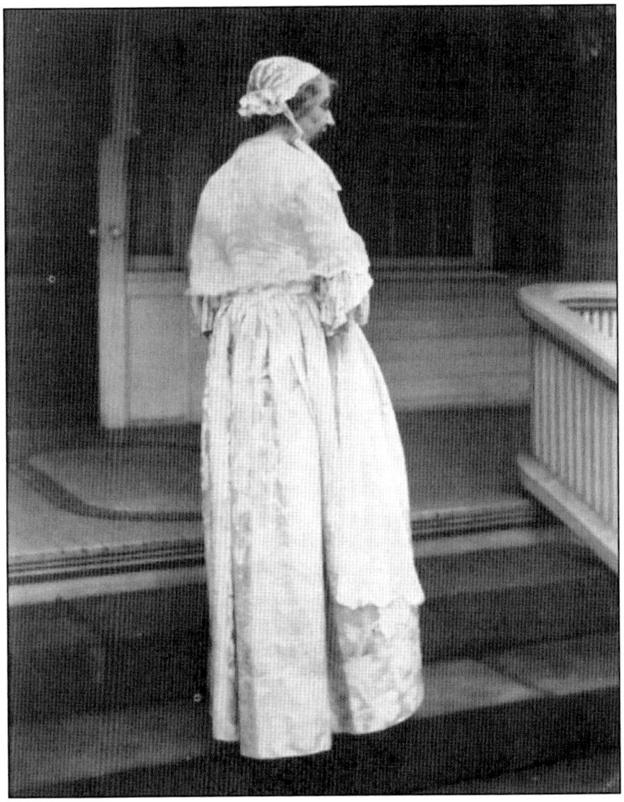

Mary L. W. Morse wears Polly Kirtland's wedding dress and point appliqué cap, worn at her wedding in Connecticut in 1792. The material is sky blue silk brocade brought from China. (Courtesy of Poland Historical Society.)

Shown below is Poland artist Chester Hunt's 1960s drawing of the first log cabin church (left) and log cabin school (right) built c. 1800 on the area now occupied by the Poland Presbyterian Church. Fowler's log cabin was closer to Yellow Creek near the area where the Route 224 bridge now crosses.

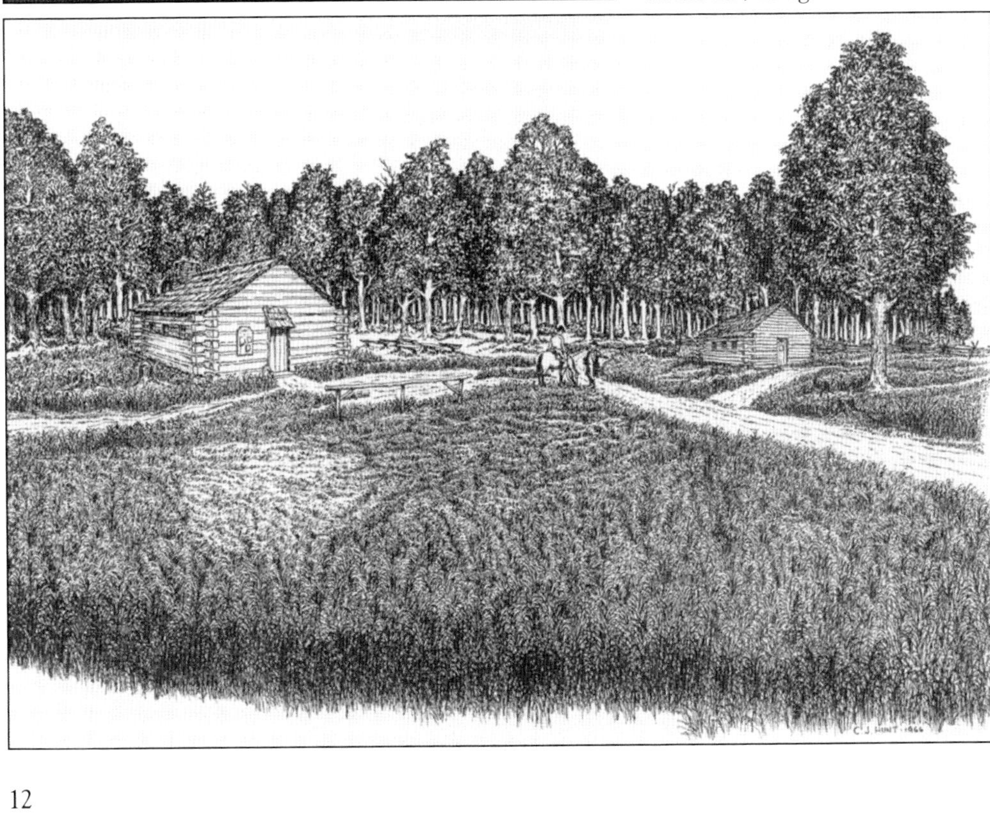

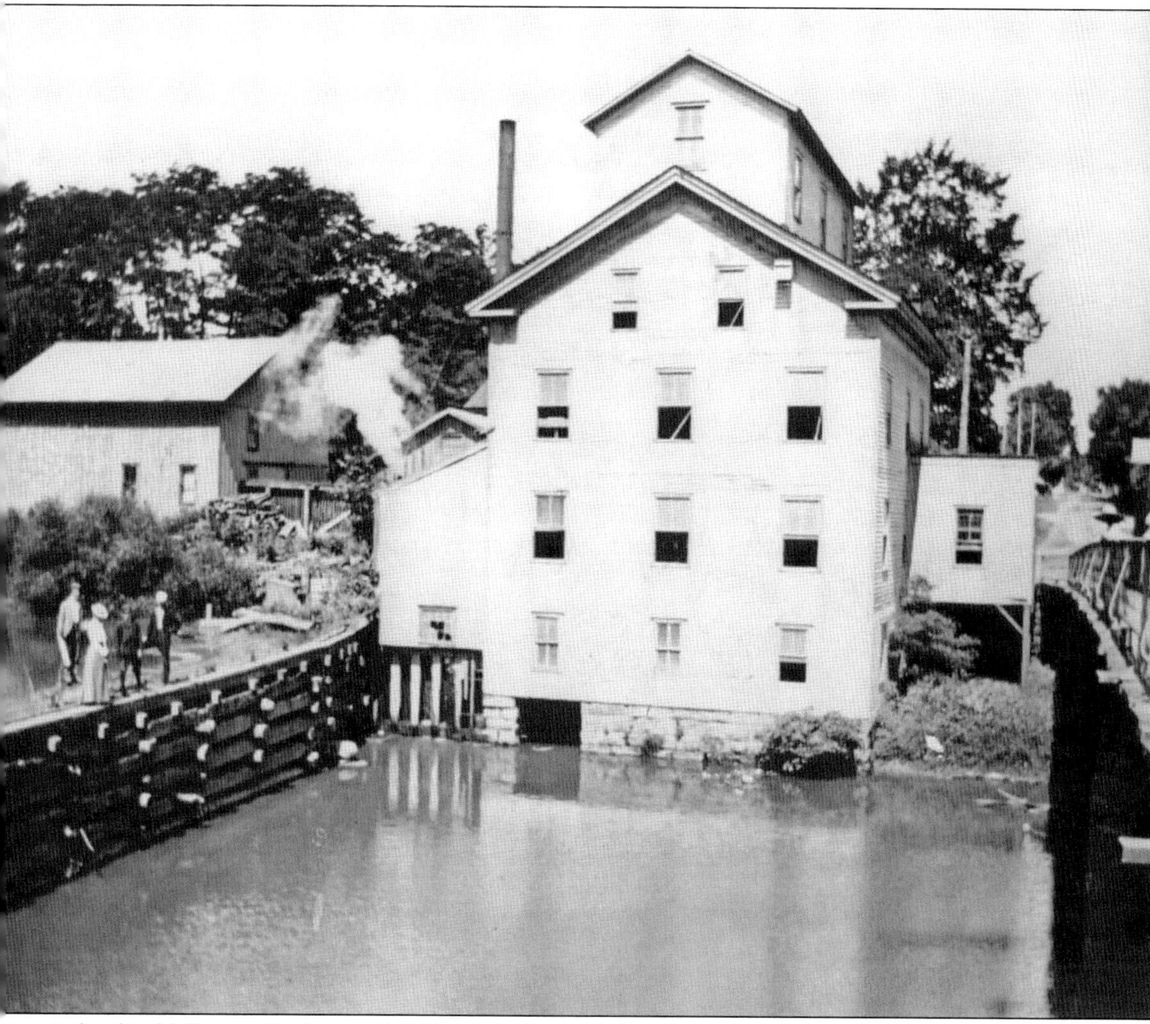

Poland's old flour mill, then called Flowler's Grist Mill in the early 1800s, was on the banks of Yellow Creek. The old wooden Main Street bridge is at the far right in the photograph. The old Poland mill was torn down in 1920. It had served the community's farmers for over 100 years. (Courtesy of Poland Historical Society.)

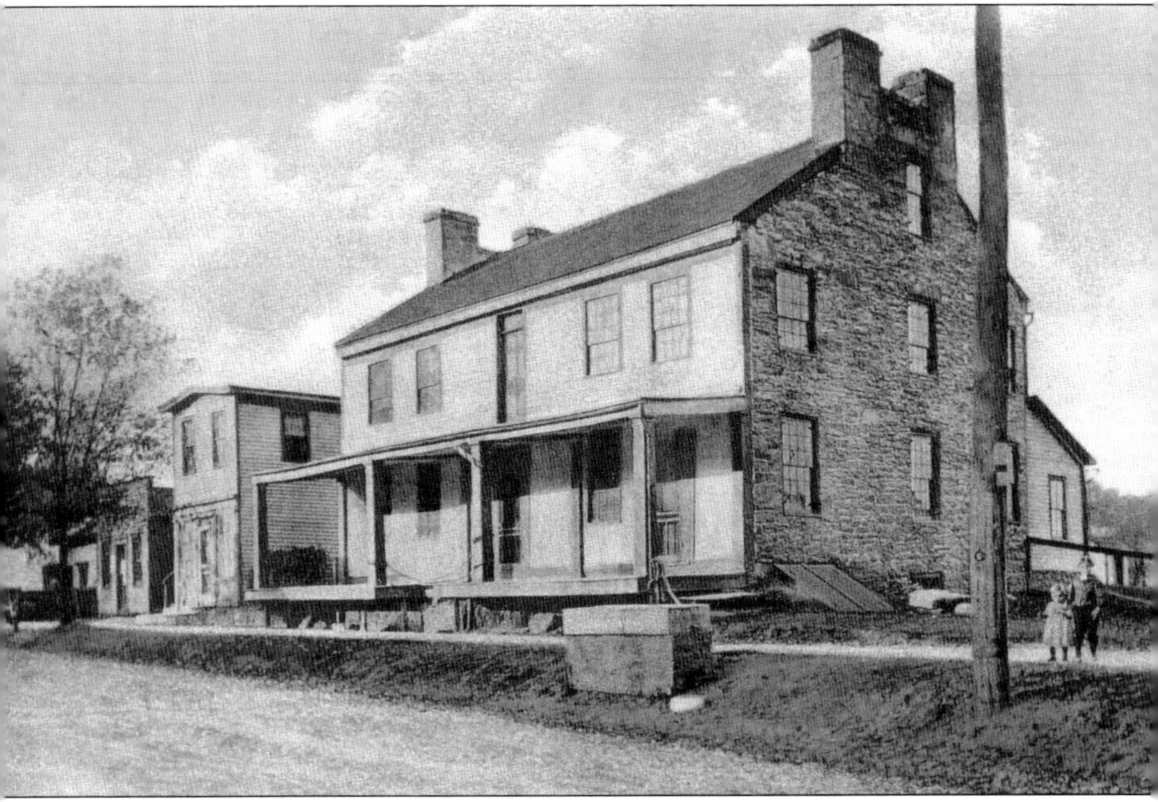

An early view is shown of Old Stone Tavern, built in 1804 by Jonathan Fowler—whose name, in the early days, was often used as the town's name. This building on South Main Street is the oldest building in Poland today. This photograph is thought to be the earliest known image of this historic building, probably taken in 1861. This building in the early and mid-1800s served as a tavern, general store, and inn for stagecoach riders stopping for the night as they traveled West. (Courtesy of Poland Historical Society.)

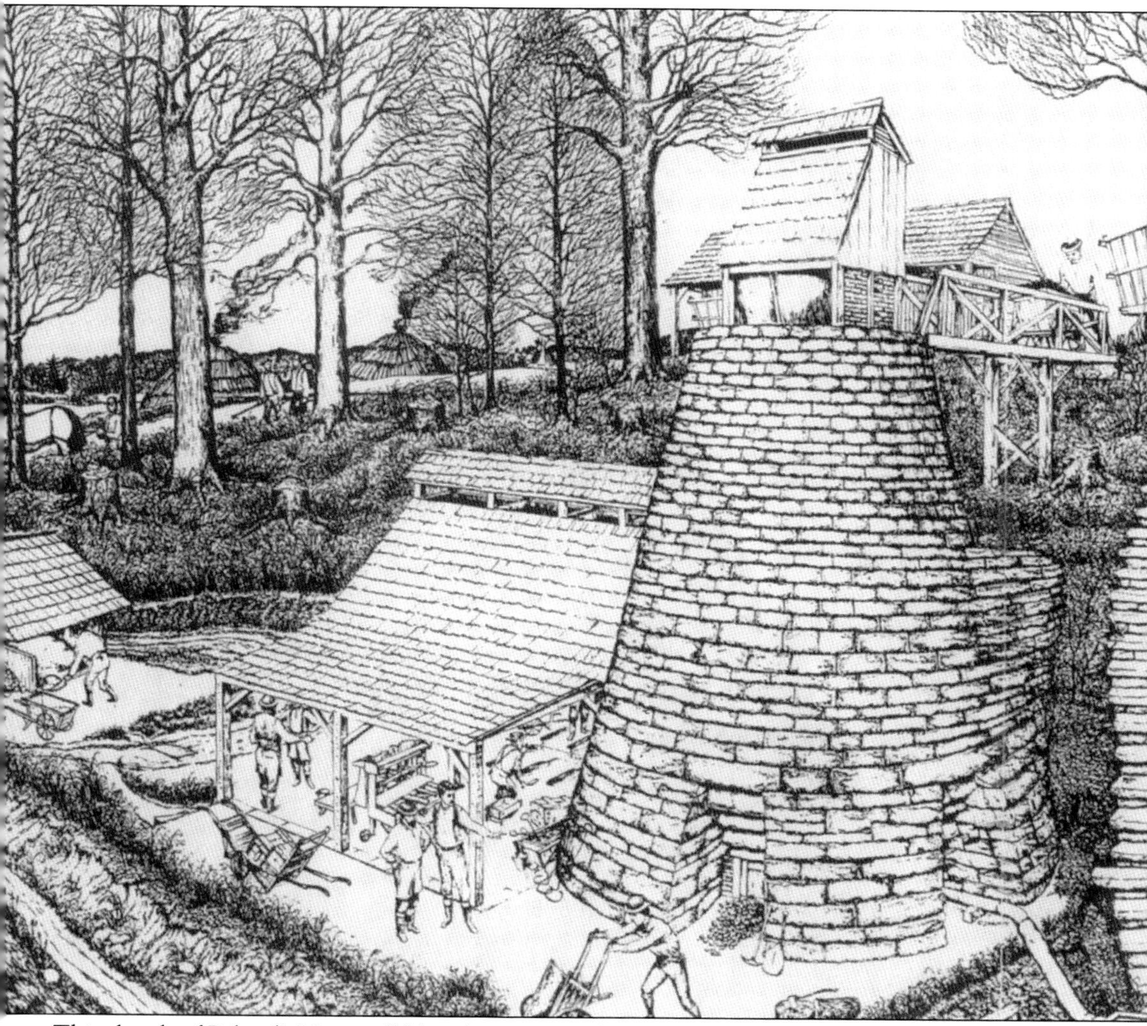

This sketch of Poland's Hopewell blast furnace was done by Poland artist, Chester Hunt, in the 1960s. It depicts the Poland furnace in full operation during 1803-12 on the banks of Yellow Creek. The furnace was abandoned in 1812 due to lack of manpower caused by the War of 1812. What is left of the old furnace today can be seen about a half-mile north of Hamilton Dam on the west bank of Yellow Creek, going toward Struthers.

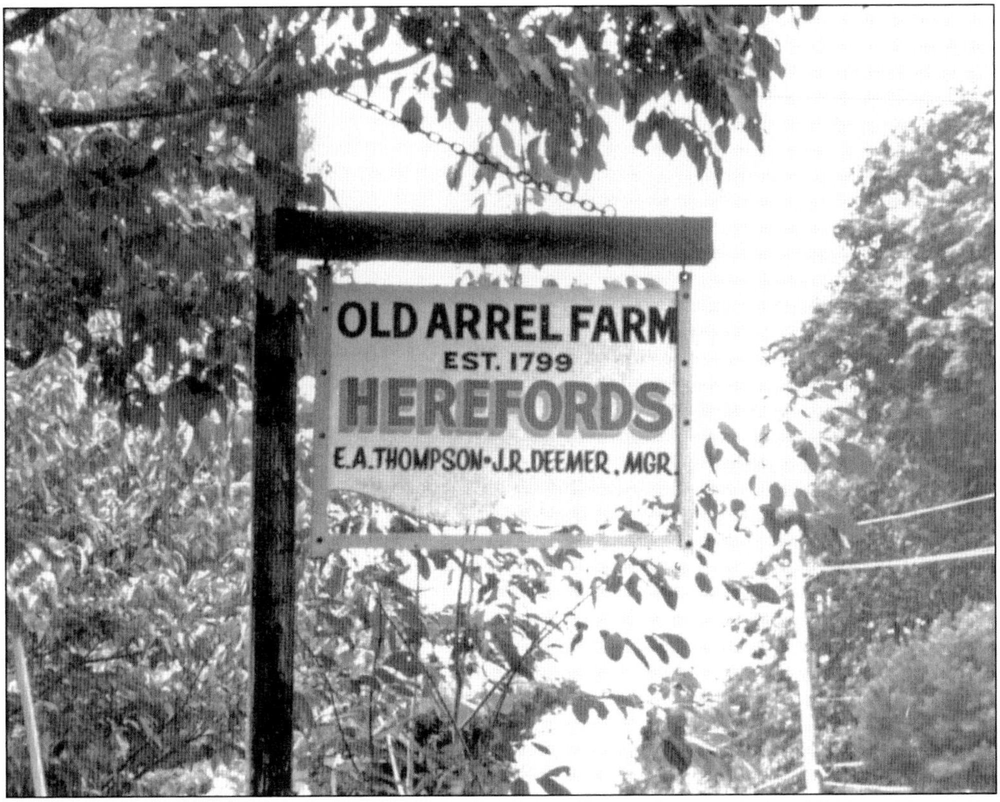

The old Arrel Farm still stands on Arrel Road in Poland Township, settled in 1799, and is still in the family today. The Arrels were among the earliest settlers in the area. A log cabin was built on the site, followed by a house. That house burned and was replaced in 1877 by the house shown in the photograph below. (Both courtesy of Jim and Claire Deemer.)

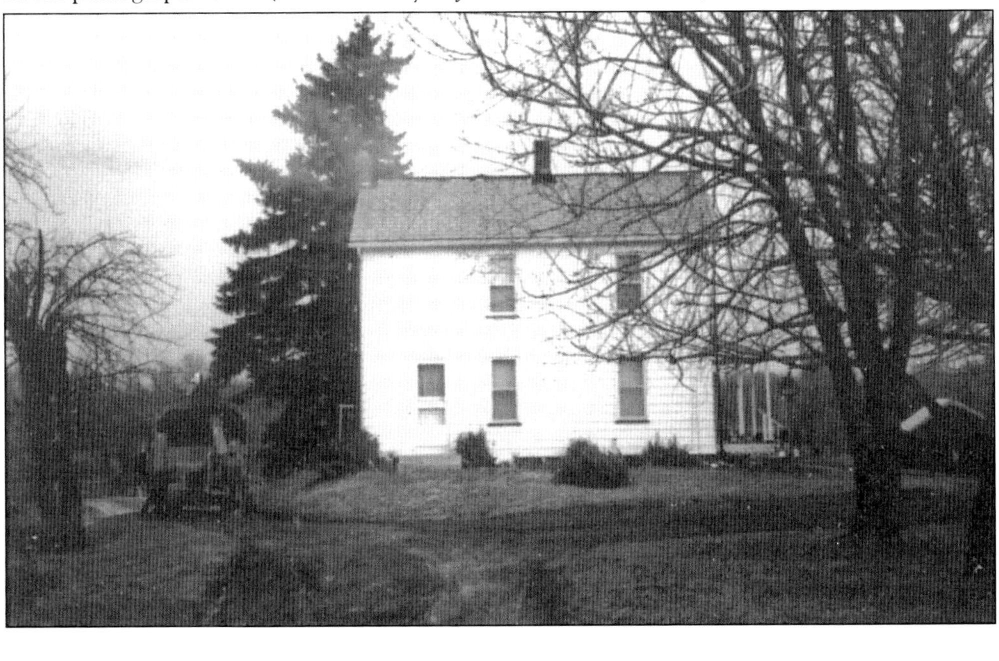

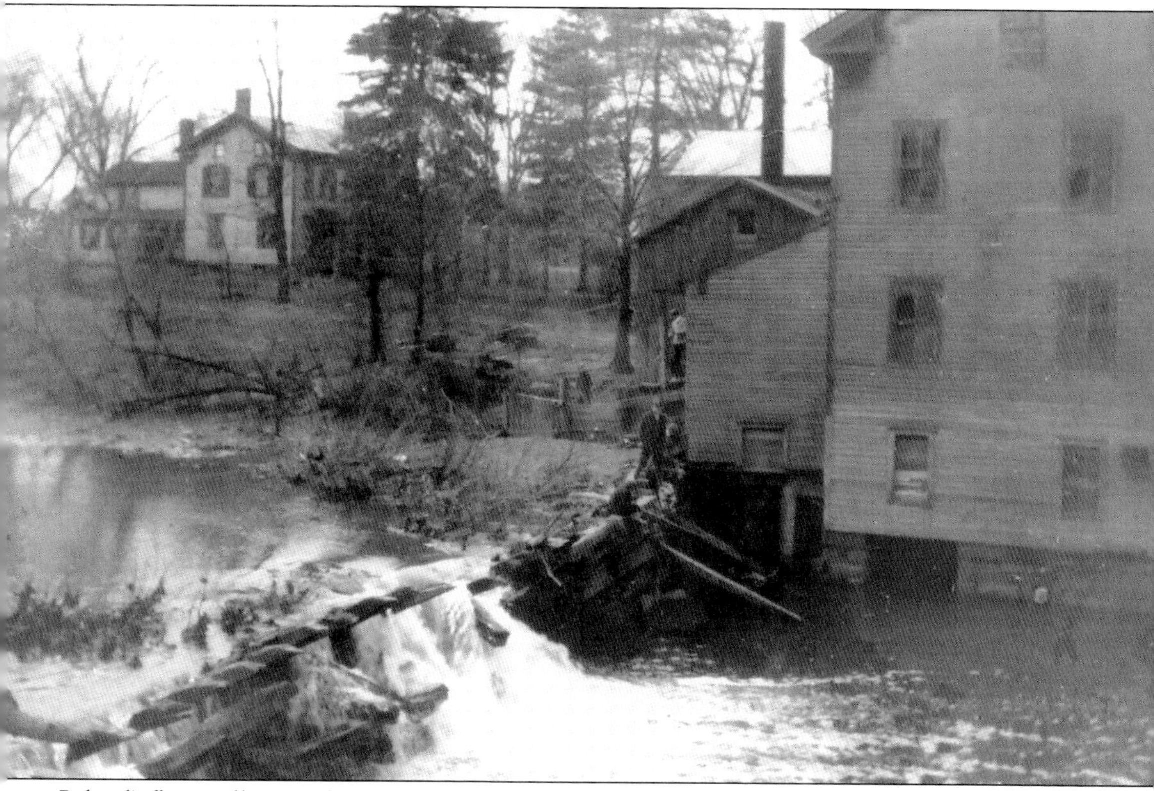

Poland's flour mill is seen here on South Main Street, just south of the bridge over Yellow Creek that was built around 1807. Note the water flowing over the dam, which was torn down in 1920. Parts of the old wooden dam could be seen in the creek as late as the 1990s. Also notice the Kennedy House in the background, now Village Hall. (Courtesy of Poland Historical Society.)

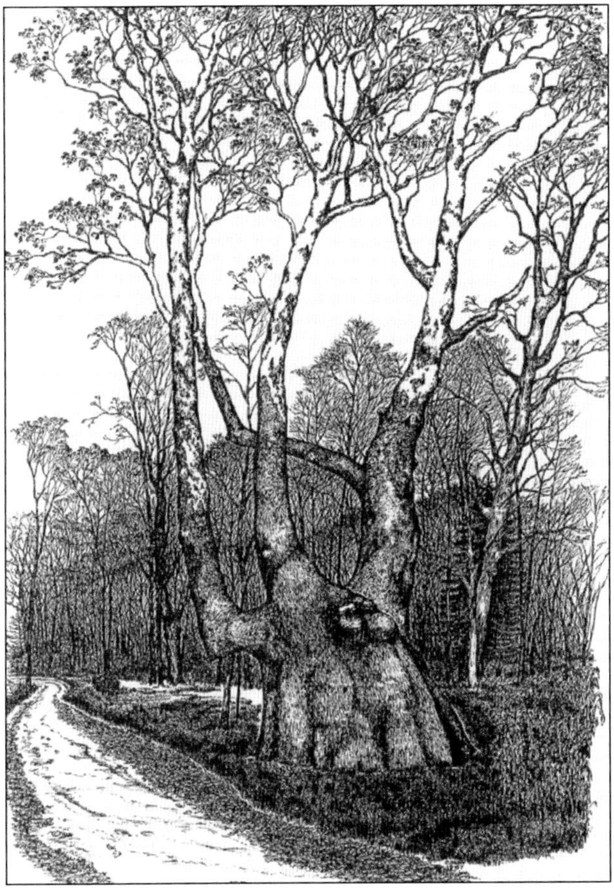

Poland artist Chester Hunt's 1960s rendering of the old sycamore tree in Poland Municipal Forest is shown at left. The forest, the first of its kind in Ohio, is run by a six-member board. The tree is said to be approximately 200 years old, dating back to when Poland was founded, and it is still standing in the Poland Woods today.

The dam at Yellow Creek bridge on South Main Street, across from where the library now stands, shows some ice on the backed-up and ponding water. The icehouse is shown in the upper left. Poland students in the 1800s loved to use this pond for ice-skating in the winter. Several fishermen are shown in lower left of the photograph. (Courtesy of Poland Historical Society.)

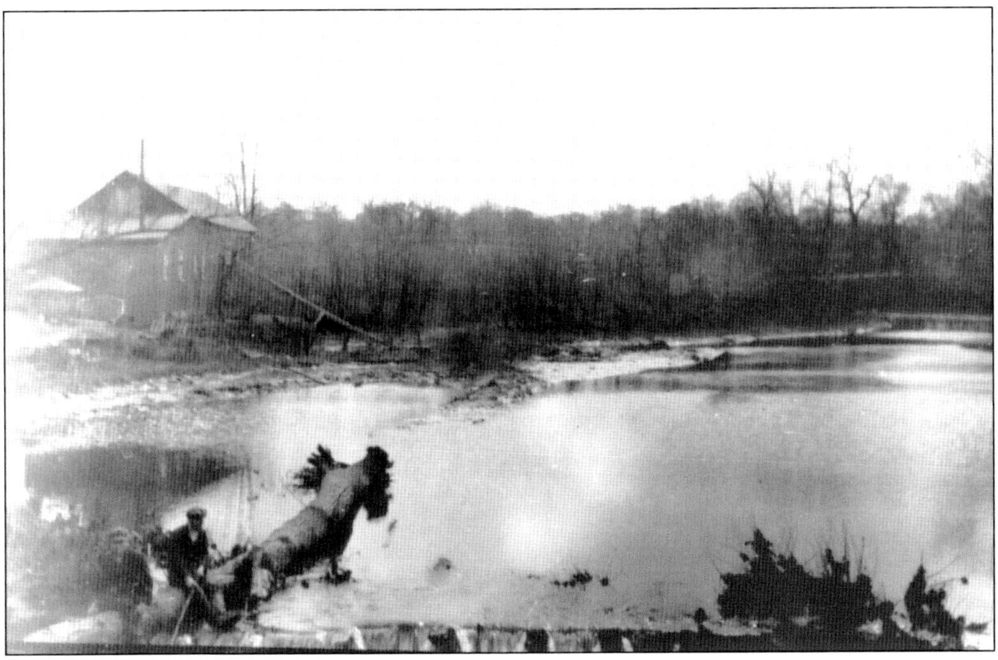

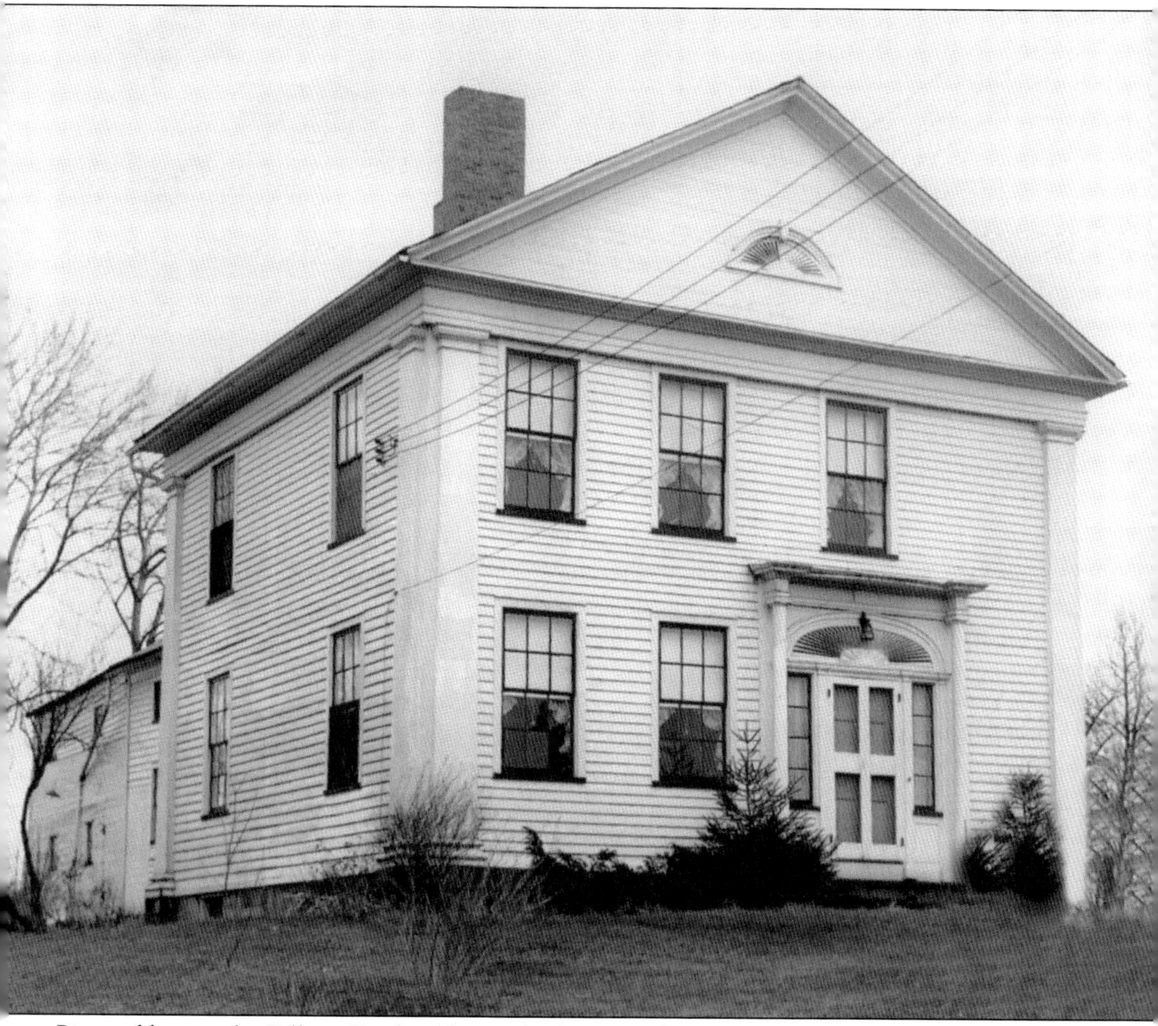

Pictured here is the Billious Kirtland house, built in 1825 by Turhand Kirtland, one of Poland's founders, for his son Billious. The house once stood on what is now the parking lot east of the current post office on Route 224. The home was moved to its present location on Audubon Lane in the early 1960s. The structure is still a residence today. (Courtesy of Janie Jenkins.)

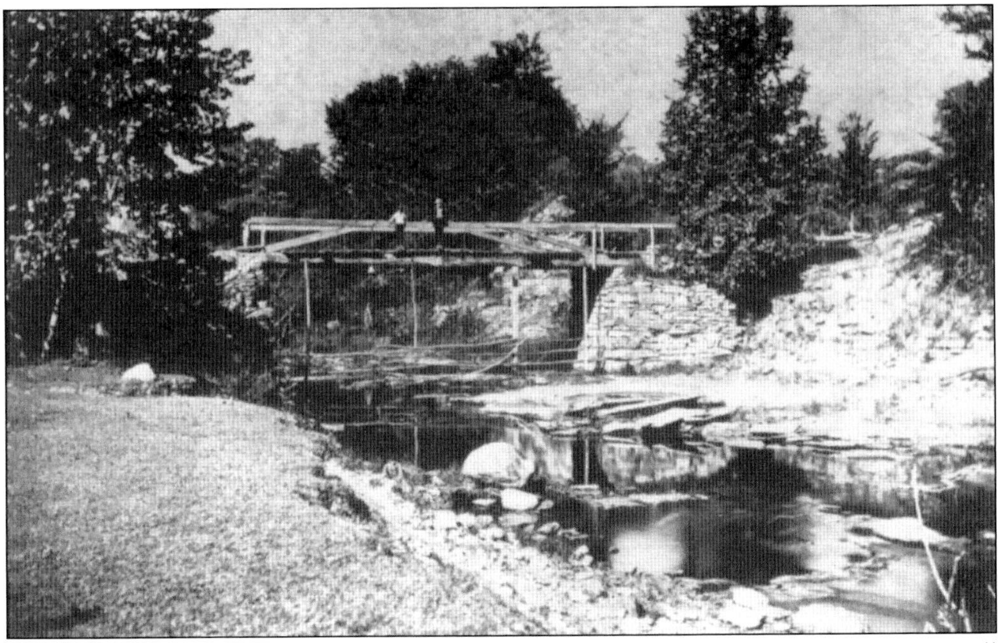

Holton's sawmill was on Yellow Creek near the site of the present Hamilton Dam. Holton's mill assisted in the sawing of wood used for the erection of Fowler's Grist Mill. Tradition relates this mill was in operation when Heaton's blast furnace was built close by on Yellow Creek in 1802. The sawmill was run by waterpower from Yellow Creek. (Courtesy of Poland Historical Society.)

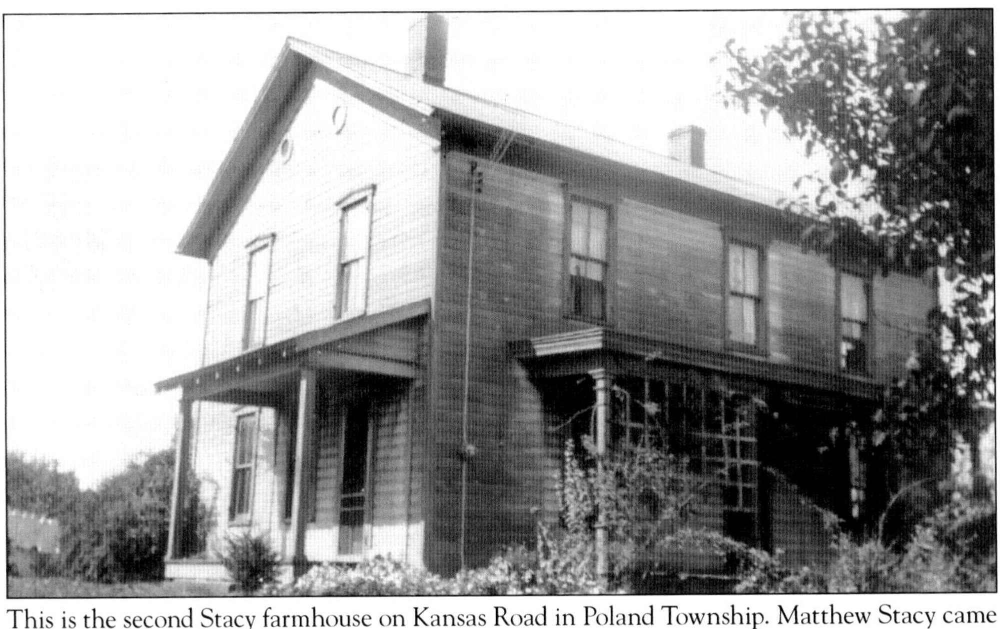

This is the second Stacy farmhouse on Kansas Road in Poland Township. Matthew Stacy came to Poland from Virginia in 1806 with his wife, Jane, and settled on this property. Their 1806 farmhouse, shown here, was torn down in the 1960s when a new home on the same site was built by the Stacy descendants. It is still in the Stacy family today. (Courtesy of Laura Stacy.)

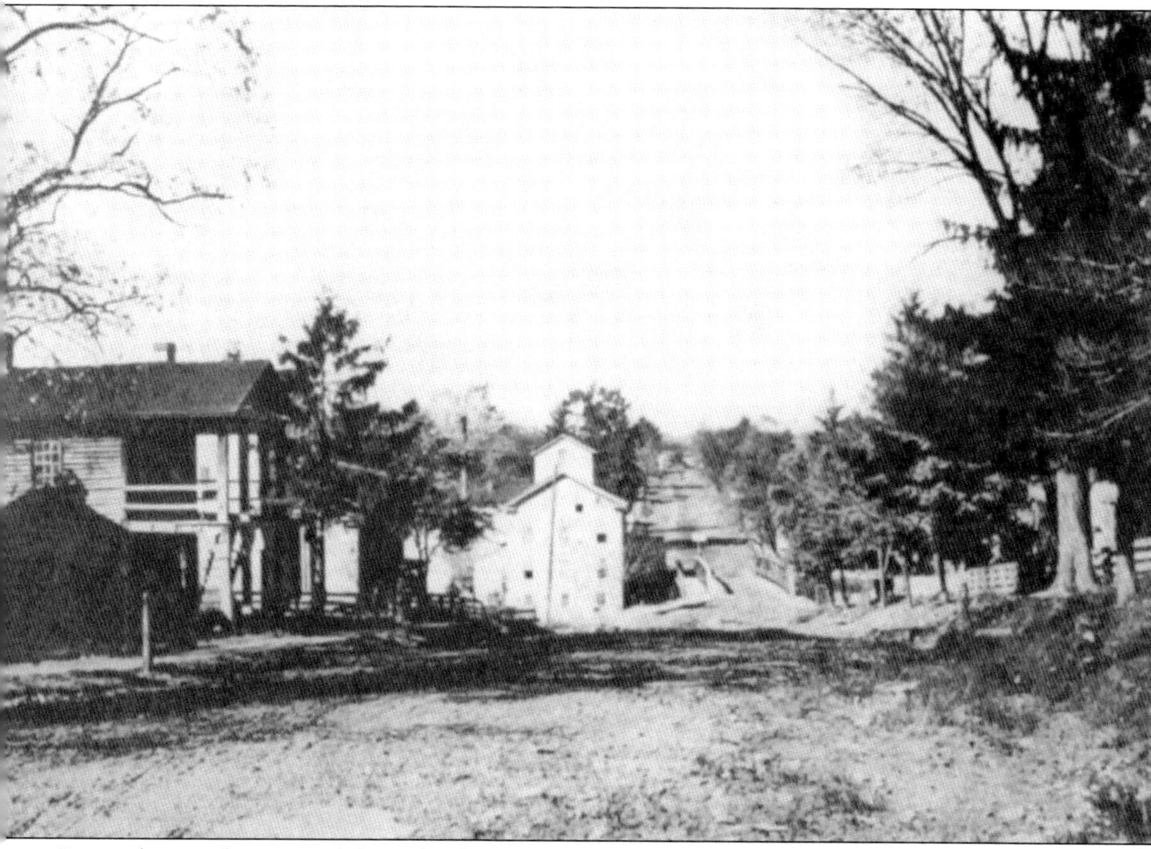

Pictured is another view of the Poland Flour and Grist Mill in the late 1800s, as seen looking west from what is now the intersection of Riverside Drive and South Main Street. In later years, towards the late 1800s and into the early 1900s, the mill was called Poland Mill and advertised, "Manufacturers of and Dealers in Flour, Food, and Grain of all Kinds." (Courtesy of Poland Historical Society.)

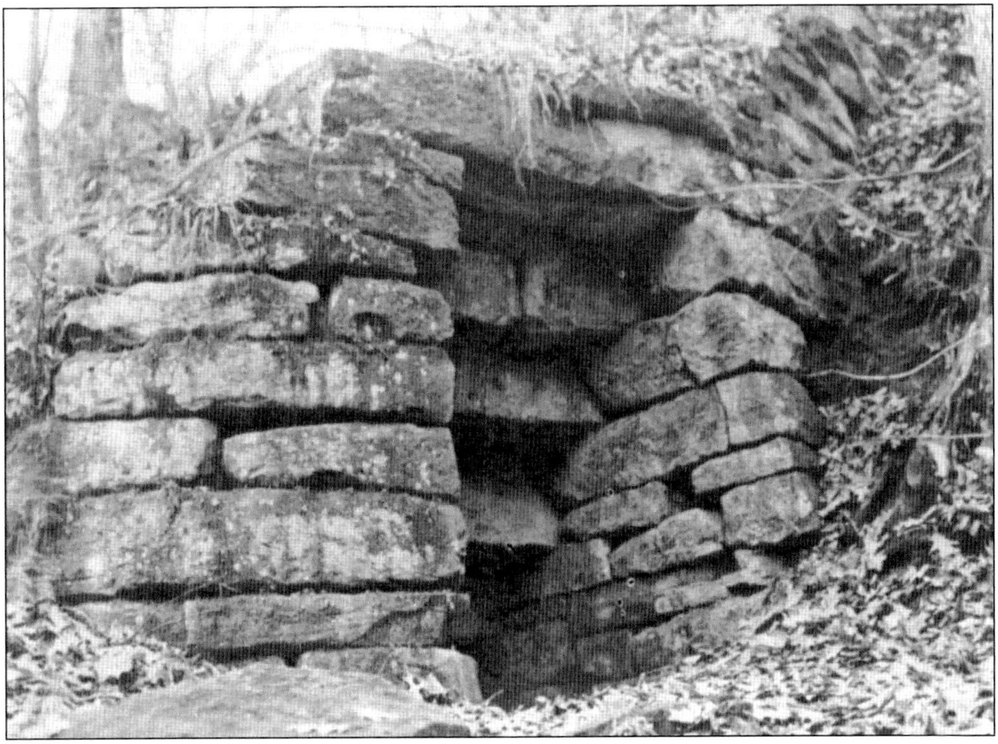

The Poland blast furnace was built in 1802 on the banks of Yellow Creek, south of what is now a dam at Lake Hamilton. Completed in 1803, the furnace was abandoned in 1812. It was built by Daniel and John Eaton, who later changed their name to Heaton, and they bravely named their charcoal iron-making furnace, "The Hopewell." It was the first blast furnace west of the Alleghenies and the first blast furnace in the Western Reserve. It was the forerunner of the great steel blast furnaces to come later in Youngstown, Campbell, and Struthers. (Courtesy of Poland Historical Society.)

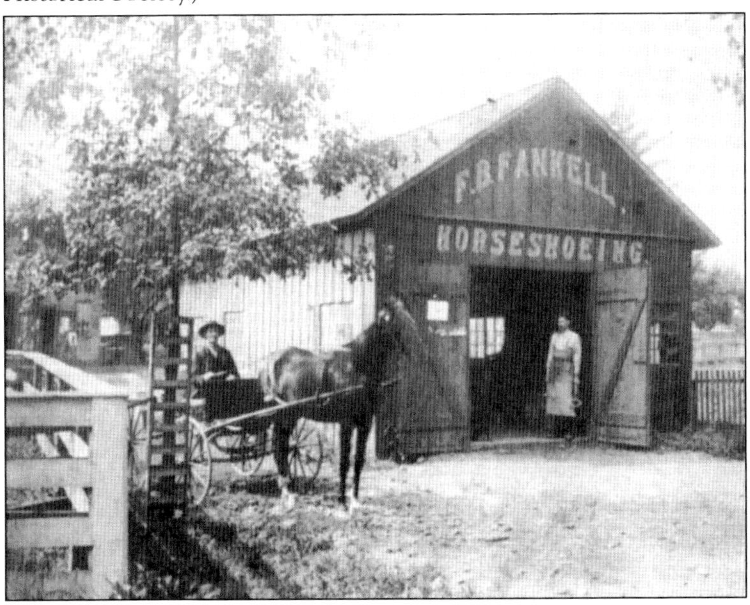

There were three blacksmith shops in Poland at one time. They were kept busy shoeing horses and repairing stagecoaches and buggies stopping in Poland, the midpoint between Pittsburgh and Cleveland. This blacksmith shop and forge were thought to be near the area of what is now Poland Union School. (Courtesy of Poland Historical Society.)

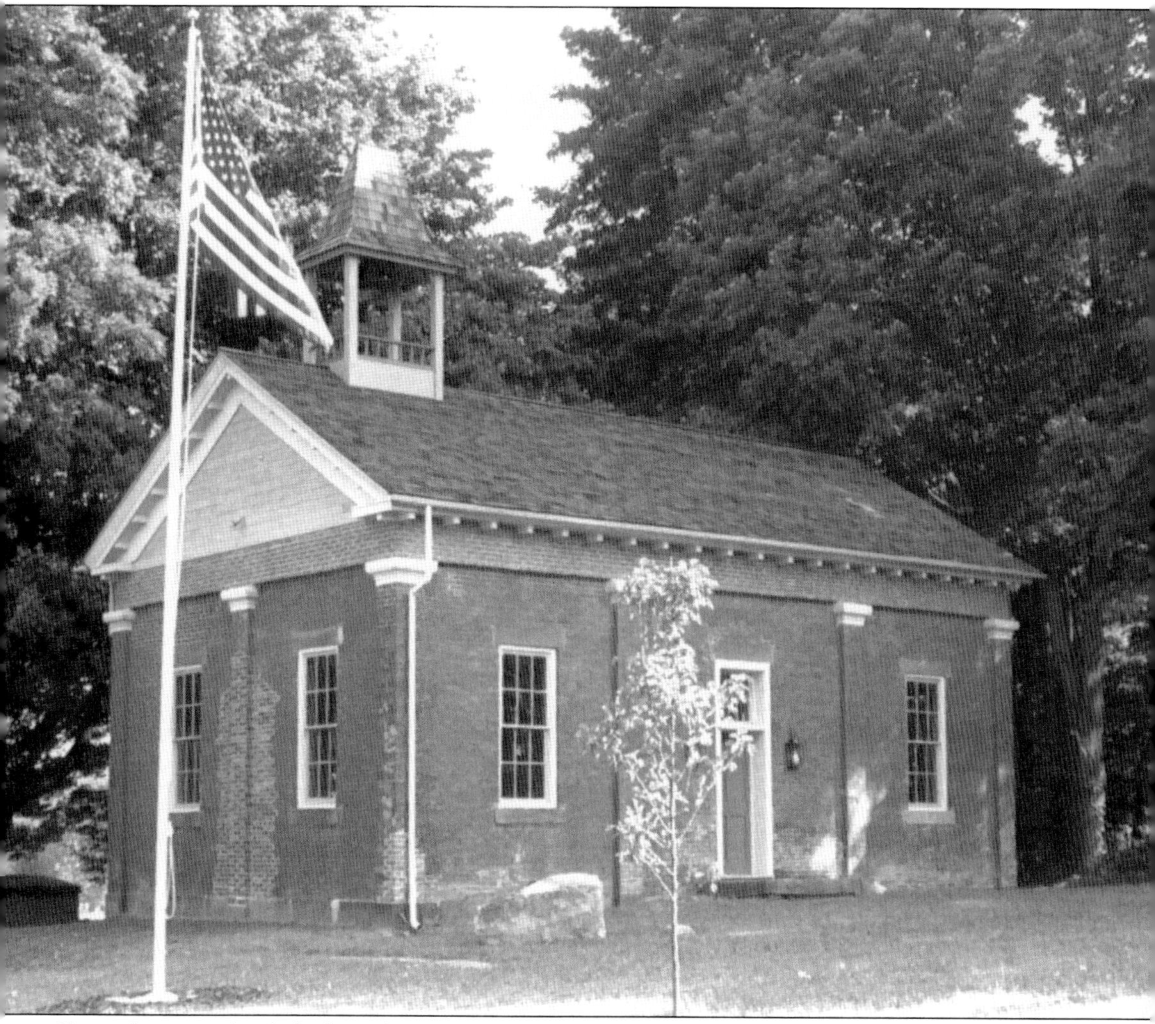

Shown here is Poland's little, red, one-room schoolhouse on Route 224, at the corner of Struthers Road. It was built in 1858 and operated until 1915. William McKinley taught here in 1860, walking the 2.5 miles from his home on South Main Street. Today it is a restored schoolhouse and the home of the Poland Township Historical Society. Leased to the society for 99 years at $1 per year by the Poland Board of Education, it is rumored to be the only one-room schoolhouse left in the state of Ohio that is still legally deeded to a board of education. (Courtesy of Poland schools' archives.)

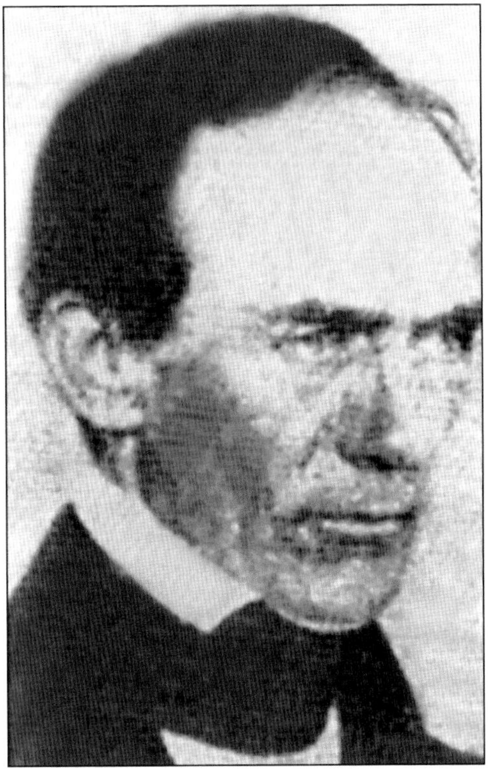

In the mid-1820s, William McGuffey, a tall young man, came to teach in one of the small one-room schoolhouses in the northern part of Poland Township located then on what is now the Poland Western Reserve north side fire station. This little schoolhouse was near McGuffey's home in Coitsville Township. At the time, McGuffey was just starting out as a teacher, but he would go on to become one of America's most famous educators. (Courtesy of Poland schools' archives.)

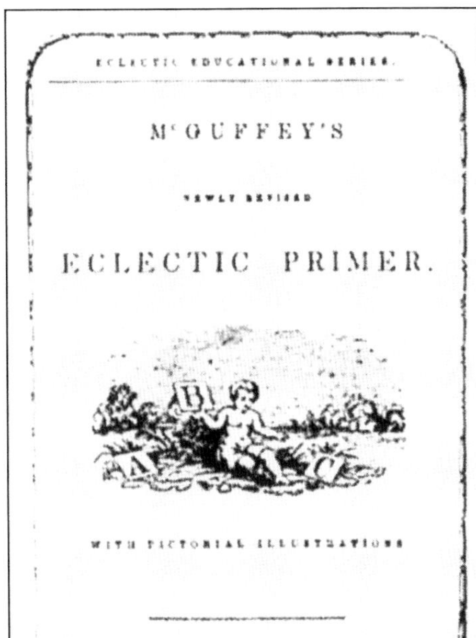

ECLECTIC EDUCATIONAL SERIES.

McGUFFEY'S

NEWLY REVISED

ECLECTIC PRIMER.

WITH PICTORIAL ILLUSTRATIONS

PUBLISHERS.
W. B. SMITH & CO., CINCINNATI.
CLARK, AUSTIN, MAYNARD & CO., NEW YORK

McGuffey's books would leave their mark on American education and American character. These books were commonly called *McGuffey Readers* and had their start in a Poland Township one-room schoolhouse. There, McGuffey made up classroom materials for students to use, as there were no textbooks back then. His books taught good, clean, wholesome living as well as morals, and they contained simple tales of American life at the time. (Courtesy of Poland schools' archives.)

Two

Academy and Seminary

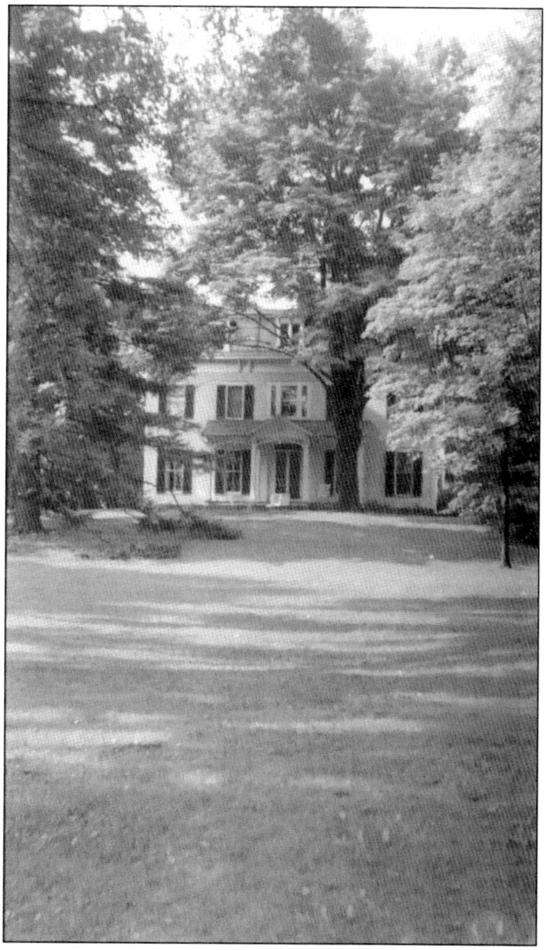

By the 1850s, Poland was becoming known for the educational institutions on College Street, so named for the elite colleges there including the Poland Law College, Poland Medical College, Poland Female College, Poland Academy, and Poland Seminary, one of the first schools in northeast Ohio to admit girls on an equal basis with boys. Shown here is Poland Law College on College Street.

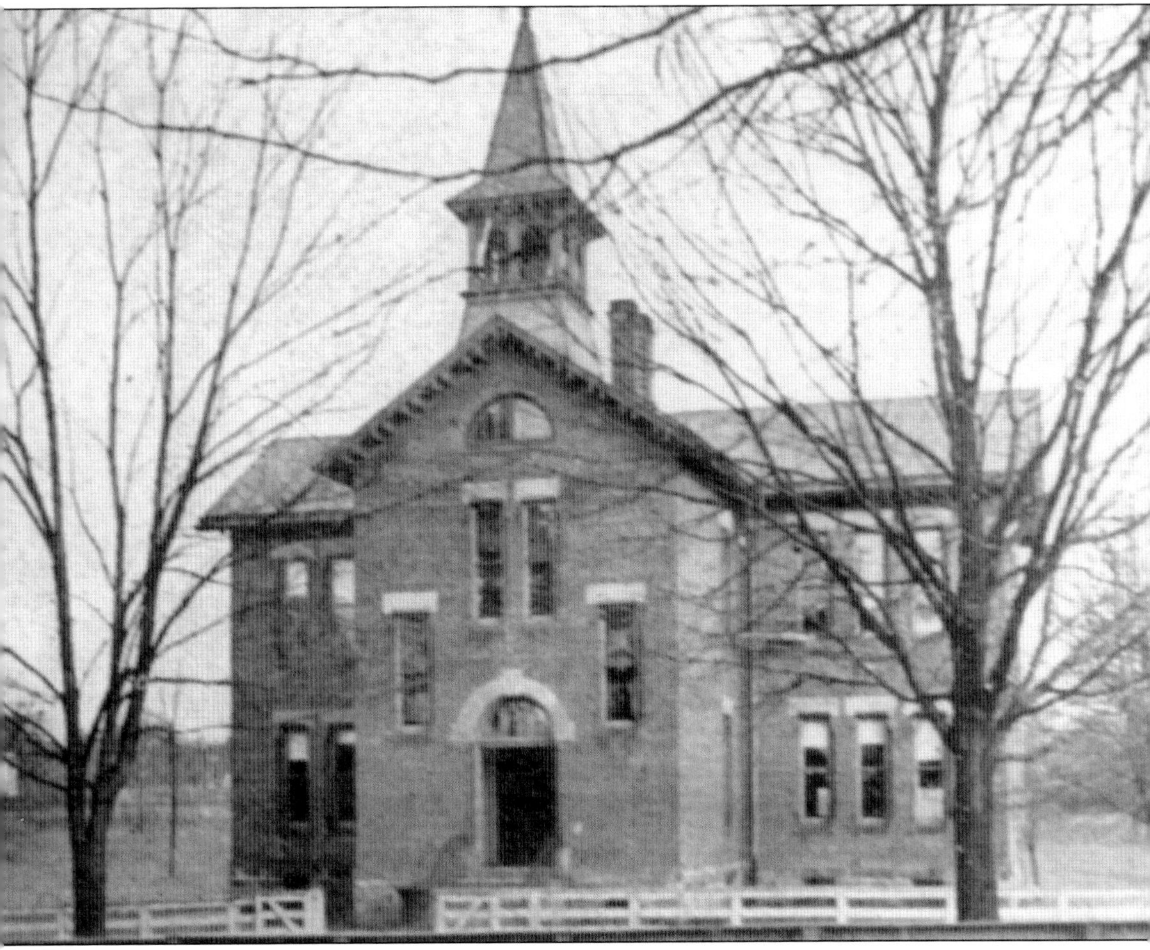

Poland Union Elementary School on Riverside Drive is shown here as it looked around 1884. At one time, this building housed all grades from kindergarten through 12th. (Courtesy of Poland schools' archives.)

A historic marker for Poland's Old Stone Tavern was erected July 2009 to commemorate the significance of this building in the Western Reserve and in the nation's history. It is the largest and oldest original Western Reserve building still standing today.

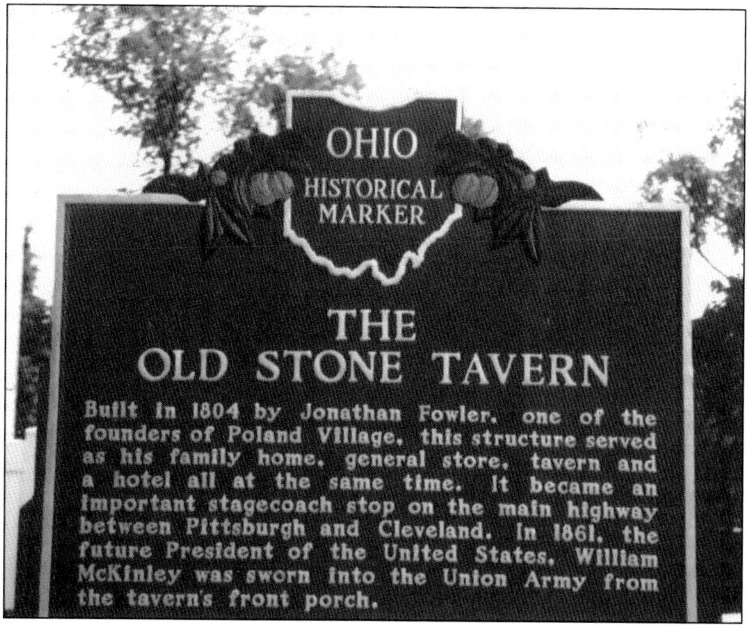

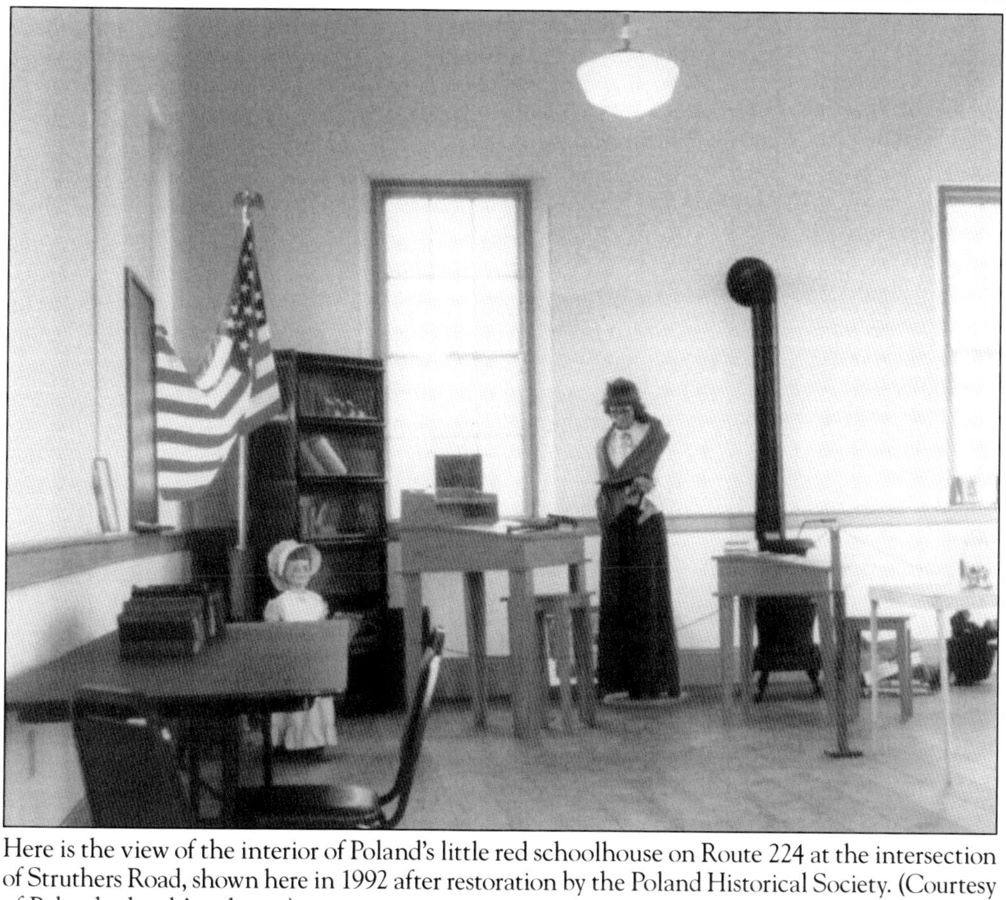

Here is the view of the interior of Poland's little red schoolhouse on Route 224 at the intersection of Struthers Road, shown here in 1992 after restoration by the Poland Historical Society. (Courtesy of Poland schools' archives.)

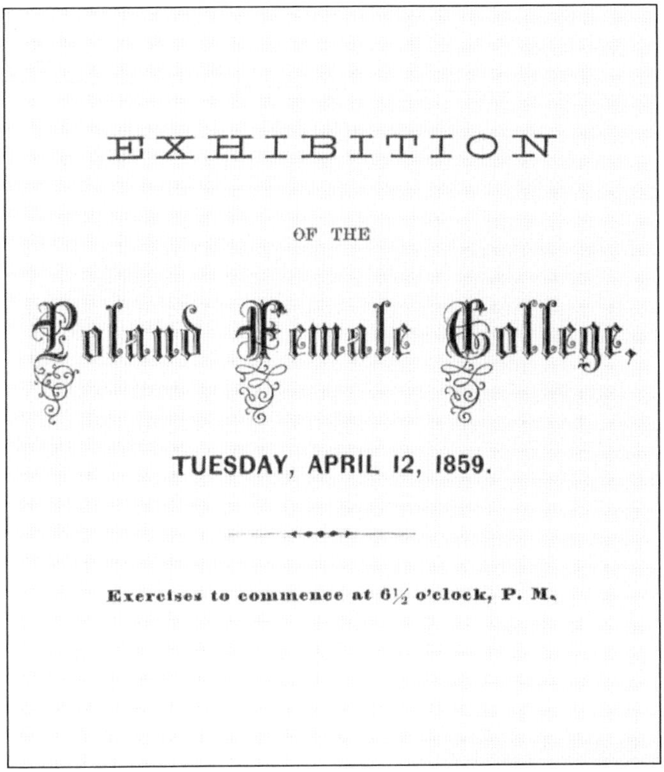

EXHIBITION

OF THE

Poland Female College,

TUESDAY, APRIL 12, 1859.

Exercises to commence at 6½ o'clock, P. M.

At left is a Poland Female College flier from 1859. The college was the building, which is now a residence, on College Street behind Wittenauer's drug store. (Courtesy of Poland schools' archives.)

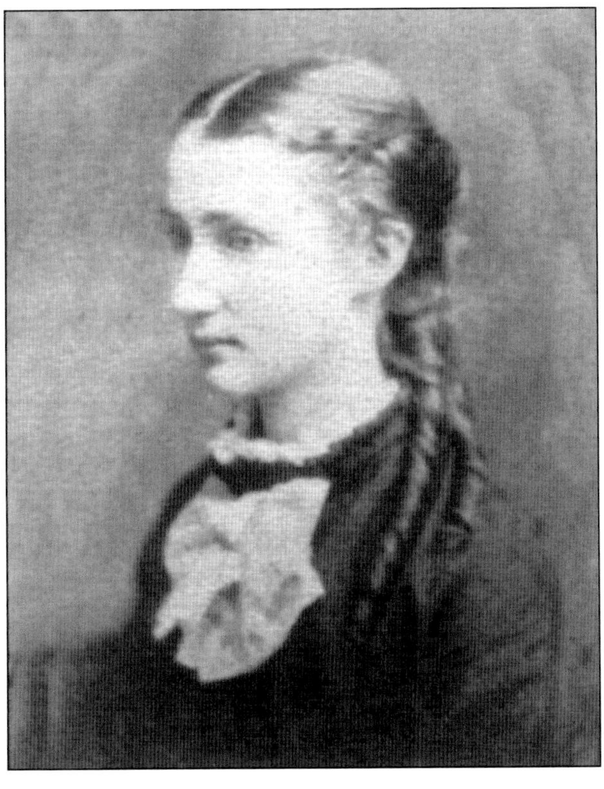

Shown is a graduation photograph of Adelaide Simpson Johnston at Poland Female College around 1859. (Courtesy of Poland schools' archives.)

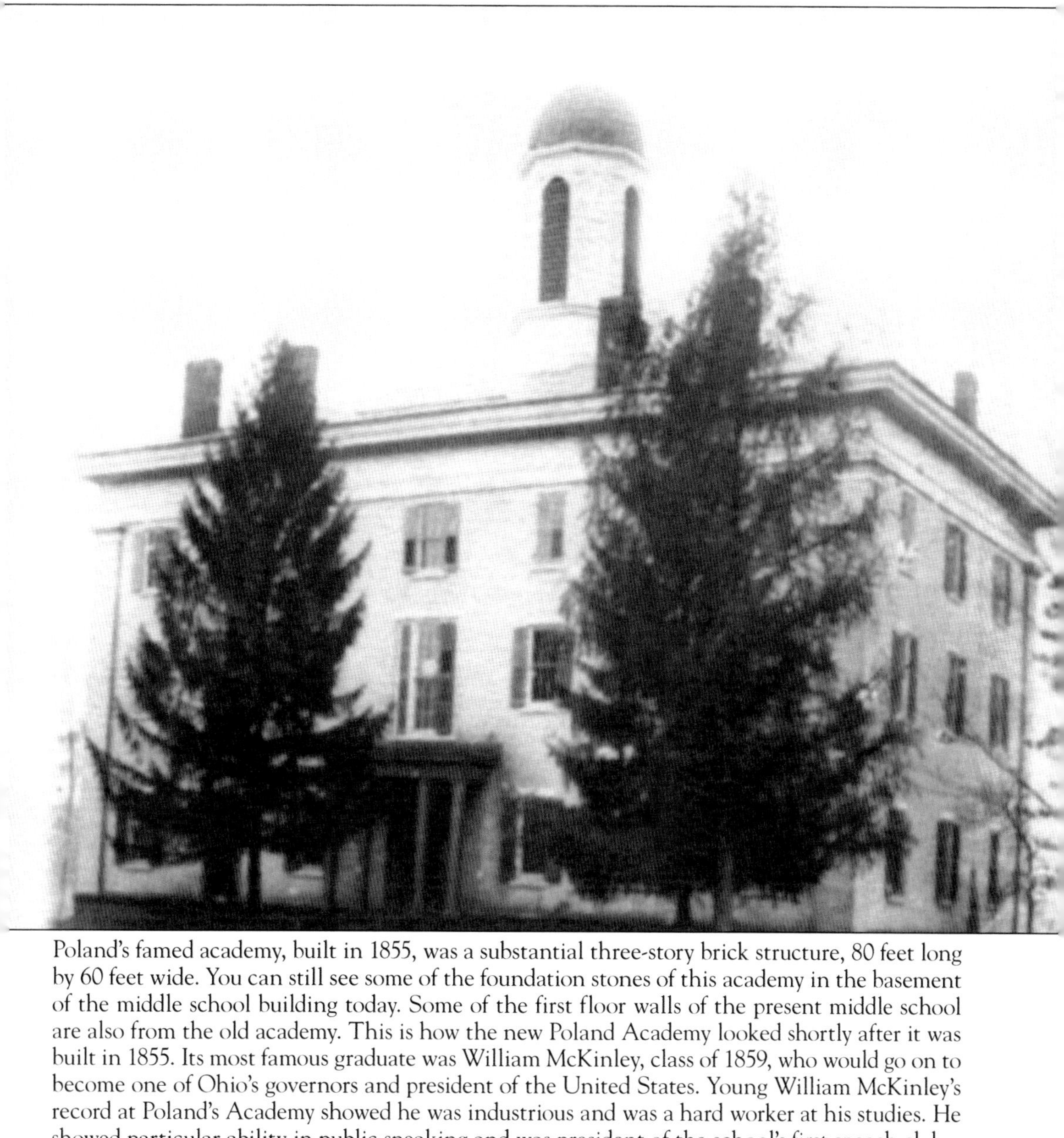

Poland's famed academy, built in 1855, was a substantial three-story brick structure, 80 feet long by 60 feet wide. You can still see some of the foundation stones of this academy in the basement of the middle school building today. Some of the first floor walls of the present middle school are also from the old academy. This is how the new Poland Academy looked shortly after it was built in 1855. Its most famous graduate was William McKinley, class of 1859, who would go on to become one of Ohio's governors and president of the United States. Young William McKinley's record at Poland's Academy showed he was industrious and was a hard worker at his studies. He showed particular ability in public speaking and was president of the school's first speech club.

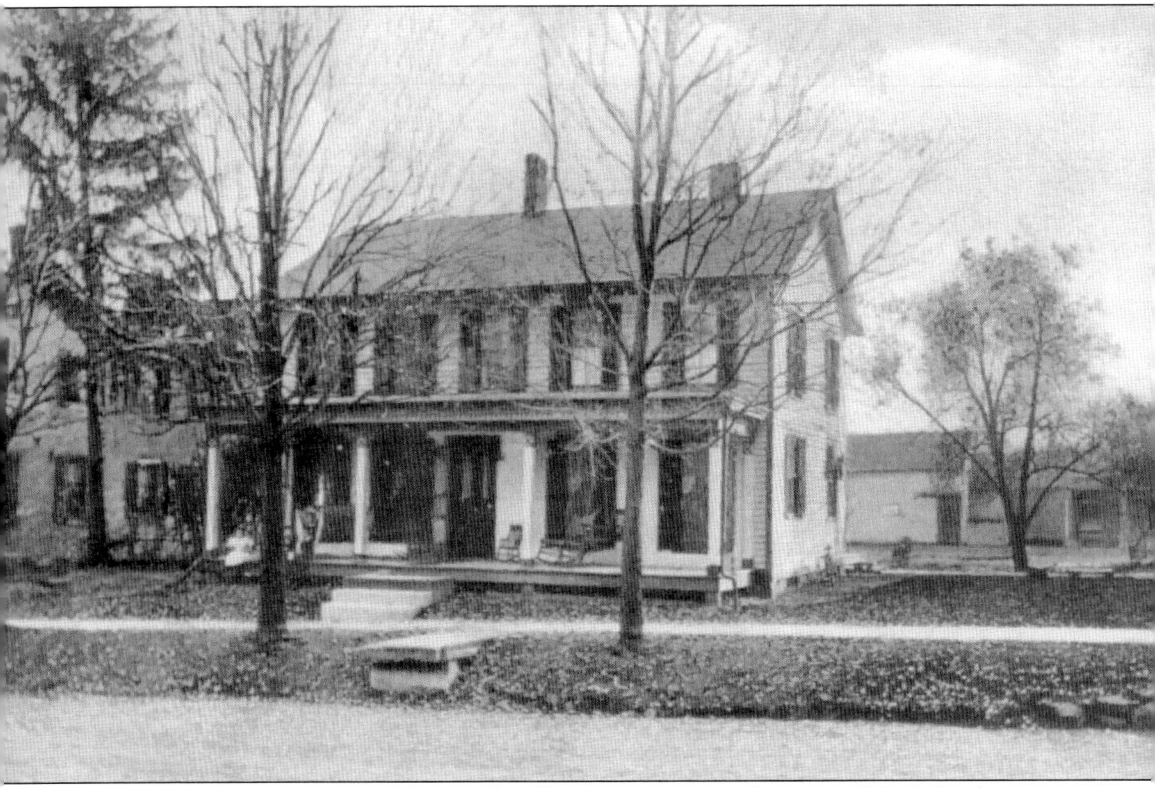

Shown here is the boyhood home of William McKinley in the early 1850s. This home once stood on South Main Street where the parking lot for the Home Savings Bank is now located. The building was torn down in 1960. As a young boy growing up in Poland, McKinley played ball on the Poland Commons, now the grassy area in front of the Presbyterian Church on South Main Street, and swam in the old swimming hole still used by Poland youth as late as the 1960s. (Courtesy of Poland Historical Society.)

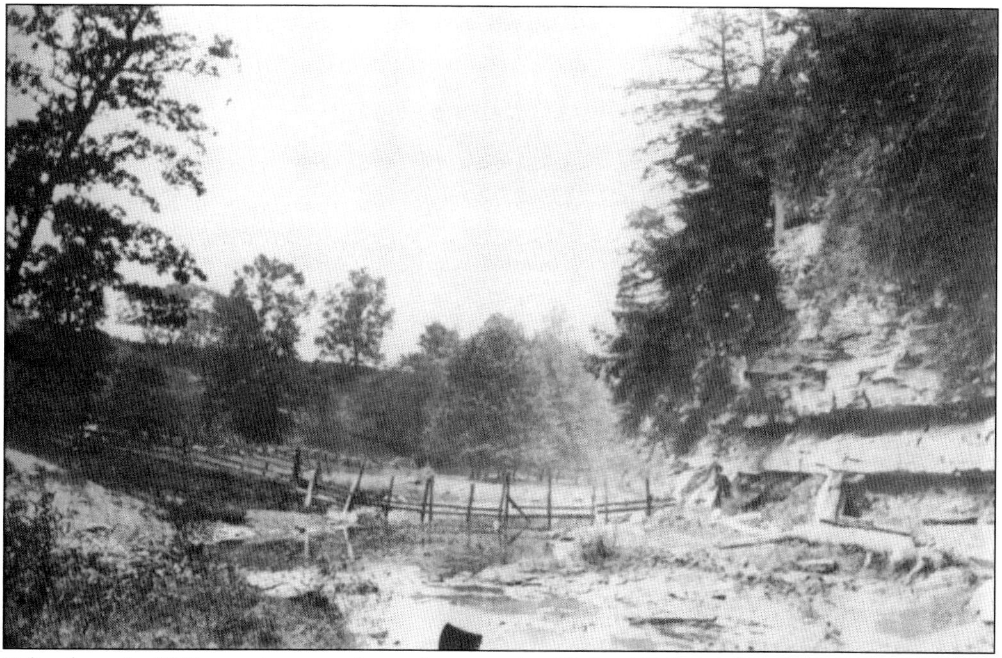

Palisade rock-cliff formations are shown here north of Poland Village along Yellow Creek, cut by years of water flowing along the creek bed. It is sometimes called "Lovers Leap" by old Polandites. (Courtesy of Poland Historical Society.)

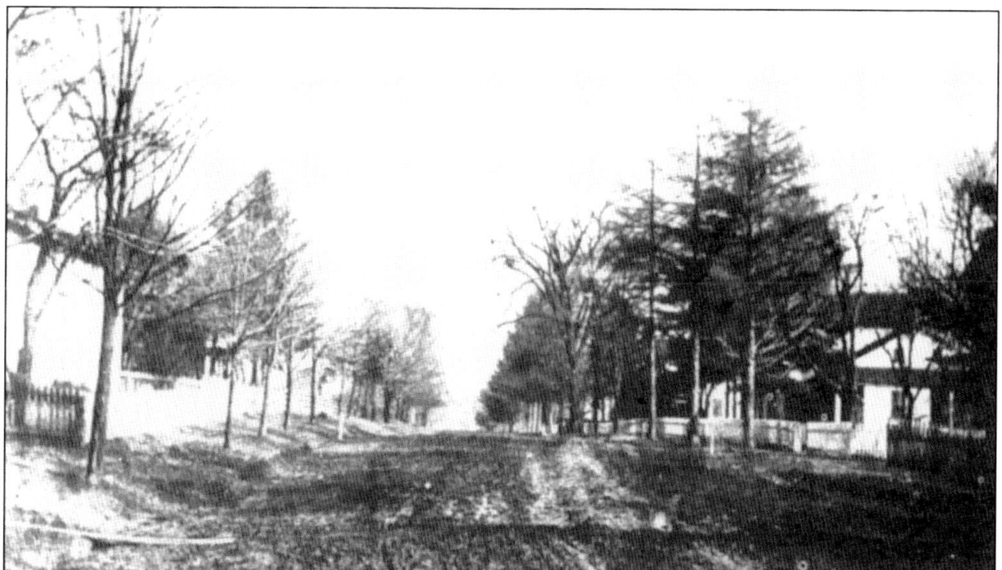

This is unpaved, muddy Water Street looking north toward Struthers around the 1870s. (Courtesy of Poland Historical Society.)

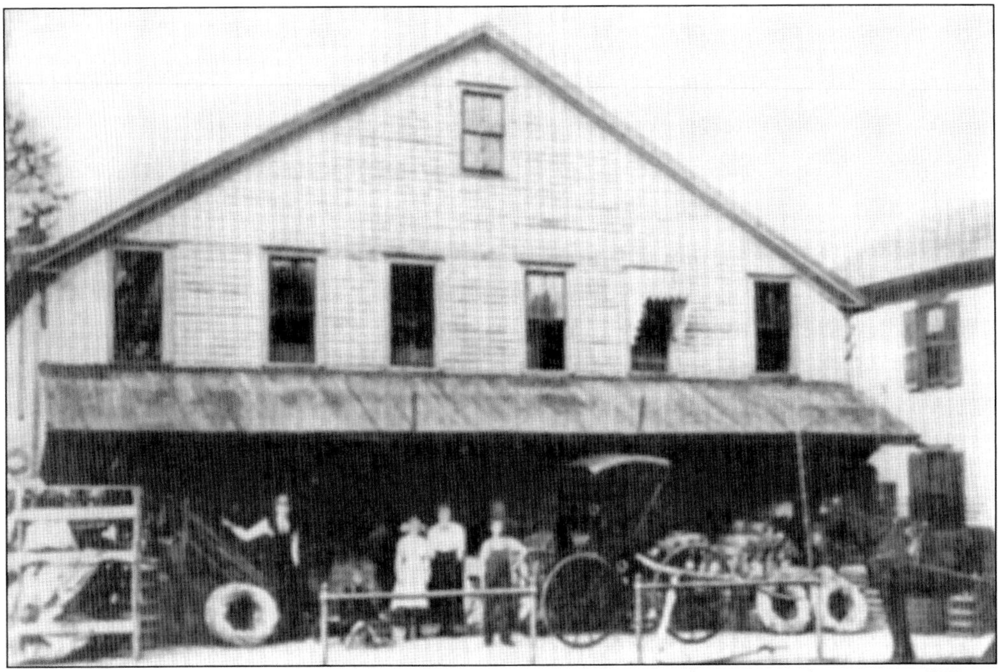

This is an early picture of Koontz's General Store, built in 1829, at what is now the corner of Water Street and South Main Street. Notice the horse and buggy in front of the store, the hitching posts to tie up the horses, and the rolls of baling wire. Reverend Bradley, in 1830, opened a small "select school" in an upstairs room over Koontz's General Store to serve as a secondary school. It became known as the Poland Academy. Several of the old foundation stones from this building are now in the front shrubbery bed at the entrance to the high school on Dobbins Road. (Courtesy of Poland schools' archives.)

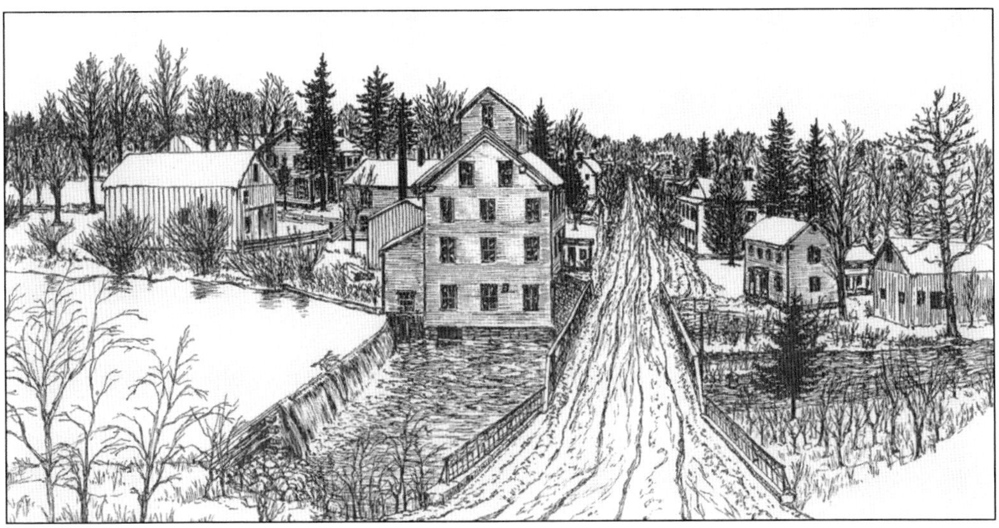

Above is Poland artist Chester Hunt's 1960s rendering of Poland in the mid-1850s showing the Poland Mill, the one-lane wooden bridge over Yellow Creek, the Kennedy House (now Village Hall), and one of the inns (far right) on Main Street.

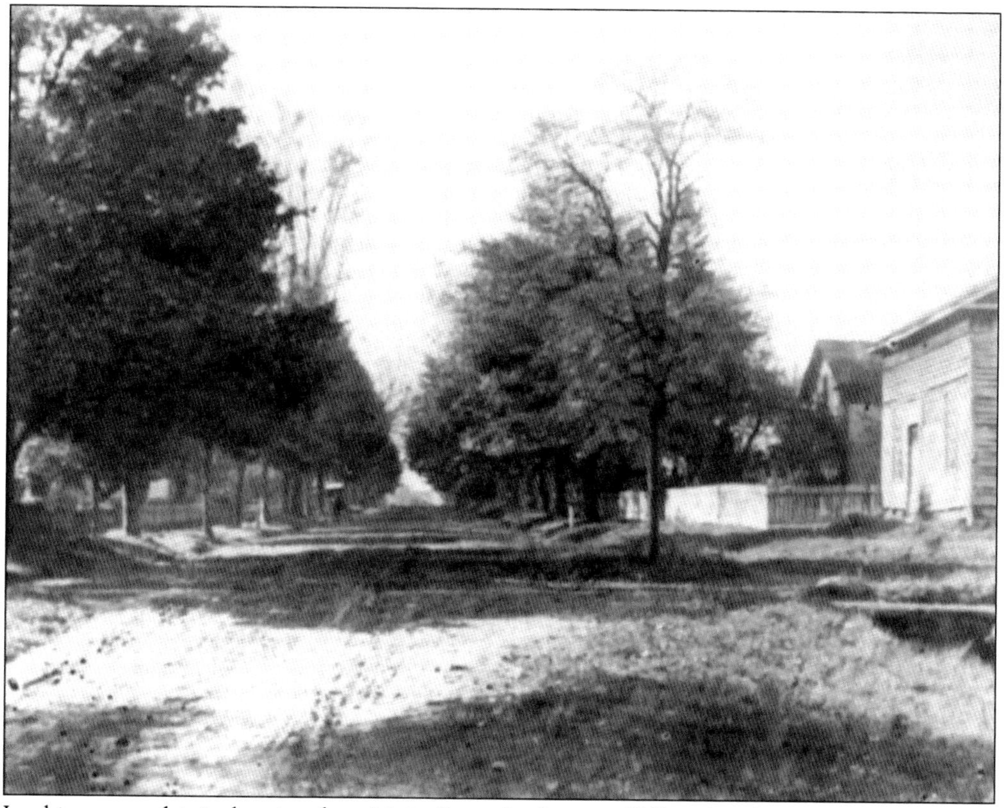

Looking west, this is the view from Main Street bridge over Yellow Creek. Note the muddy road and wooden sidewalks in this *c.* 1860 photograph. The Rice Lonergan house at the far right was built in 1835, is now 215 South Main Street, and is currently being remodeled as a residence. (Courtesy of Poland Historical Society.)

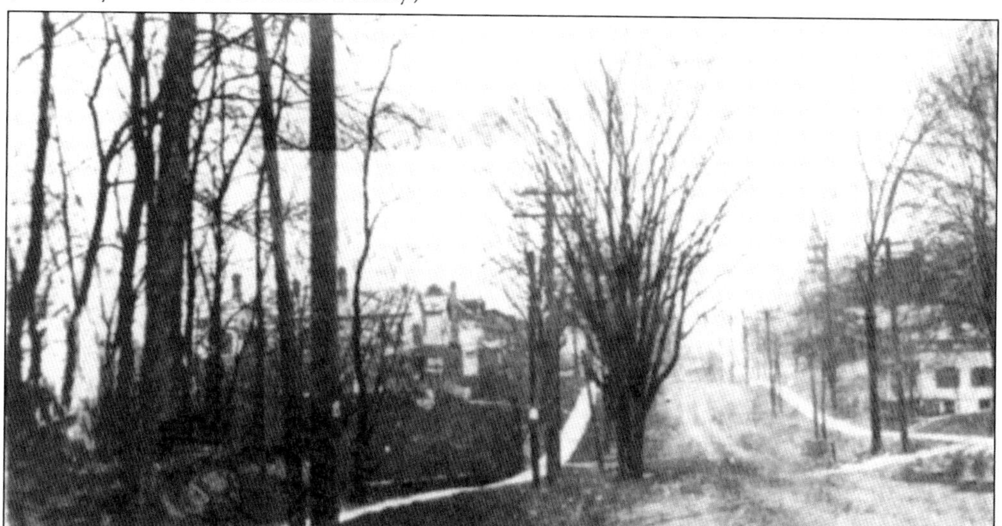

This view looks north in 1861 from what is now the intersection of Riverside Drive and South Main Street. Back then, Riverside Drive was called Center Road. Notice the bell tower steeple, right of center, which is Union Elementary. (Courtesy of Poland schools' archives.)

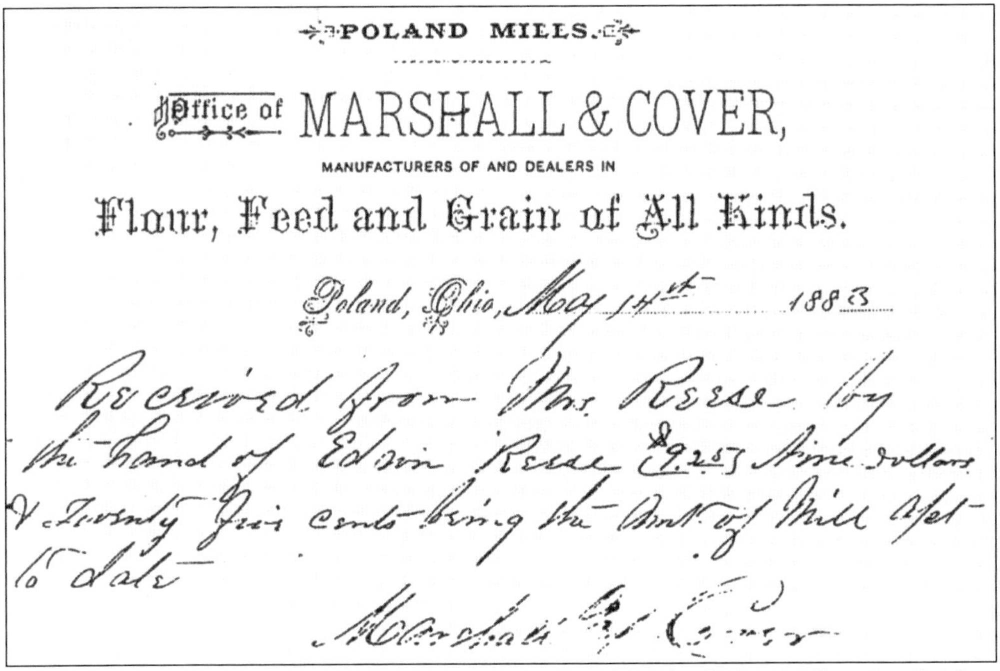
POLAND MILLS.

Office of MARSHALL & COVER,

MANUFACTURERS OF AND DEALERS IN

Flour, Feed and Grain of All Kinds.

Poland, Ohio, May 14th 1883

Received from Mrs Reese by the hand of Edwin Reese $9.25 Nine dollars & Twenty five cents being the Amt of Mill Acct to date

Marshall & Cover

This receipt for $9.25, dated May 14, 1883, was from the old Poland Flour Mill on South Main Street at the Yellow Creek bridge. (Courtesy of Poland Historical Society.)

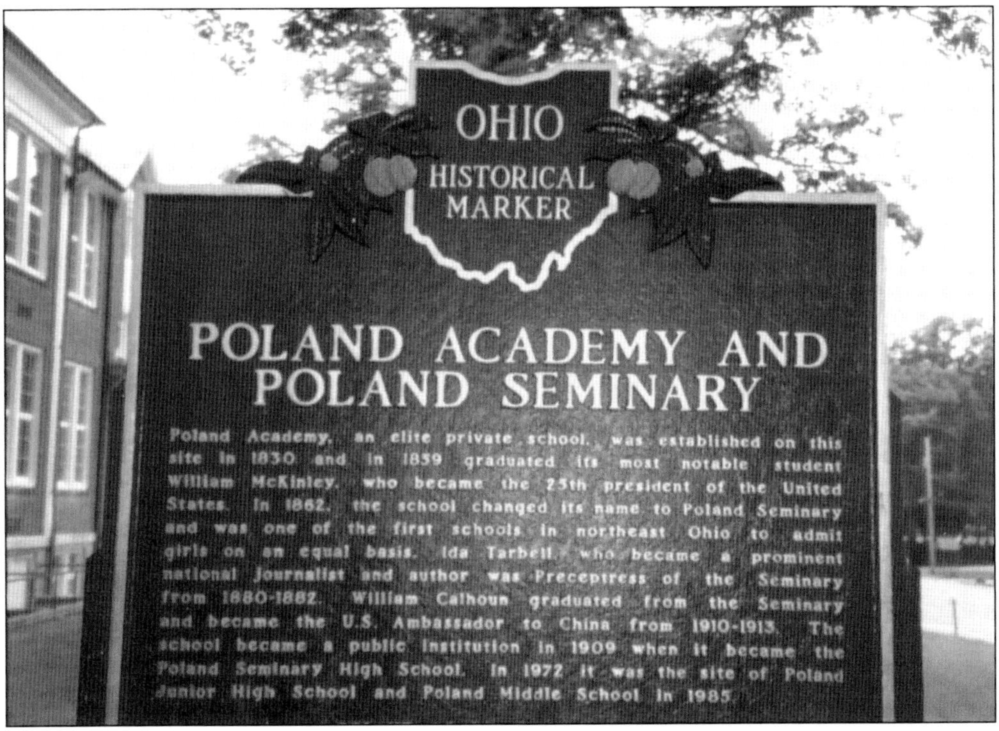

The Ohio Historical Marker in front of the Middle School on College Street was erected in 2007. It denotes the historical significance of the Poland Academy and the Poland Seminary on this site from the 1850s to the early 1900s.

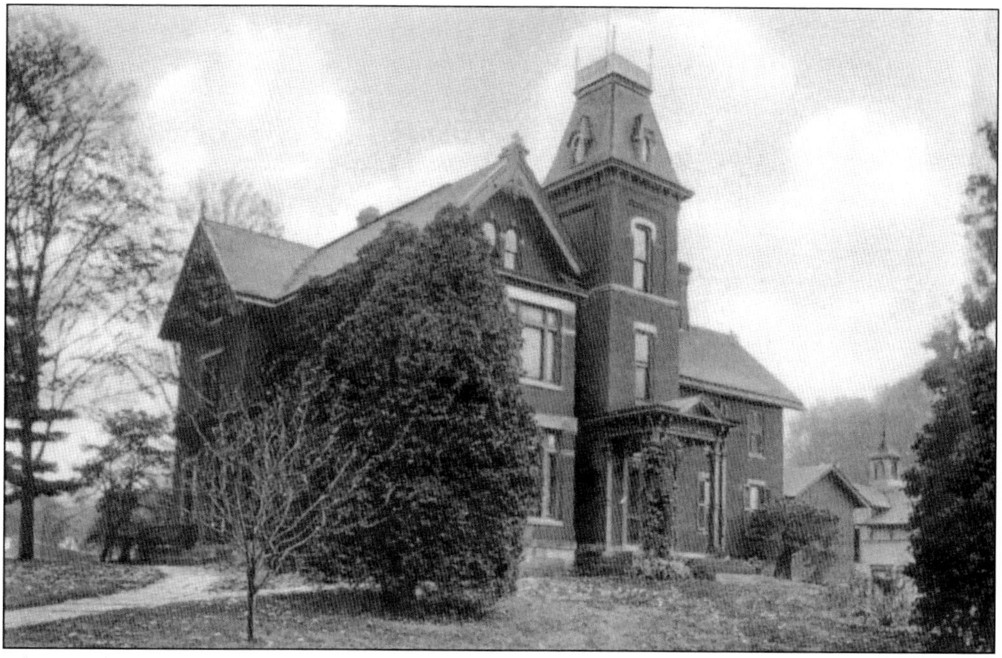

The Kirtland-Bishop house was built in 1851 by the grandson of Turhand Kirtland. It is commonly referred to today as the Bishop House and is still a residence. (Courtesy of Poland Historical Society.)

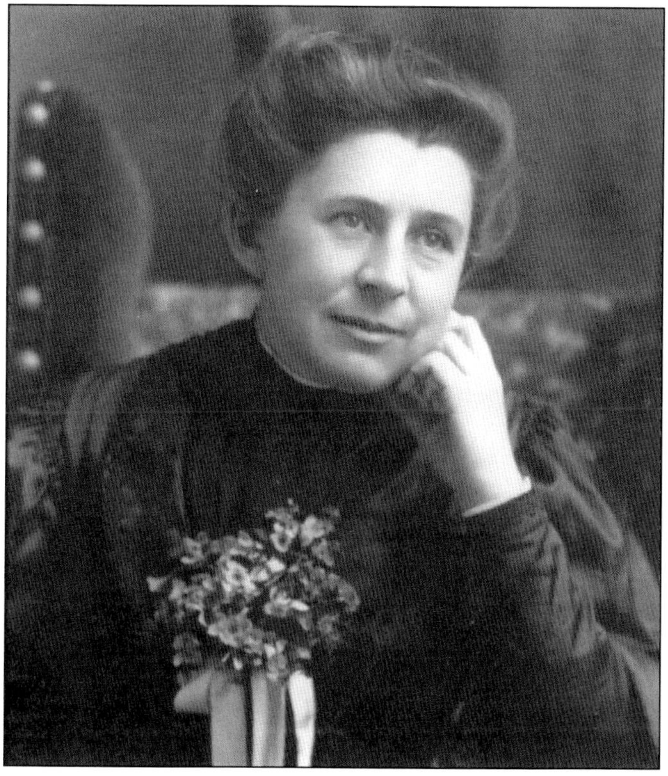

Ida Tarbell was the most famous of the distinguished faculty at the seminary. Ida Tarbell was preceptress (head) of the seminary from 1881 to 1883 and taught English composition. She would go on to national prominence as editor of *McClure's Magazine* and the *American Magazine*. She also won national recognition for her two-volume series, *The Early Life of Abraham Lincoln*, which was a national best seller, and a two-volume work, *The History of the Standard Oil Company*. (Courtesy of Poland schools' archives.)

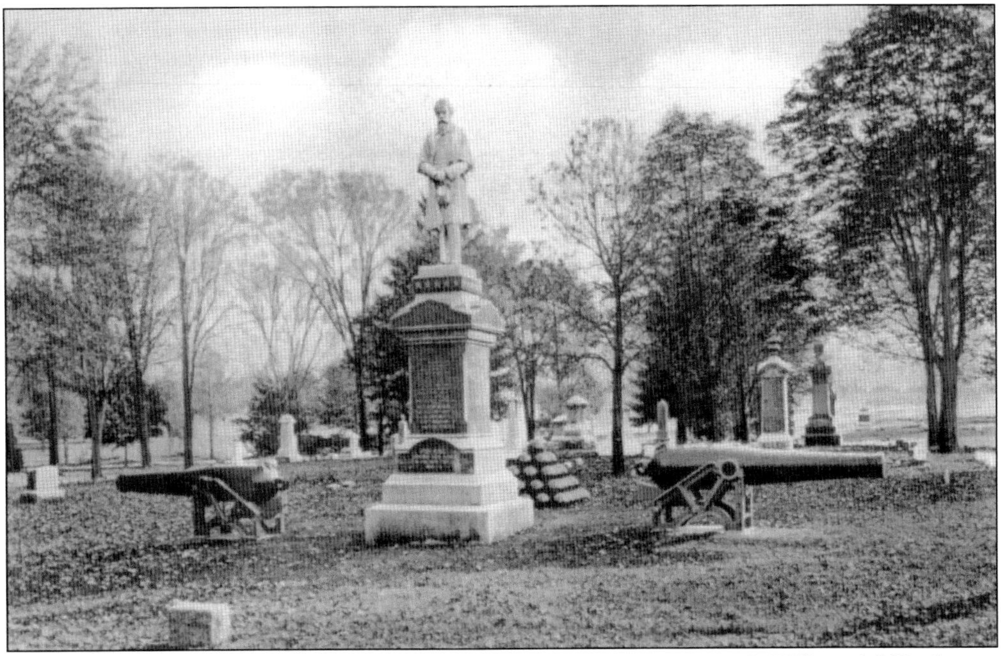

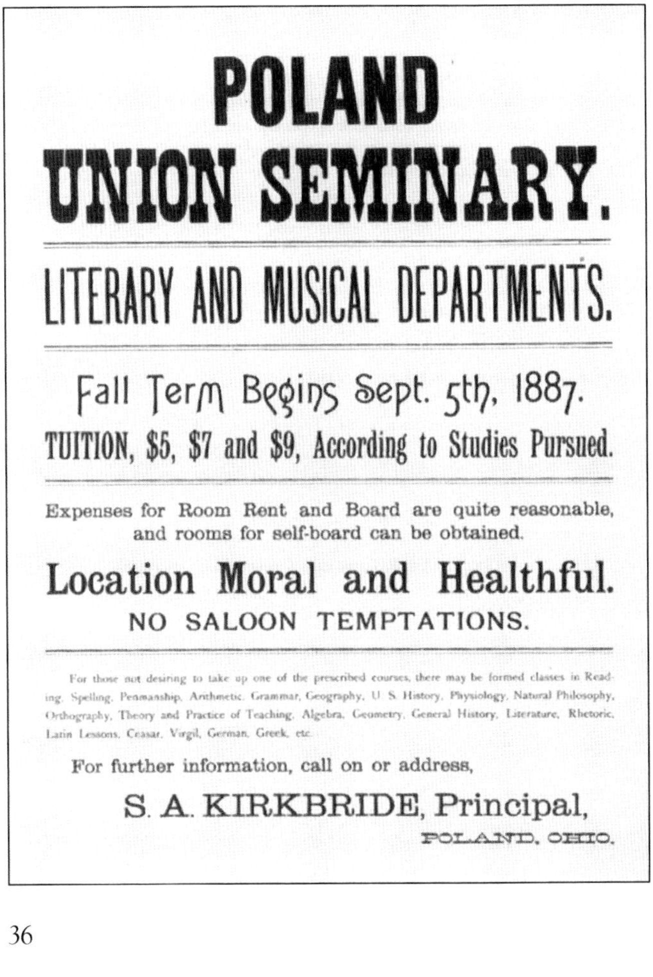

POLAND

UNION SEMINARY.

LITERARY AND MUSICAL DEPARTMENTS.

Fall Term Begins Sept. 5th, 1887.

TUITION, $5, $7 and $9, According to Studies Pursued.

Expenses for Room Rent and Board are quite reasonable, and rooms for self-board can be obtained.

Location Moral and Healthful.

NO SALOON TEMPTATIONS.

For those not desiring to take up one of the prescribed courses, there may be formed classes in Reading, Spelling, Penmanship, Arithmetic, Grammar, Geography, U. S. History, Physiology, Natural Philosophy, Orthography, Theory and Practice of Teaching, Algebra, Geometry, General History, Literature, Rhetoric, Latin Lessons, Ceasar, Virgil, German, Greek, etc.

For further information, call on or address,

S. A. KIRKBRIDE, Principal,

POLAND, OHIO.

In 1887, William McKinley spoke at the dedication of the Soldiers Monument in Poland Cemetery, now known as Poland's Riverside Cemetery. A reception of tea and cookies following the ceremony was put on by the ladies of the Poland community. Poland still celebrates Memorial Day at this monument. (Courtesy of Poland Historical Society.)

An 1887 flier for the Poland Seminary shows tuition was only $5 for the semester. The community was advertised as moral and healthful with no saloon temptations for the students. (Courtesy of Poland schools' archives.)

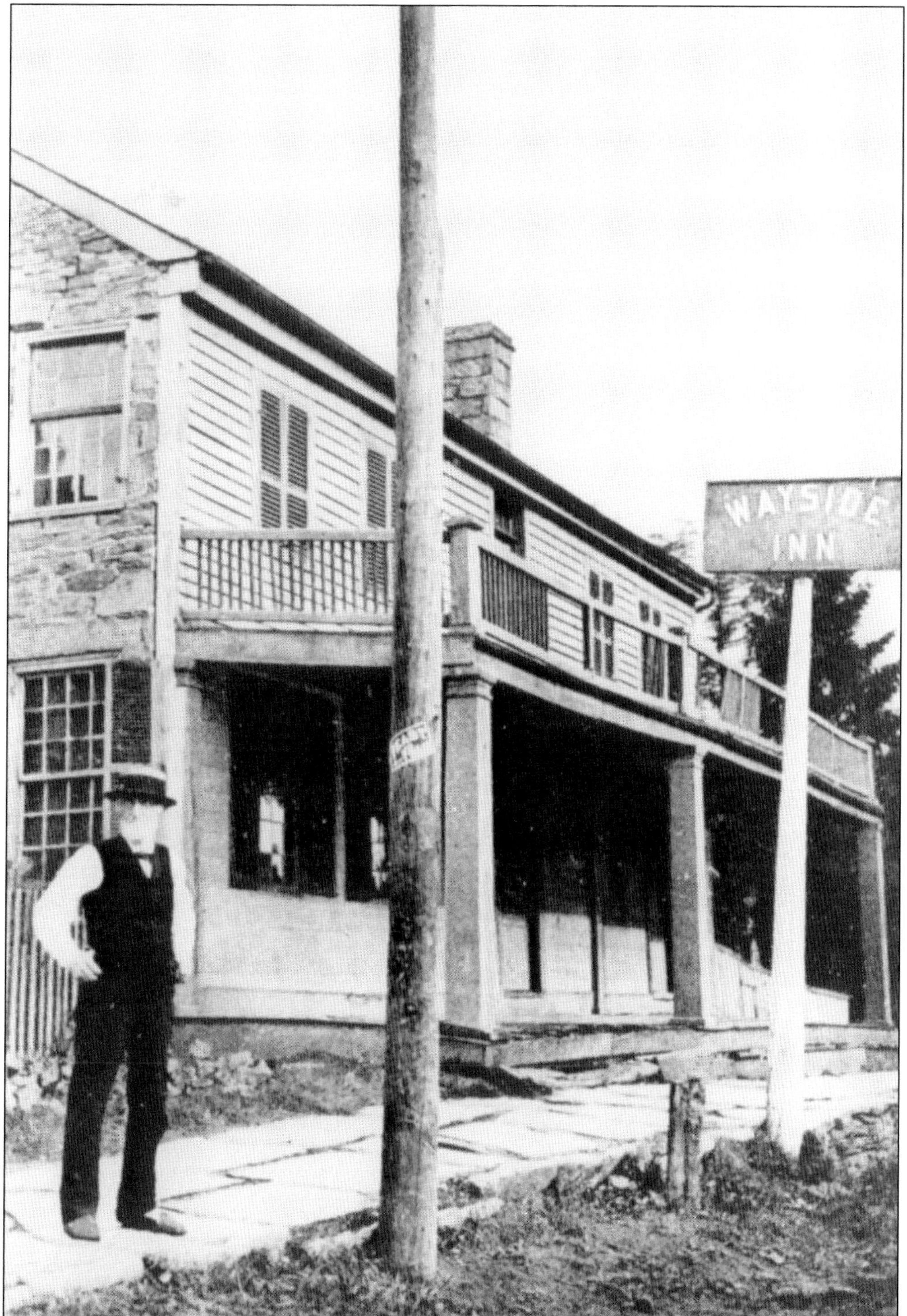

The Wayside Inn is seen here sometime between 1880 and 1890 and is now the Old Stone Tavern on South Main Street. (Courtesy of Poland Historical Society.)

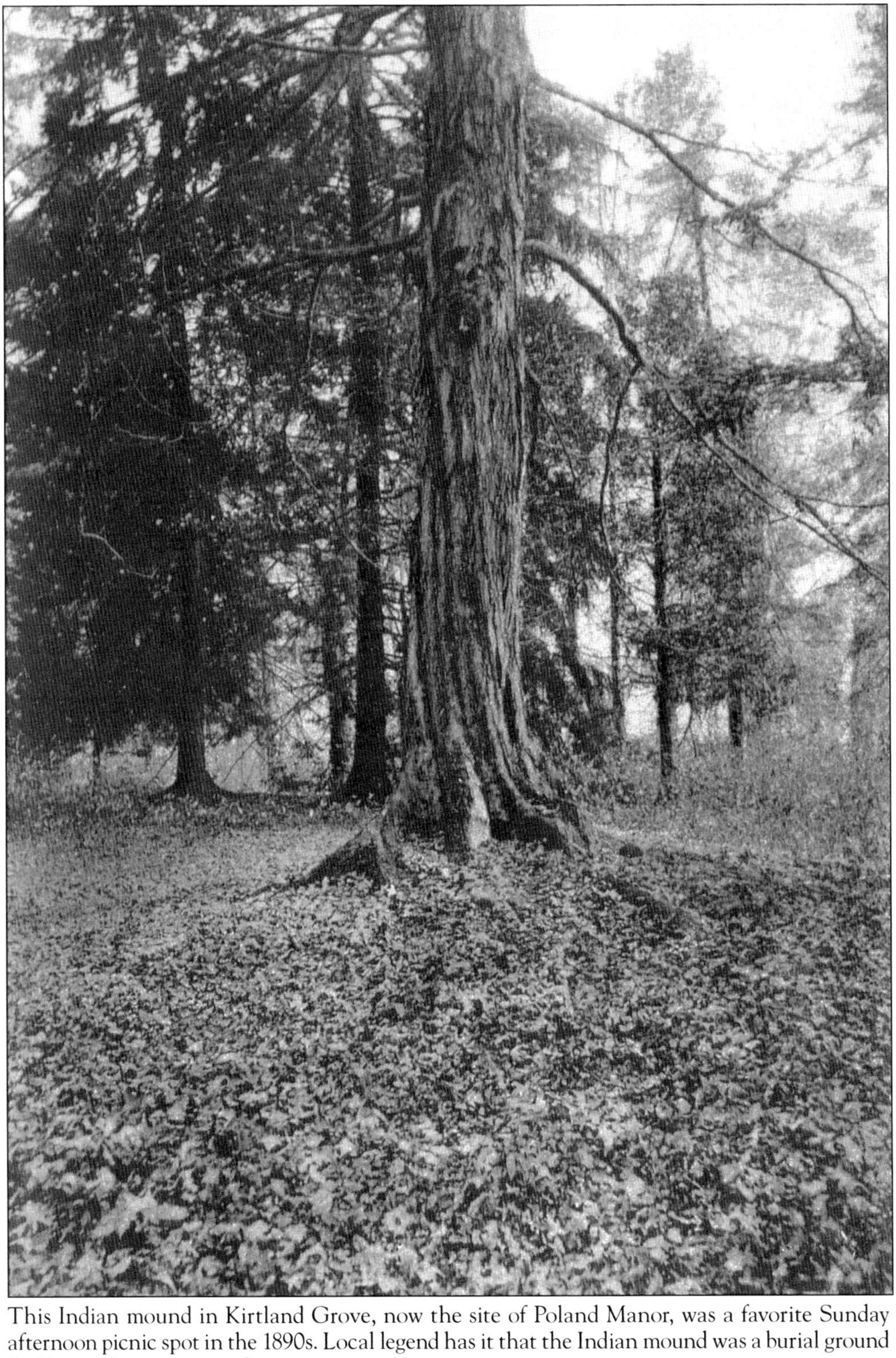

This Indian mound in Kirtland Grove, now the site of Poland Manor, was a favorite Sunday afternoon picnic spot in the 1890s. Local legend has it that the Indian mound was a burial ground for Native Americans in the area.

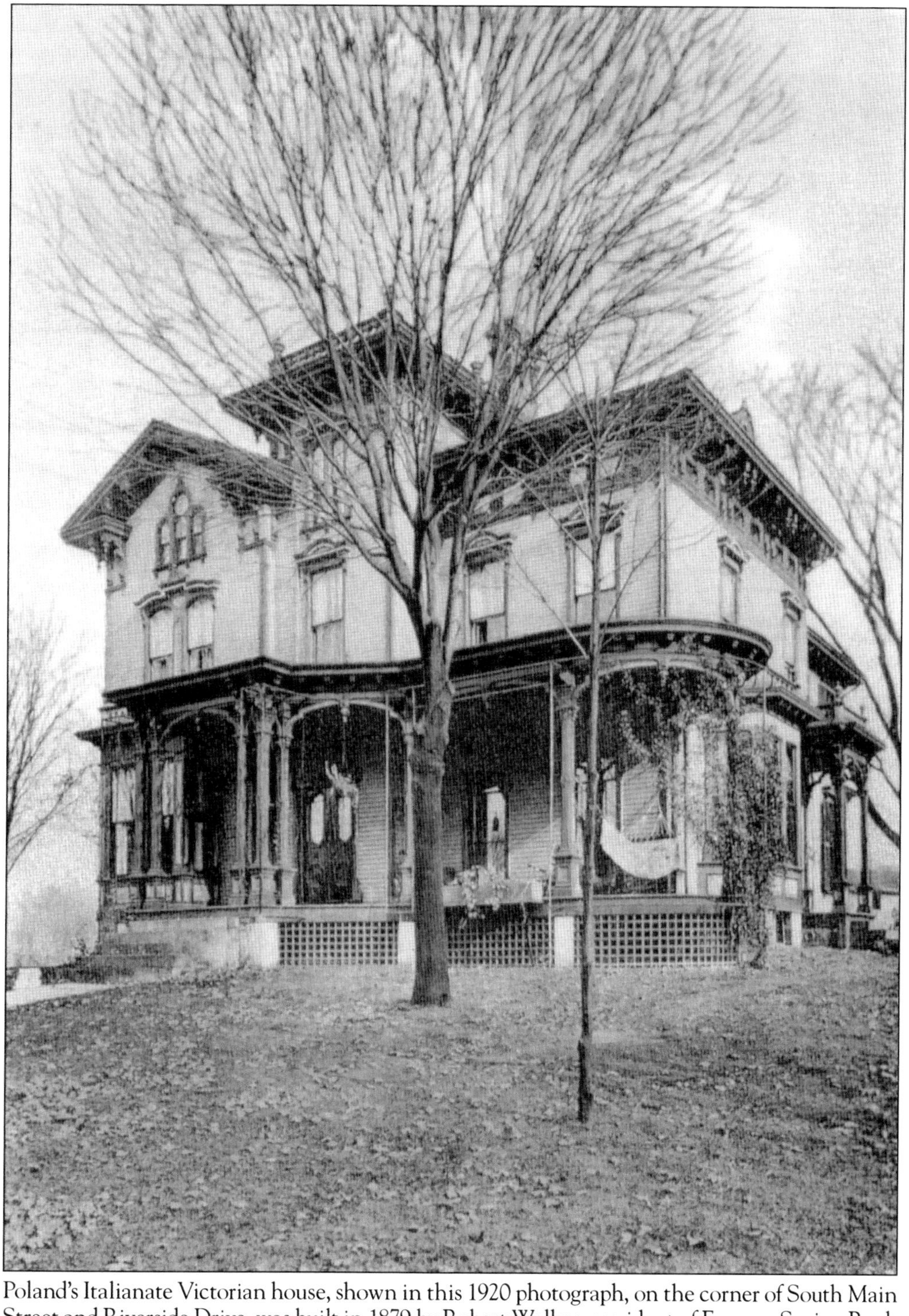

Poland's Italianate Victorian house, shown in this 1920 photograph, on the corner of South Main Street and Riverside Drive, was built in 1879 by Robert Walker, president of Farmers Saving Bank next door. It has been extensively restored in recent years to its original appearance. (Courtesy of Poland Historical Society.)

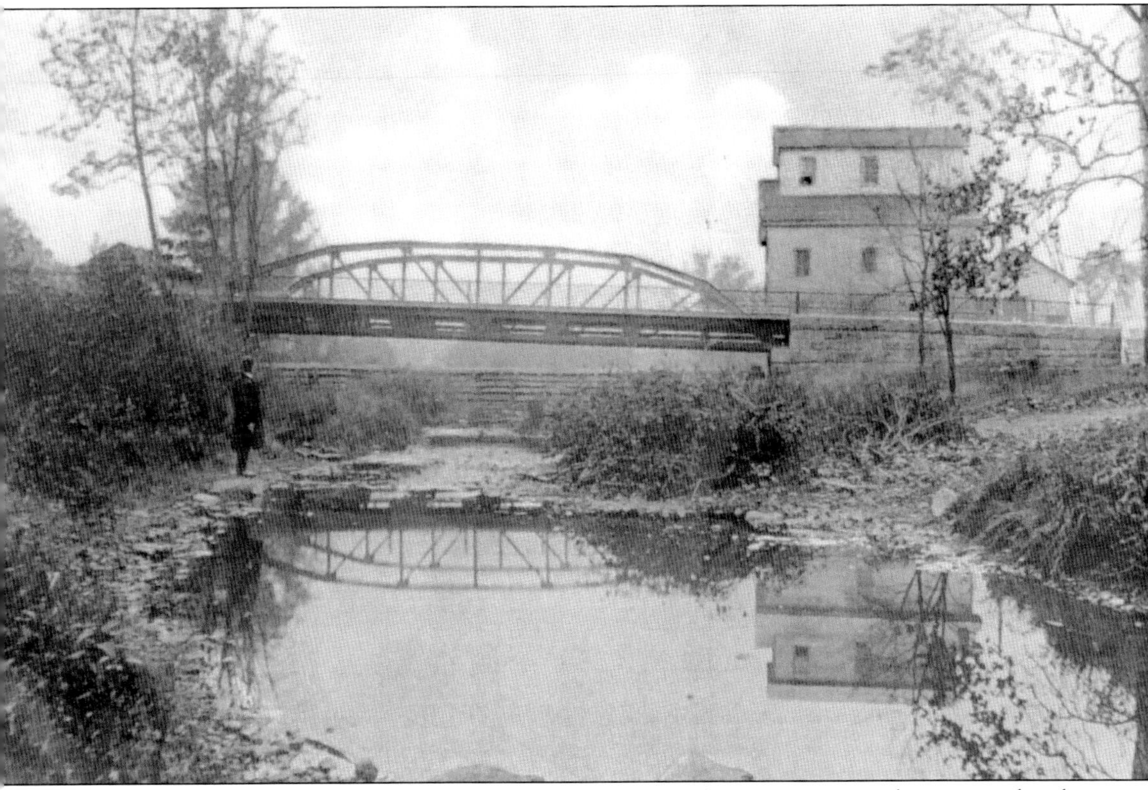

The new Main Street bridge over Yellow Creek is shown above just as it was being completed in 1920 as part of the widening of Main Street from one lane. The photograph is labeled "Mill and Dam, Poland, Ohio." The town grew around this point of Yellow Creek, not only for the water source in early times, but because it was the lowest point to ford the creek. (Courtesy of Poland Historical Society.)

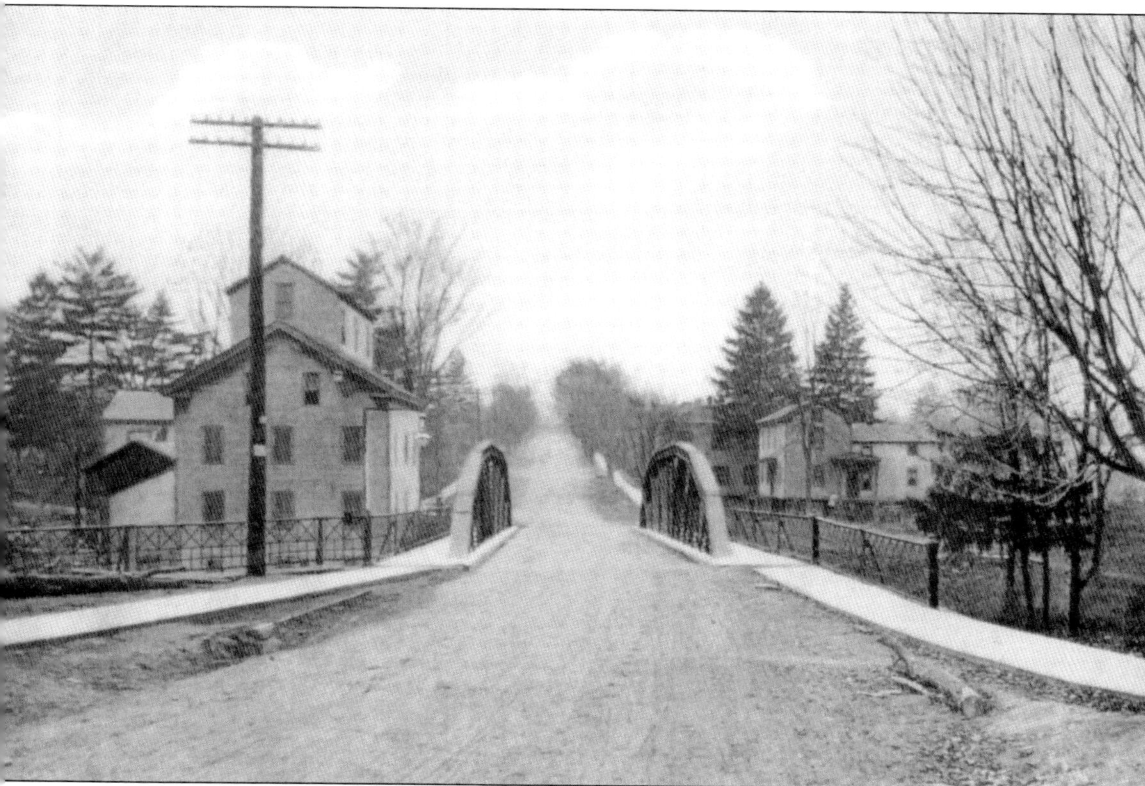

The Yellow Creek Bridge on South Main Street in 1919 still shows dirt roads just before the 1920 paving. (Courtesy of Poland Historical Society.)

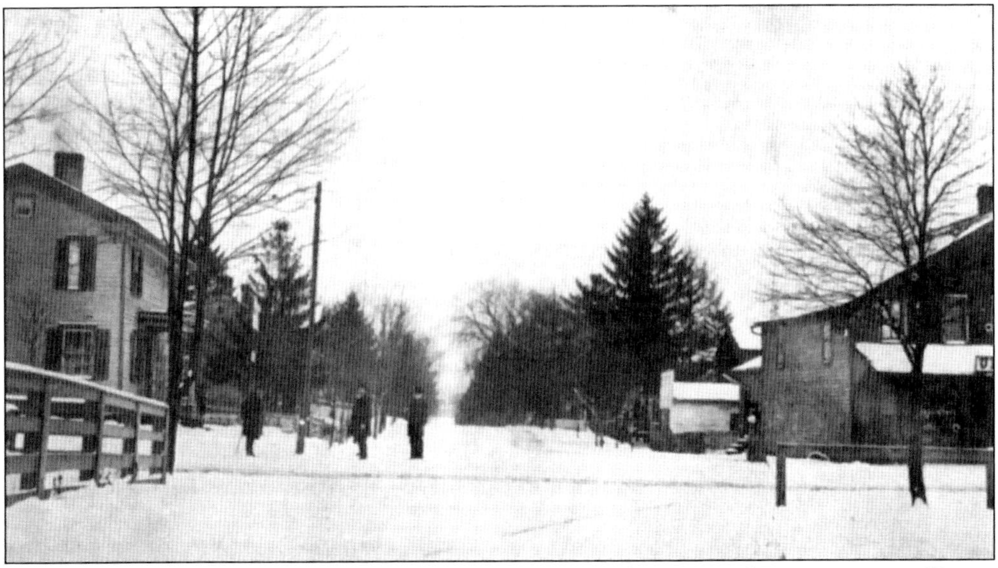

This picture shows men standing roadside, around 1890, at what is now the intersection of Route 224 and Water Street. (Courtesy of Poland Historical Society.)

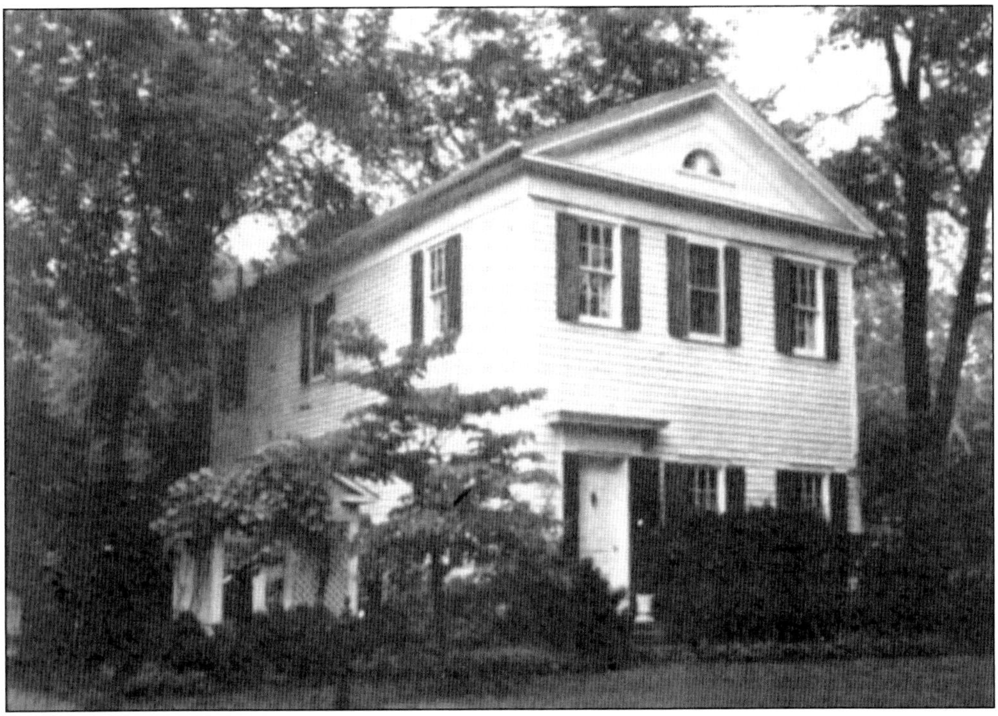

This is Poland's old historic dormitory on South Main Street as it looked in the 1960s. It once housed the boys attending the academy and then the Seminary on College Street. Built in 1846 to be a residence and store of John Hunter, in 1862 it became a boys dormitory until the early 1900s. The old wooden mantel over the fireplace in the main living room still carries initials carved by the boys who boarded there. Later in the mid 1900s it was the long time residence of the Steinfeld family. In the 1970s it became the corporate headquarters of Panelmatic and in 2001 the old structure was incorporated into the new public library building.

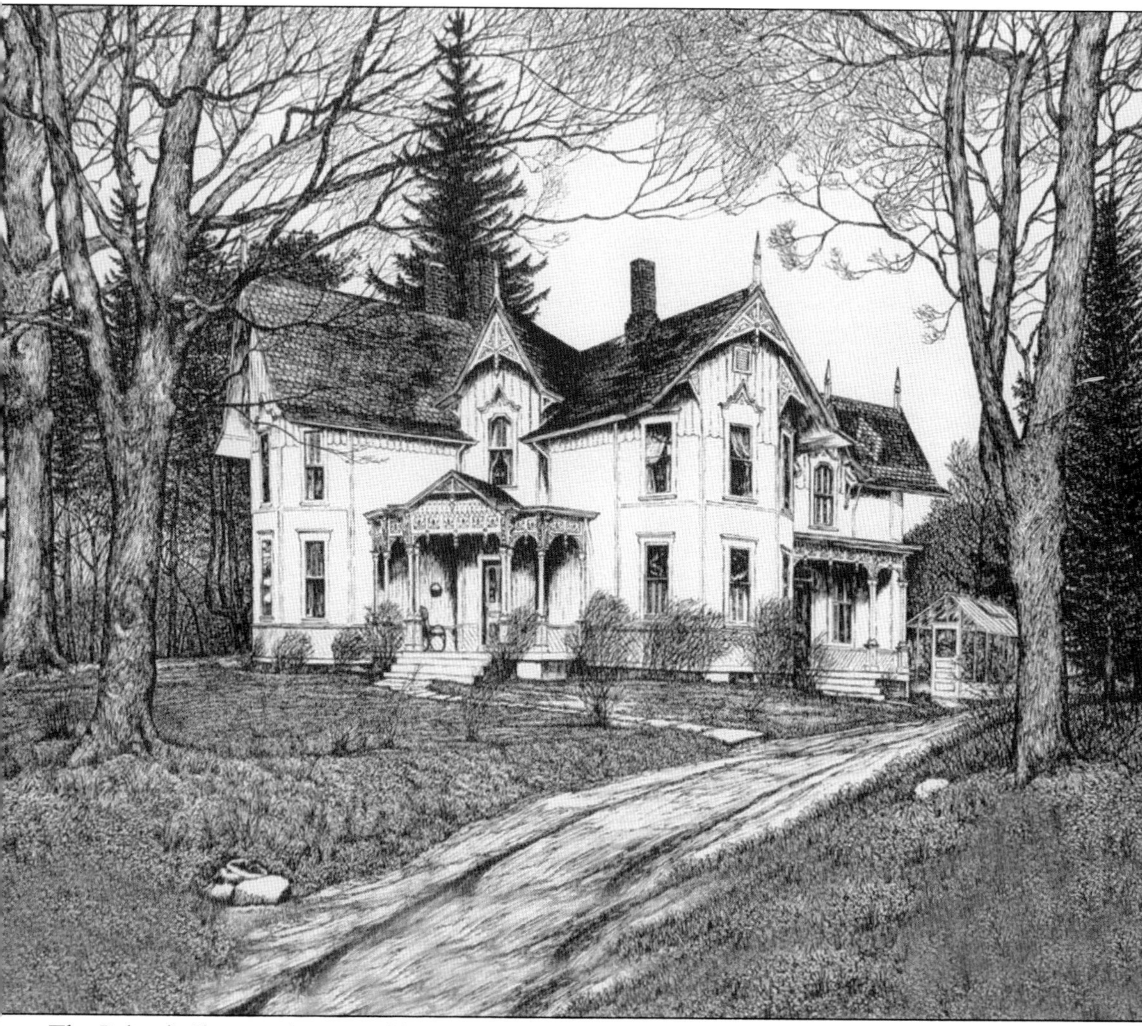

The Poland's "house of seven gables" once stood on the site of what is now the Farmer's Bank Building. Built in the Victorian Age, around the 1870s, it was torn down in the early 1960s. Five of seven gables are shown here, two were on the back side of the house. In the early 1950s, this residence was a very popular bed and breakfast.

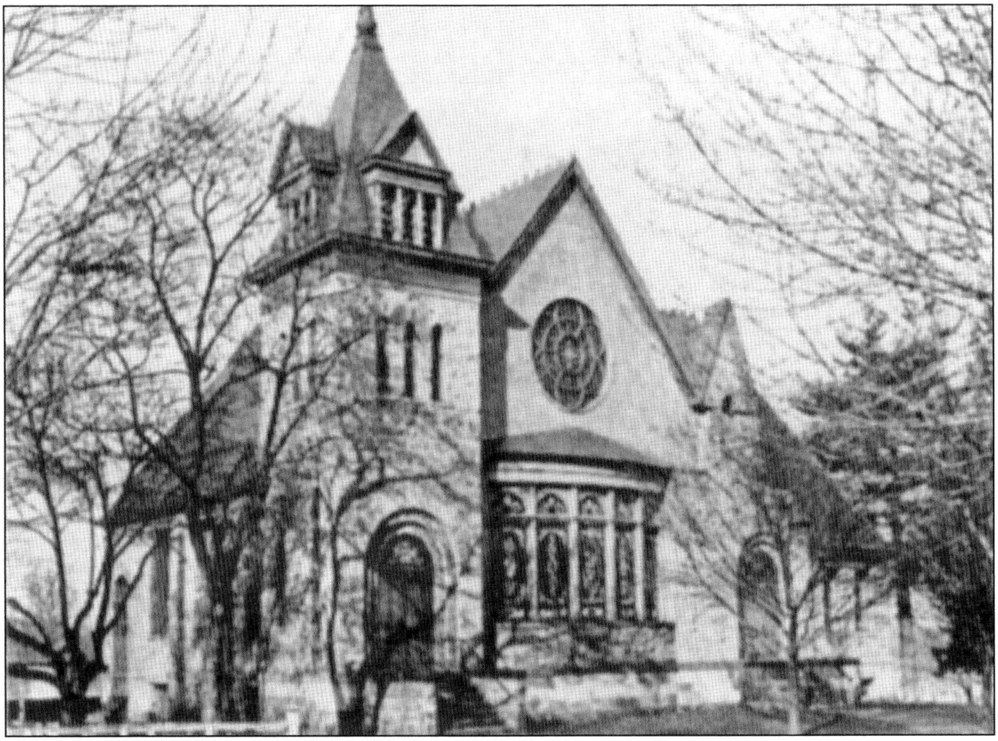

Here is how the Poland Presbyterian Church looked when it was built in 1897. (Courtesy of Poland Historical Society.)

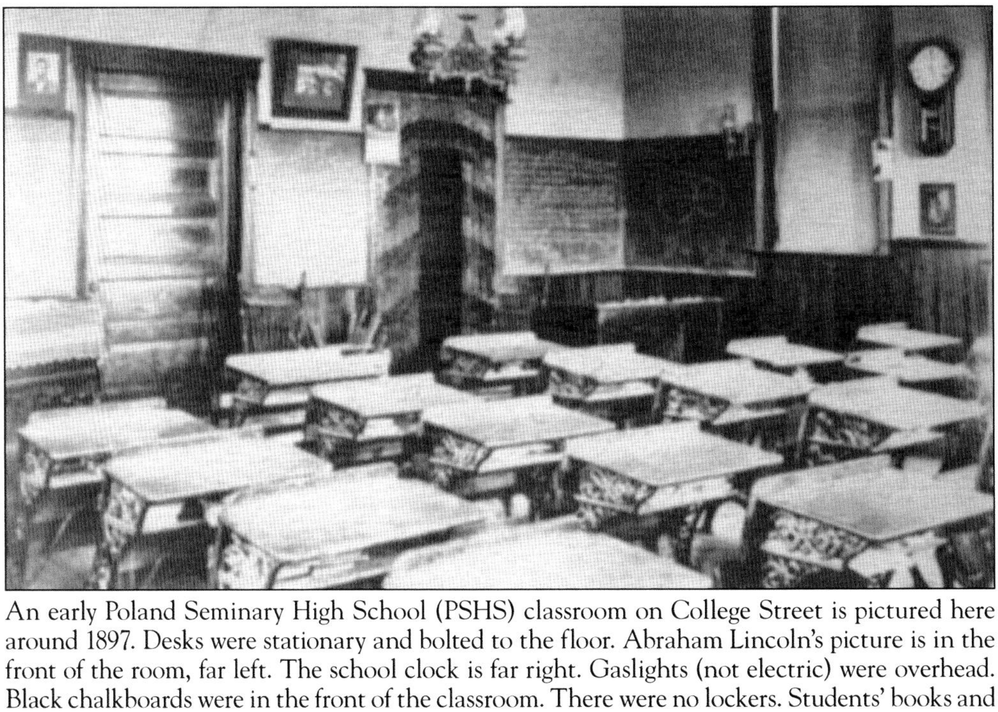

An early Poland Seminary High School (PSHS) classroom on College Street is pictured here around 1897. Desks were stationary and bolted to the floor. Abraham Lincoln's picture is in the front of the room, far left. The school clock is far right. Gaslights (not electric) were overhead. Black chalkboards were in the front of the classroom. There were no lockers. Students' books and personal items were placed on a shelf under each desk. (Courtesy of Poland schools' archives.)

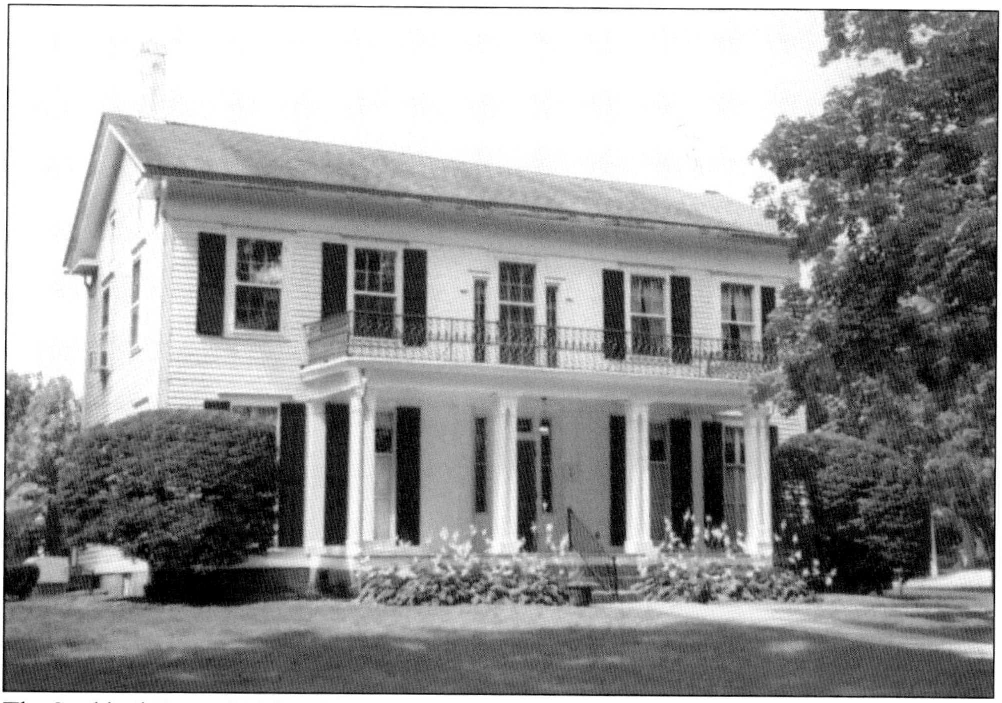

The Stoddard House, 308 South Main Street, was built in 1845 for Charles Stoddard, who owned and operated a tannery on the south side of Yellow Creek near the dam and bridge. It was a private residence until 1960, when it was acquired from the estate of Judge Kennedy for use as Village Hall.

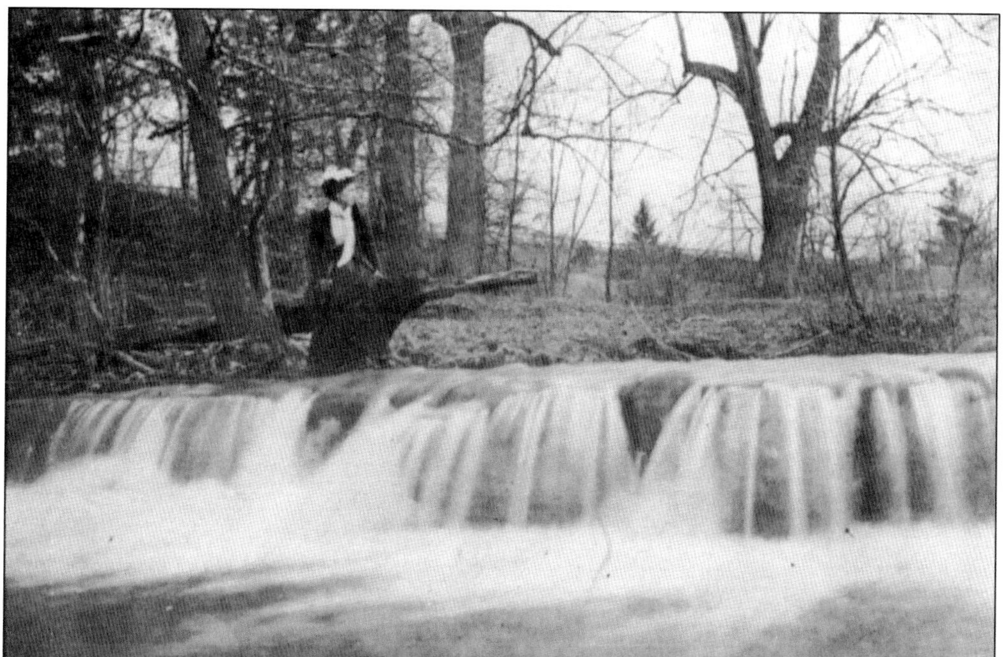

This 1900 photograph shows a pretty view of a Victorian lady by Yellow Creek "Falls," near what is today known as Cemetery Bridge. (Courtesy of Poland Historical Society.)

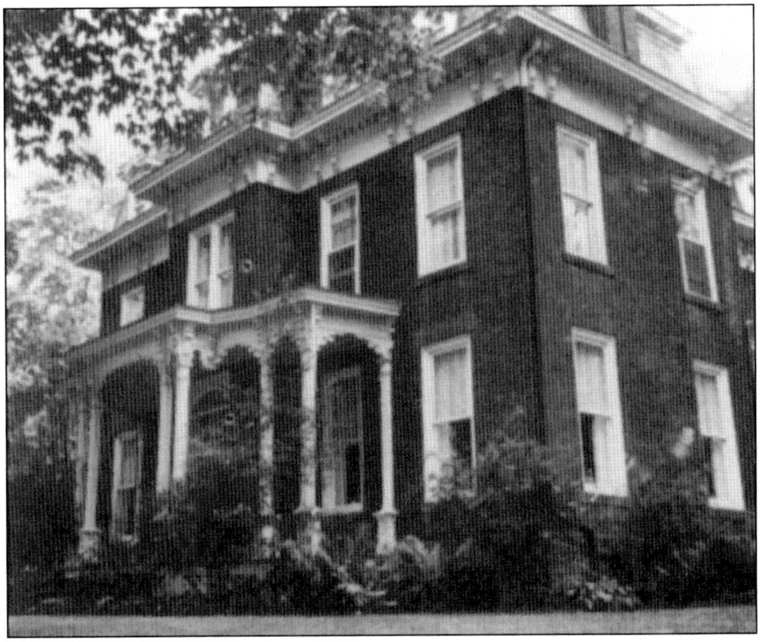

The Walter Arrel House, 500 South Main Street today, was built about 1876 as a brick Victorian by Walter Arrel for his wife, who preferred life in the village to the Arrel Farm. For a brief time in the 20th century, it was the "Tally Ho Tavern." Since 1986, it has been The Inn at the Green Bed and Breakfast. (Courtesy Poland Historical Society.)

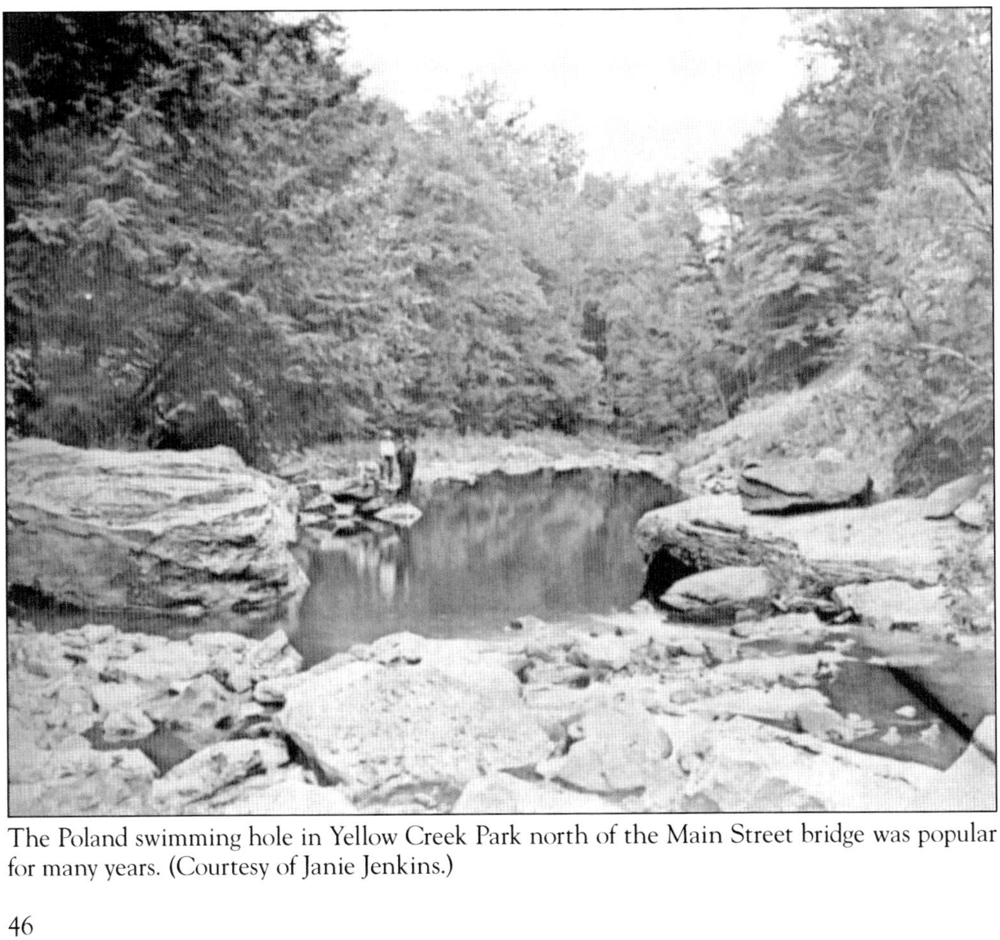

The Poland swimming hole in Yellow Creek Park north of the Main Street bridge was popular for many years. (Courtesy of Janie Jenkins.)

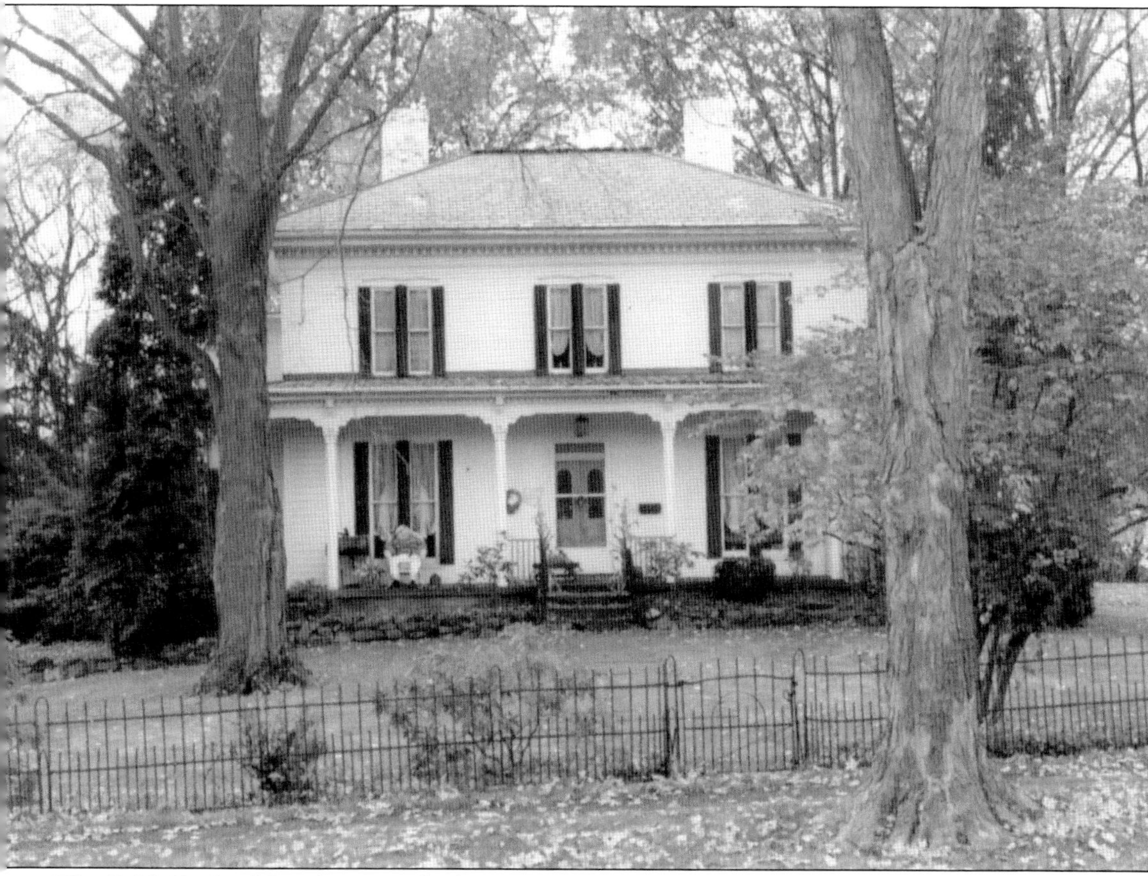

The C. N. Kirtland Residence was built in 1873 on North Lima Road. The Kirtland Woods are now the site of Poland Manor and were behind this home. The Indian Burial Mound was also behind this home in the woods close to Yellow Creek. In more recent times it was the home of prominent Attorney Osborne Mitchell.

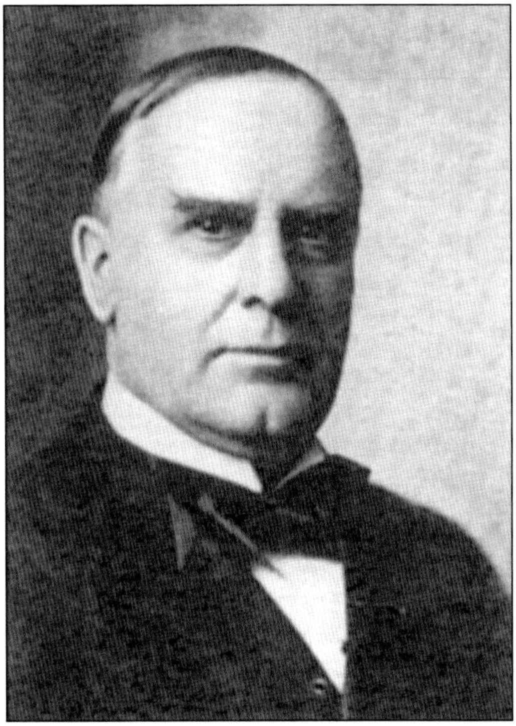

William McKinley is seen here as he appeared in the late 1890s when he was president of the United States. In 1876, he was elected to the Ohio House of Representatives, as Ohio's governor in 1891, and as the 25th president in 1896. He was the last veteran of the Civil War to be elected president. After attending Poland Academy, he went to Allegheny College, returning to teach in Poland Township in what is now referred to as "Poland's little red schoolhouse," which is still on Route 224 east of Poland. His salary was $25 monthly. He would walk the two and a half miles to the school from his home on South Main Street. (Courtesy of Poland Historical Society.)

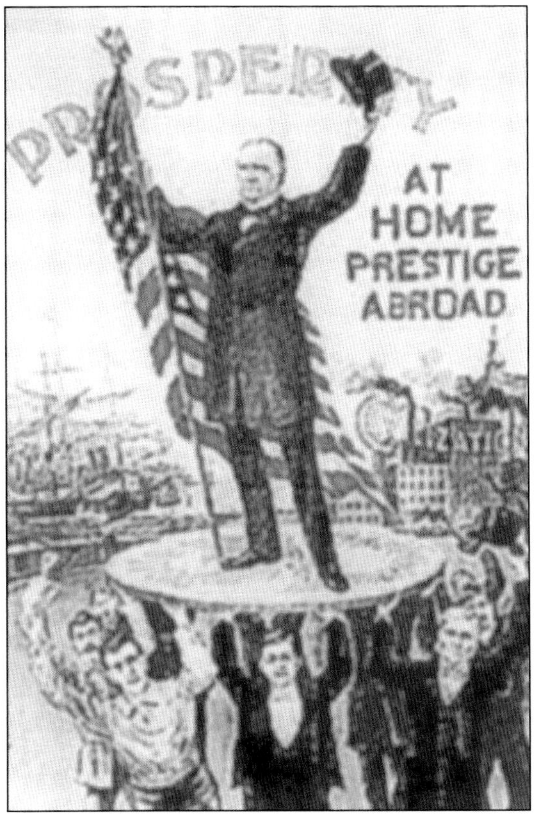

William McKinley, the 25th President of the United States is shown here in a 1900 photograph. He was the first president to use telephones and telegraphs with the new media. At the age of 58, he was shot by an assassin's bullet when attending the Pan American Exposition in Buffalo, New York, on September 6, 1901. (Photograph by Charles Parker.)

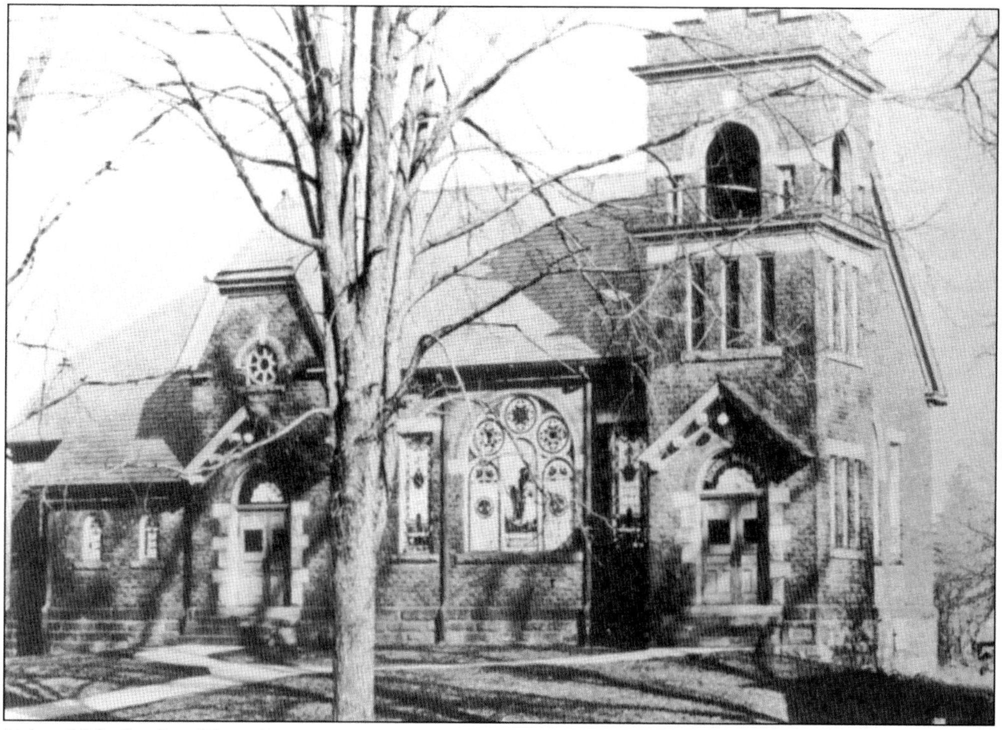

Poland Methodist Church on North Main Street was built in 1904 but burned down in 1957. It is now the site north of Chase Bank. (Courtesy of Poland Historical Society.)

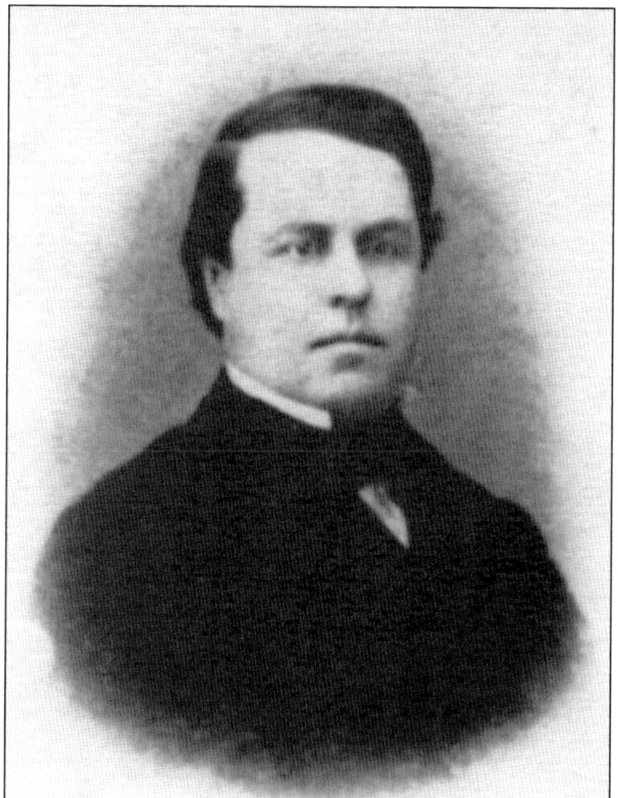

Judge Charles Glidden, a professor at the Poland Law School and one of William McKinley's law teachers following the Civil War, is shown here. (Courtesy of Poland schools' archives.)

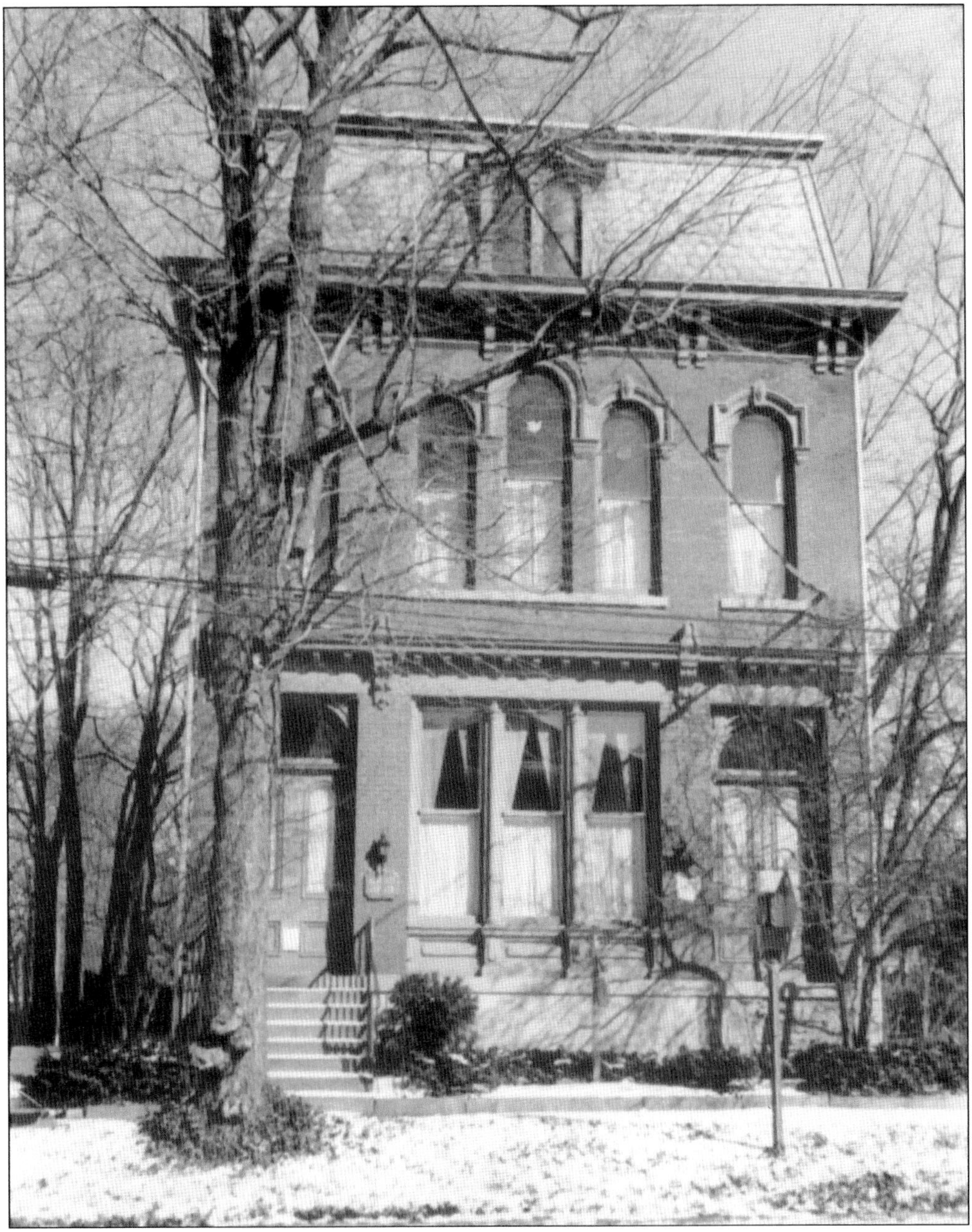

Poland's old bank is shown in this 1920 photograph. The three-story red brick structure on South Main Street was built in 1874 as the Farmers Deposit and Savings Bank. The ceiling of the vault was made of seven huge stones, each a foot thick and 16 inches wide. The bank president was Robert Walker, who lived next door in the large Victorian house. The bank was liquidated in 1874 and the building today houses several apartments. (Courtesy of Poland Historical Society.)

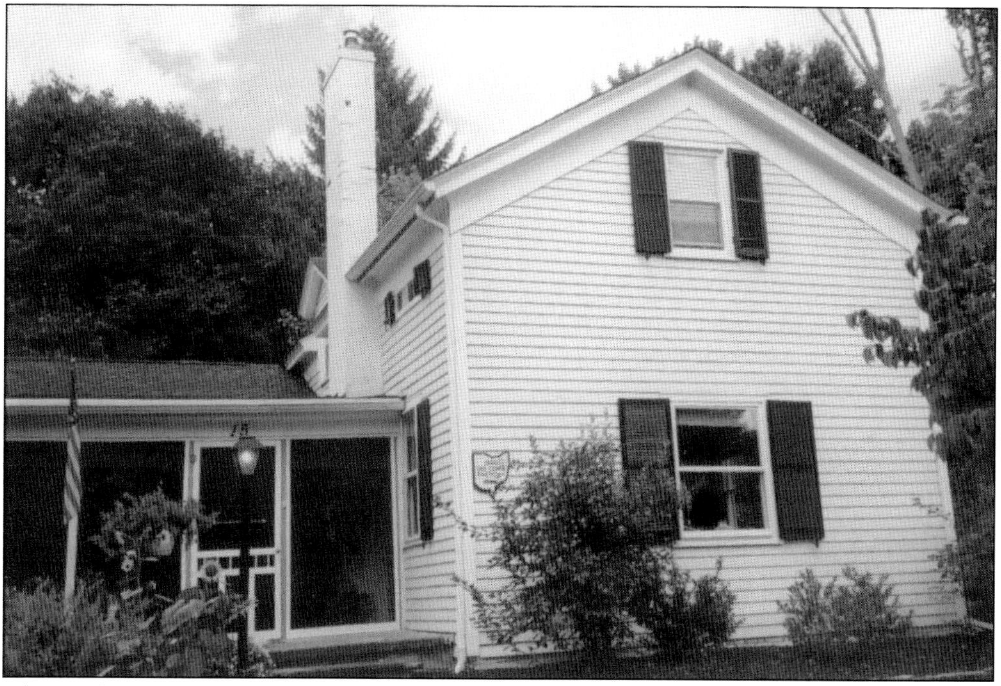

This residence at 15 Water Street was built around 1826 as a "comb factory" in Poland's business district. It is now a residence. The original building is on the right. The screened-in porch on the left is, of course, a recent addition.

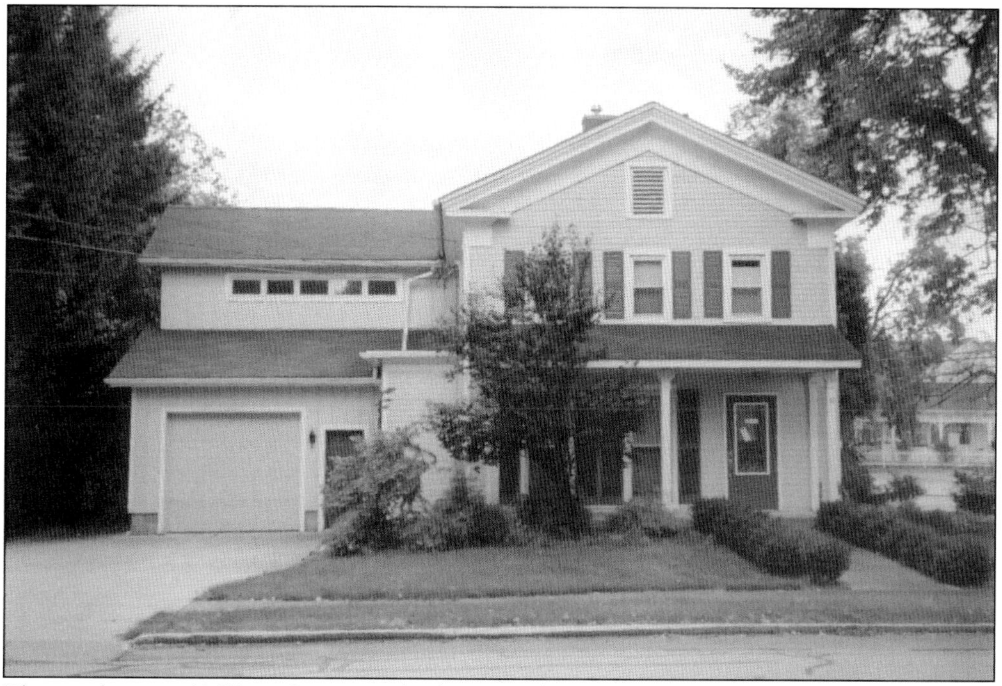

This residence at 10 Water Street was built in 1876 by Adam Case as a tailor shop, bringing the first Singer sewing machine to Poland. The original home is on the right, and the attached garage on the left is a recent addition.

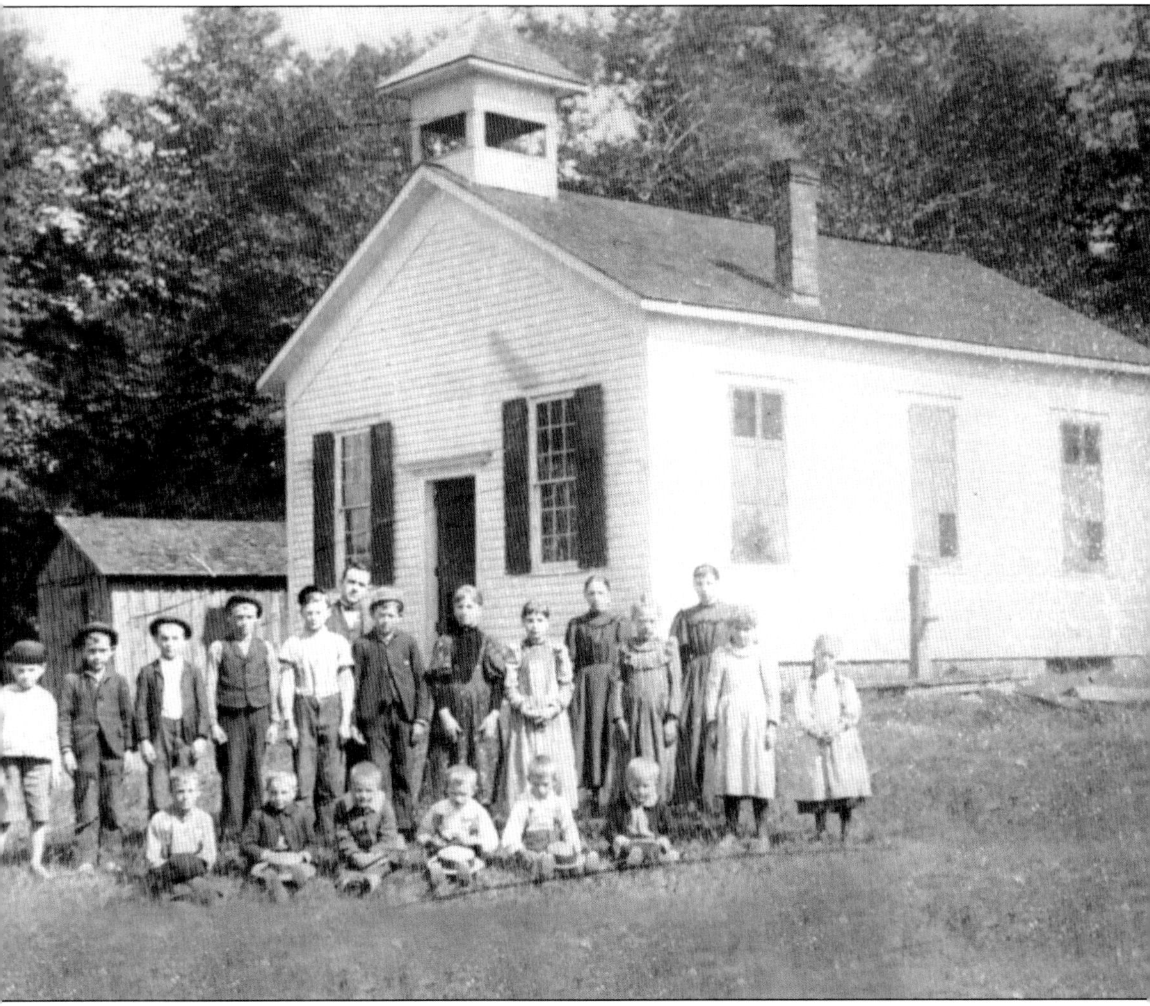

Poland had many one-room schoolhouses such as Kansas Corners, shown here in 1908 with Mr. Faust, the teacher. Notice the varying ages of pupils, as all grade levels were taught together in the same schoolroom. This school was located on Kansas Road at the corner of Moore Road. (Courtesy of Poland schools' archives.)

Mr. and Mrs. Cleland, who lived on Water Street, pose in this 1900 photograph. The Cleland home is still a residence today. (Courtesy of Poland Historical Society.)

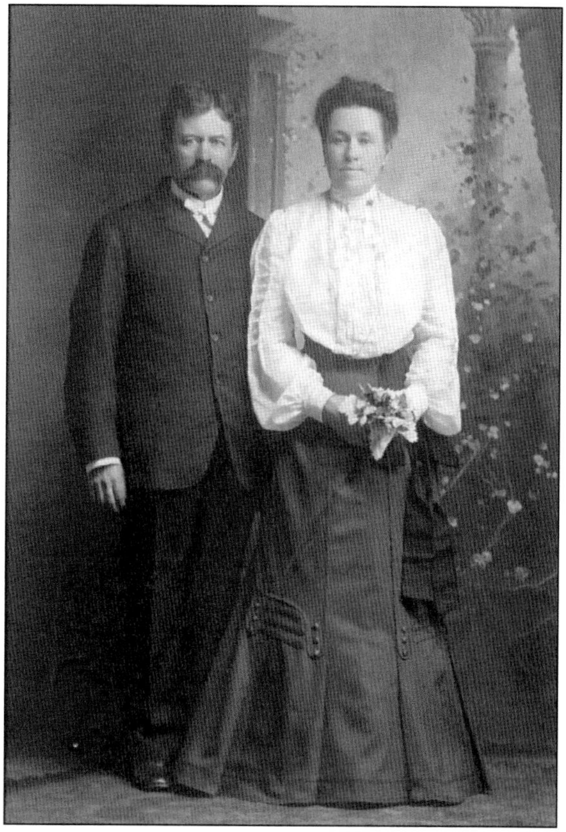

Mollie Cleland stands in front of their home, which still stands today, on Water Street in this 1900 photograph. Mr. Cleland was clerk of Poland Village in 1900. (Courtesy of Poland Historical Society.)

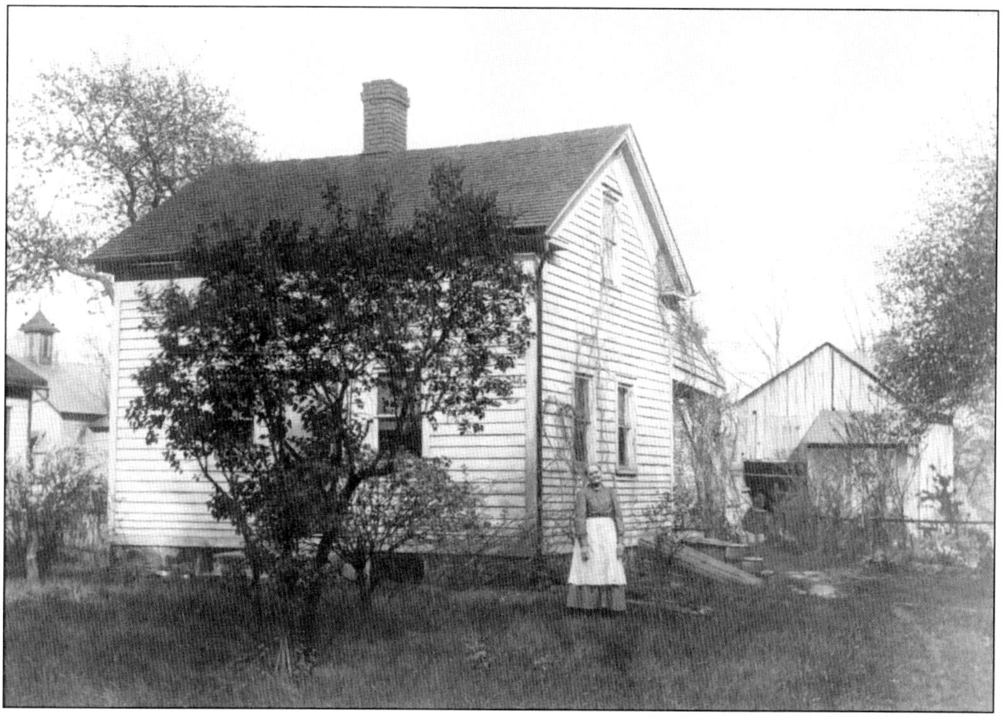

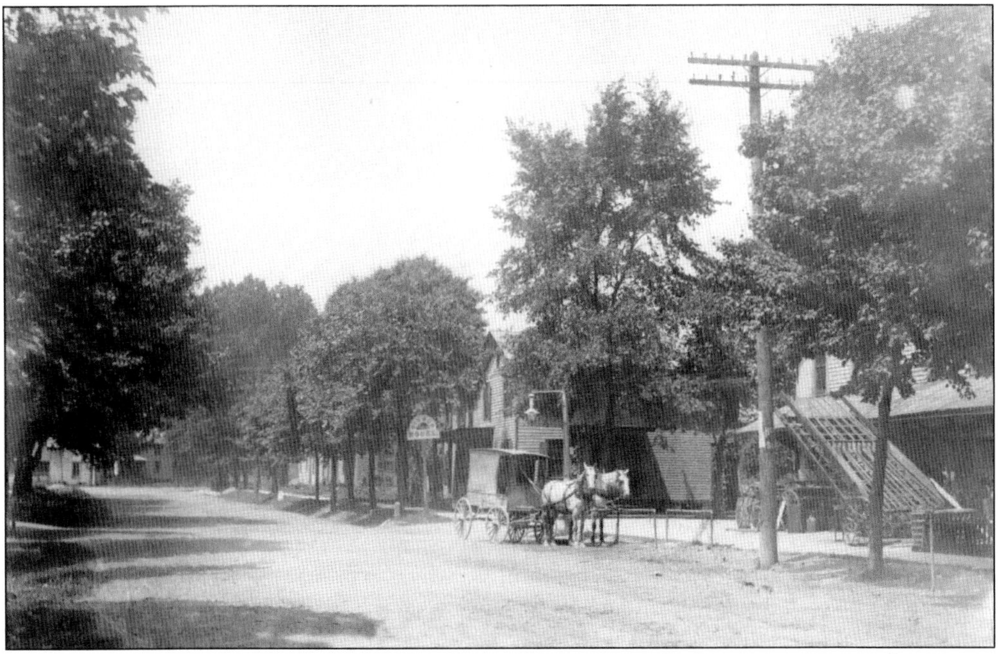

Poland's Main Street is shown in the 1890s. This is the same location as the 1945 cover photograph. (Courtesy of Poland Historical Society.)

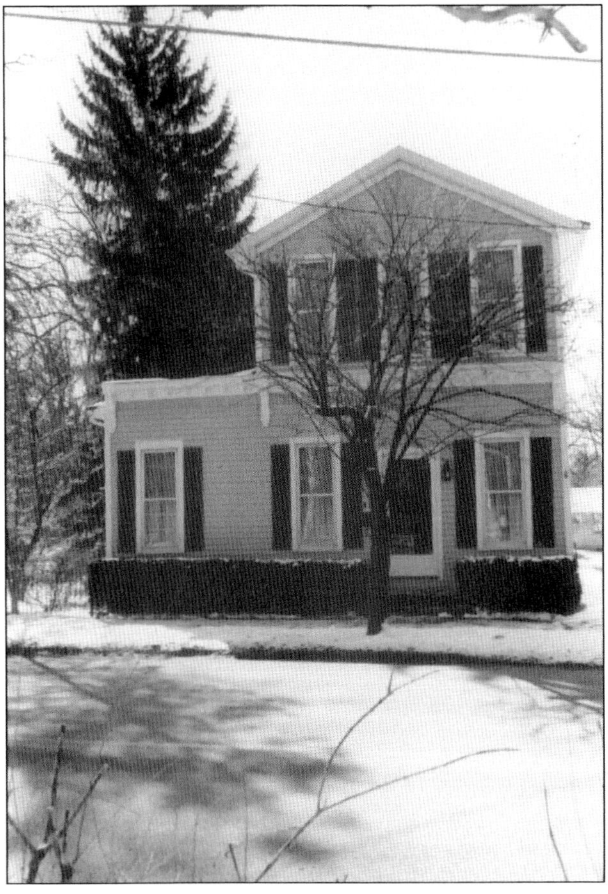

This building was constructed in 1855 as a drug store with the druggist's residence in the back of the store. Prior to its remodeling in 1969, it was a grocery store known to Poland kids in the 1960s as Schwartz's, where candy was a penny a piece. (Courtesy of Poland Historical Society.)

Membership cards in the William McKinley Memorial Association were sold in Poland to support the McKinley Memorial Building to be constructed in Niles, Ohio, the slain president's birthplace. This membership card is dated March 7, 1911. (Courtesy of Poland Historical Society.)

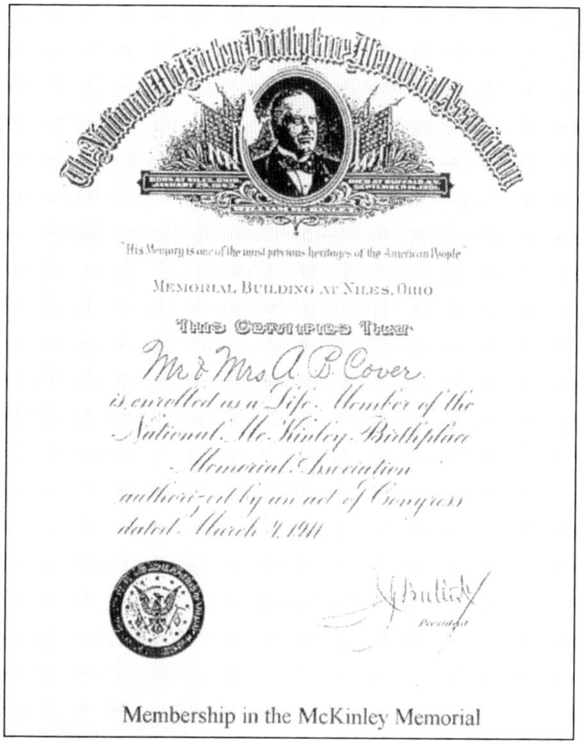

The National McKinley Birthplace Memorial Association

"His Memory is one of the most precious heritages of the American People"

Memorial Building at Niles, Ohio

This Certifies That

Mr & Mrs A. B. Cover

is enrolled as a Life Member of the National McKinley Birthplace Memorial Association authorized by an act of Congress dated March 4, 1911

Butler
President

Membership in the McKinley Memorial

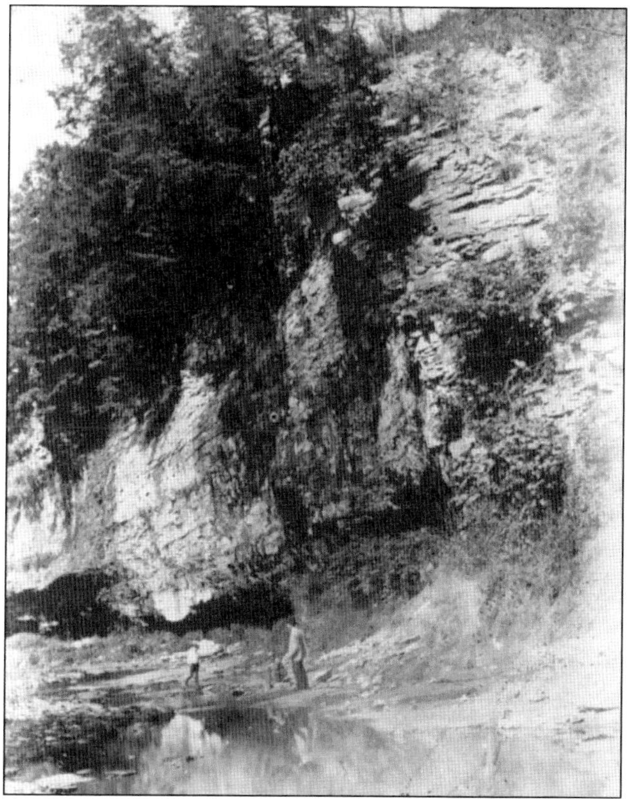

The palisades along Yellow Creek, north of Poland Village going toward Lake Hamilton, are very picturesque. Notice the father and son by the creek's edge (bottom center of photograph). (Courtesy of Poland Historical Society.)

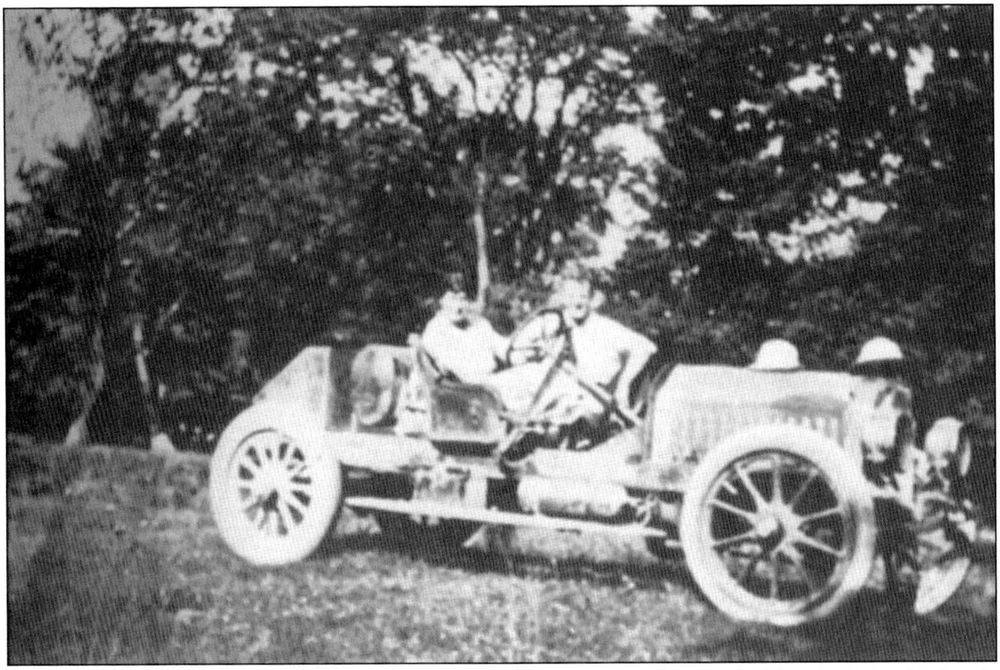

One of Poland's earliest cars, the "Peerless" automobile, is shown here in 1915 with Helen Richards and Jim Johnston. (Courtesy of Poland Historical Society.)

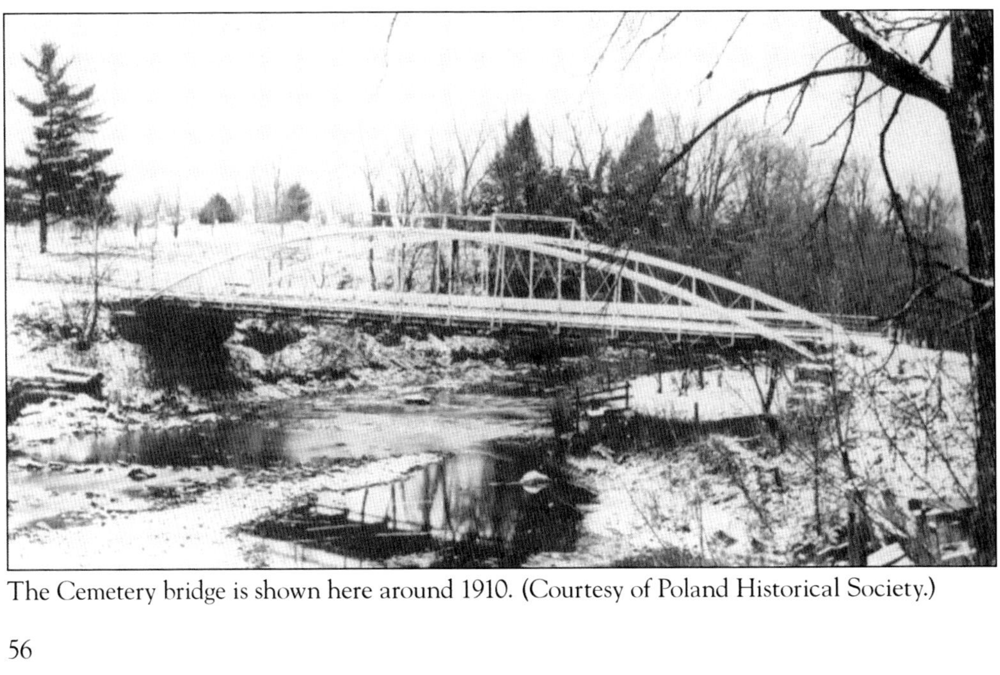

The Cemetery bridge is shown here around 1910. (Courtesy of Poland Historical Society.)

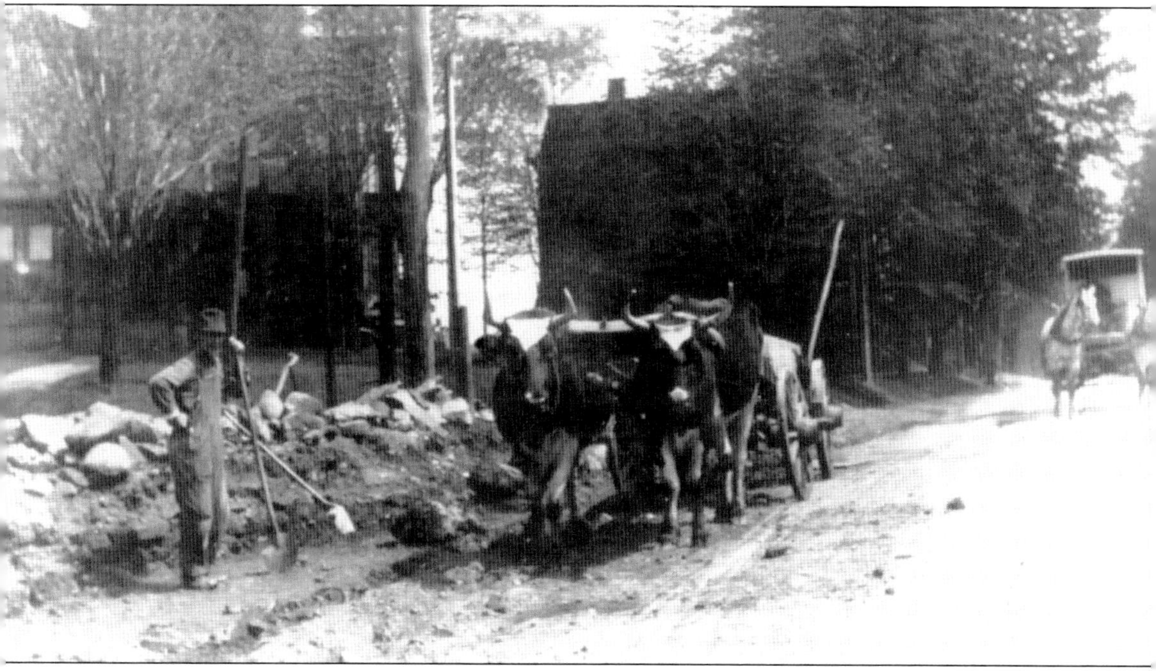

A pair of oxen is being used in the 1920 widening of Main Street at the intersection of what is now Riverside Drive. Notice the horses pulling a wagon on the right. The old bank is in the center of the photograph and the Victorian house is on the left. Main Street was widened to accommodate more traffic. The worker with the shovels, left of the center, is doing roadwork by hand. (Courtesy of Poland Historical Society.)

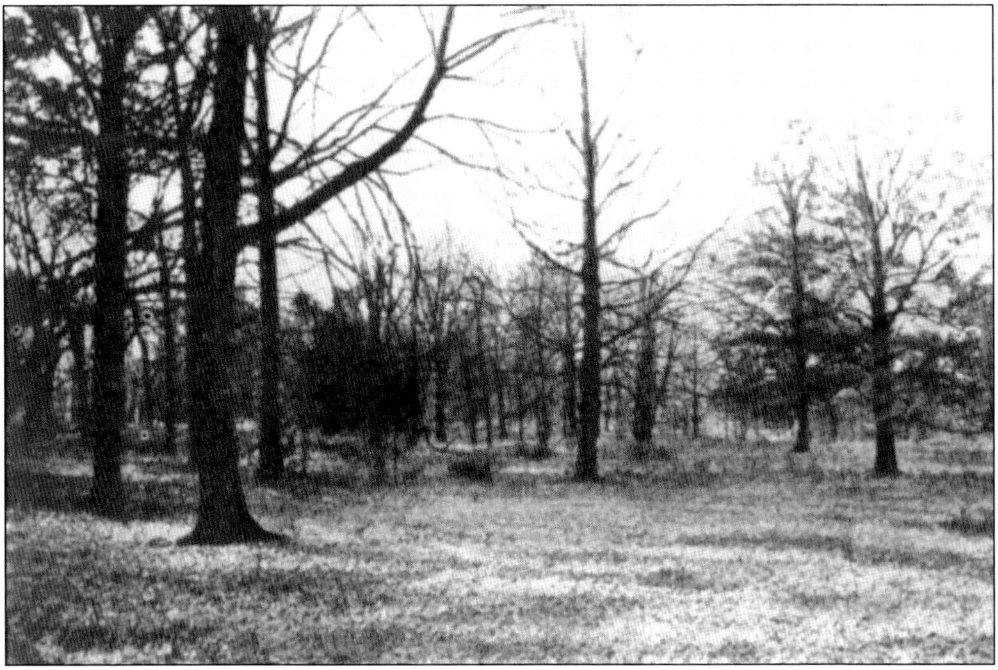

Kirtland Grove looking toward Yellow Creek in 1899 is now Poland Manor. (Courtesy of Poland Historical Society.)

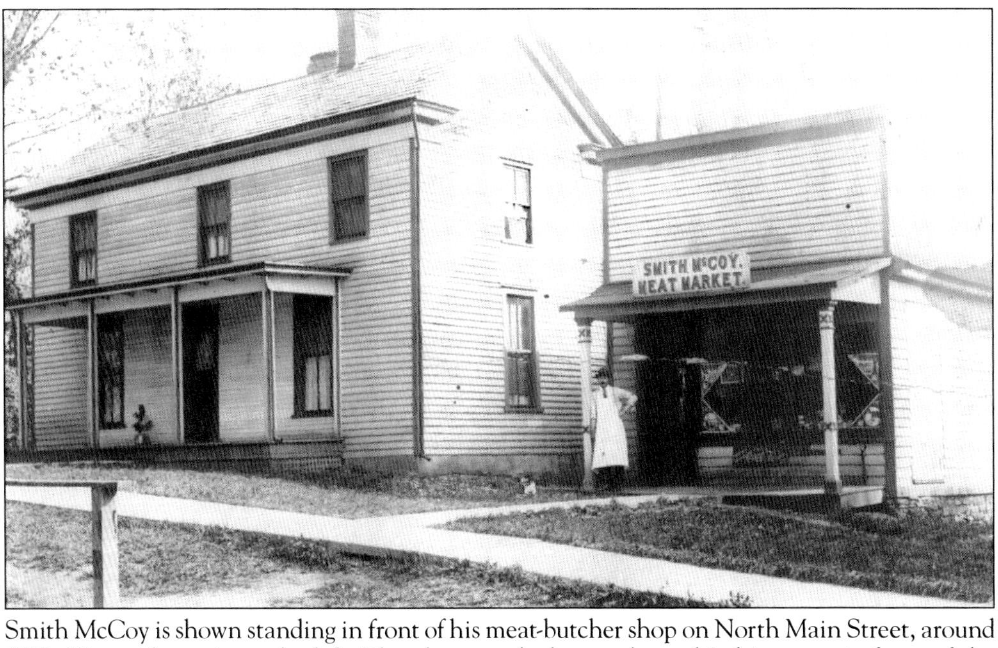

Smith McCoy is shown standing in front of his meat-butcher shop on North Main Street, around 1913. His residence is on the left. The photograph shows a horse hitching post in front of the store, lower left. (Courtesy of Poland Historical Society.)

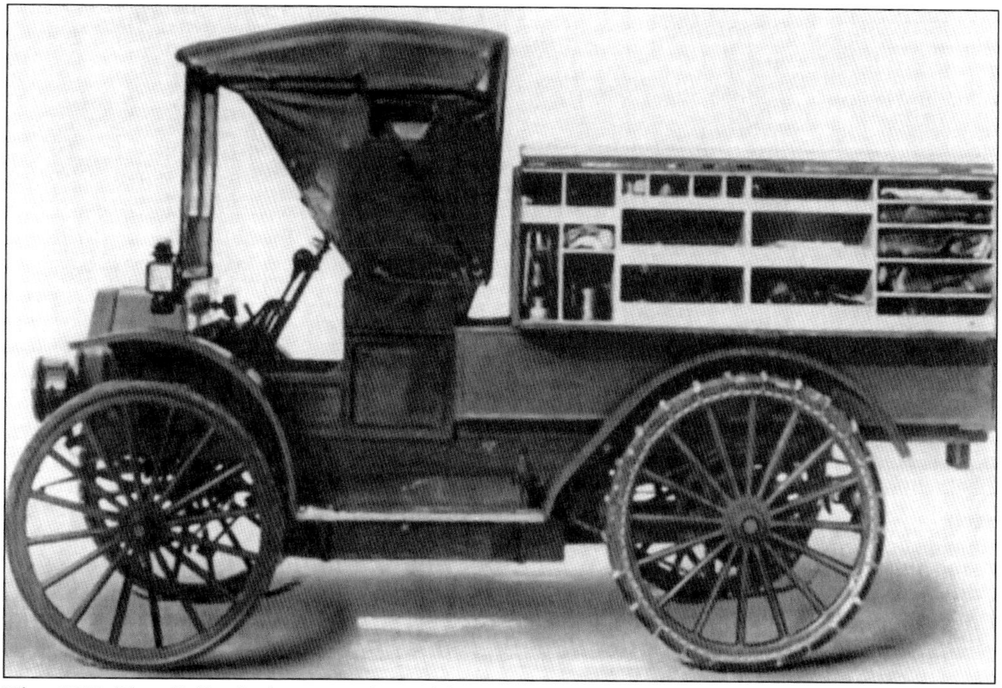

This 1917 Ohio Bell telephone truck would come from Youngstown to service the dozen phones in Poland at that time. (Courtesy of Poland Historical Society.)

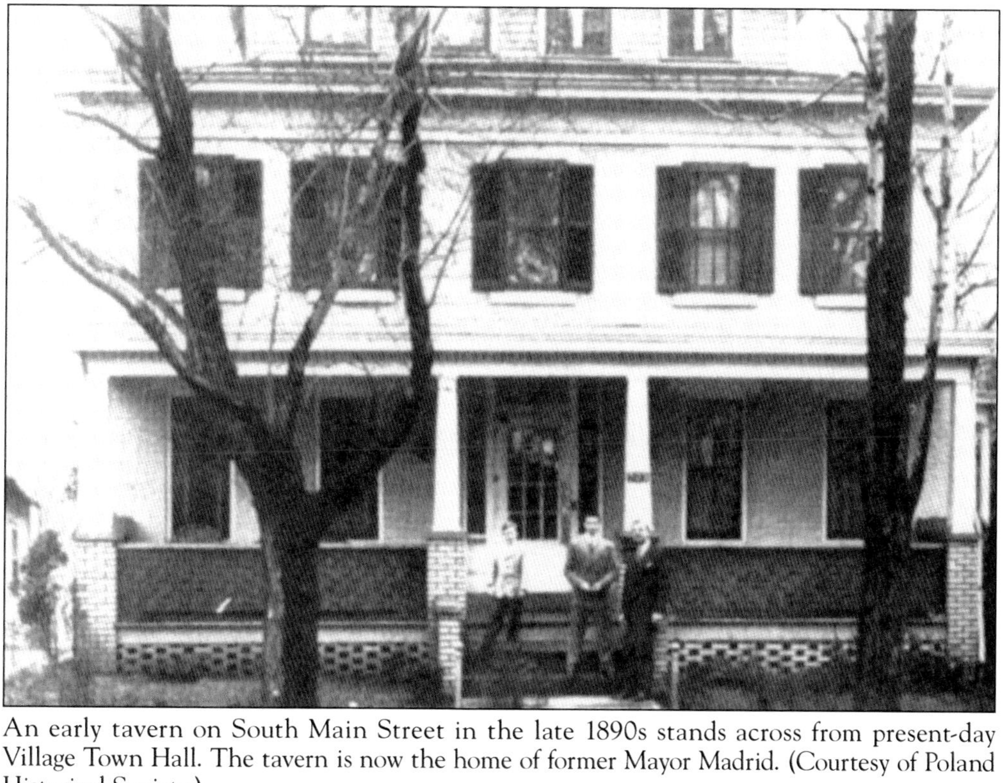

An early tavern on South Main Street in the late 1890s stands across from present-day Village Town Hall. The tavern is now the home of former Mayor Madrid. (Courtesy of Poland Historical Society.)

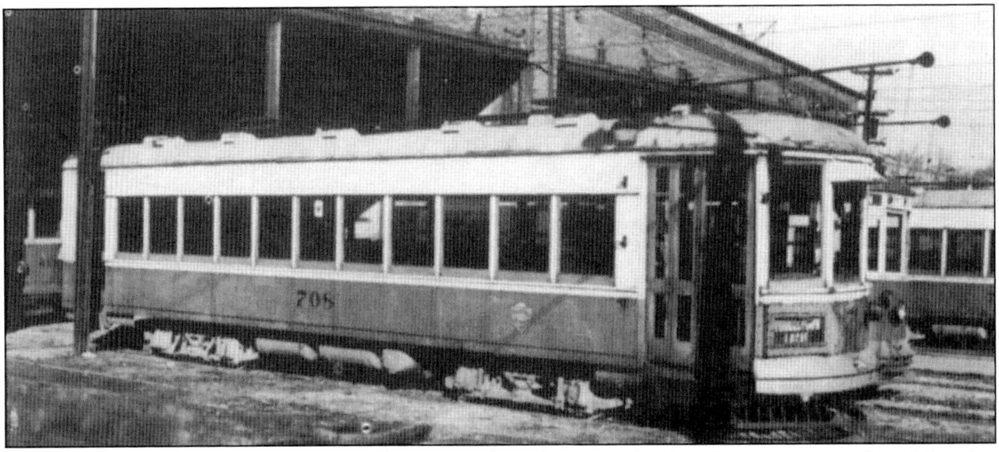

Poland's electric trolley No. 708 is shown in this photograph. Grading was completed for the right-of-way in 1913 for a streetcar trolley line from Youngstown to Poland, via Poland Avenue, Powers Way, and Sheridan Road. In 1940, the rails and trolley lines were removed and gasoline buses introduced. The main end-of-line and most popular stop on the Poland route was at the side street of what now is called The Inn at the Green. A sign there today reads, "Trolley Bus Stop 1913–1973." The bus route was discontinued when automobiles replaced mass transportation in 1973. This photograph shows the "Poland Trolley" in 1940 about to make its last run.

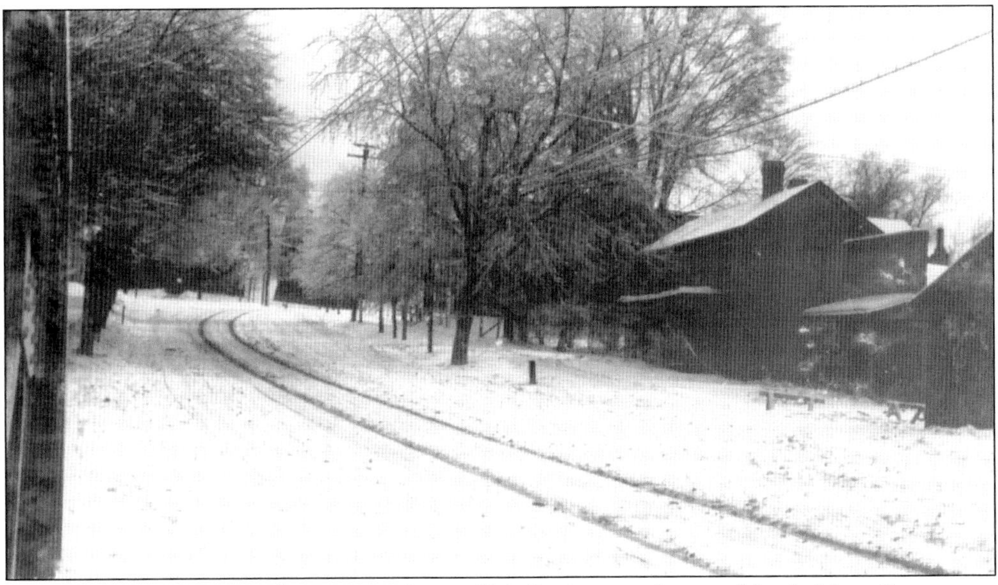

Rails of steel are seen in the snow in front of McCoy's meat shop on North Main Street near what is now the location of the Chase bank. The streetcar of "trolley," as it was called then, ran on these ribbons of steel in the roadway. The streetcar line ran from Youngstown to Poland via Powers Way to Sheridan Road to Main Street. This photograph was taken in 1913. (Courtesy of Poland Historical Society.)

A rare photograph of Poland's flour mill shows it being torn down in 1920. Note the windows are out and the pile of debris in the front of the mill as it is being dismantled. (Courtesy of Poland Historical Society.)

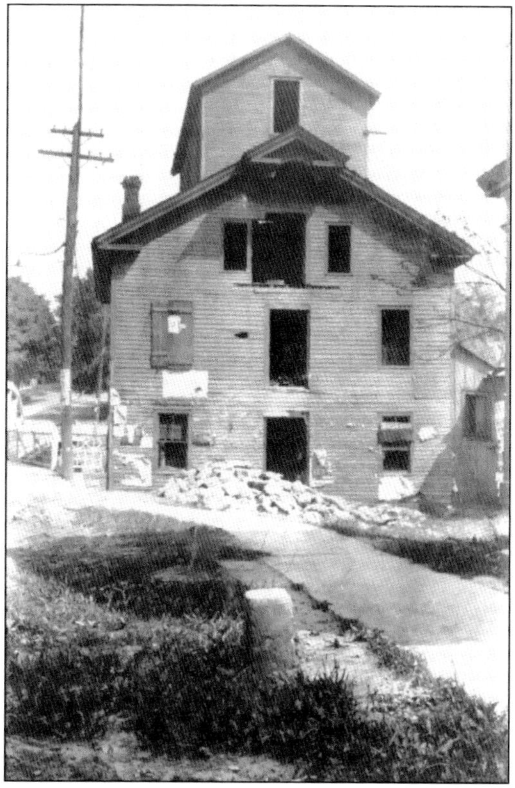

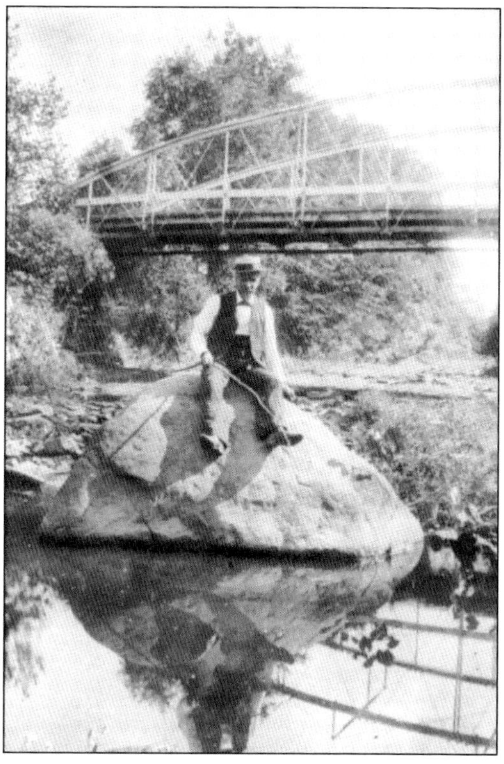

Frank Mansfield sits on the "Big Rock" in Yellow Creek before it was moved to Poland Cemetery by the Morse family. The cemetery bridge is in the background of this 1885 photograph. The rock today can be seen behind the Soldier Monument as the gravestone for Civil War veteran Morse.

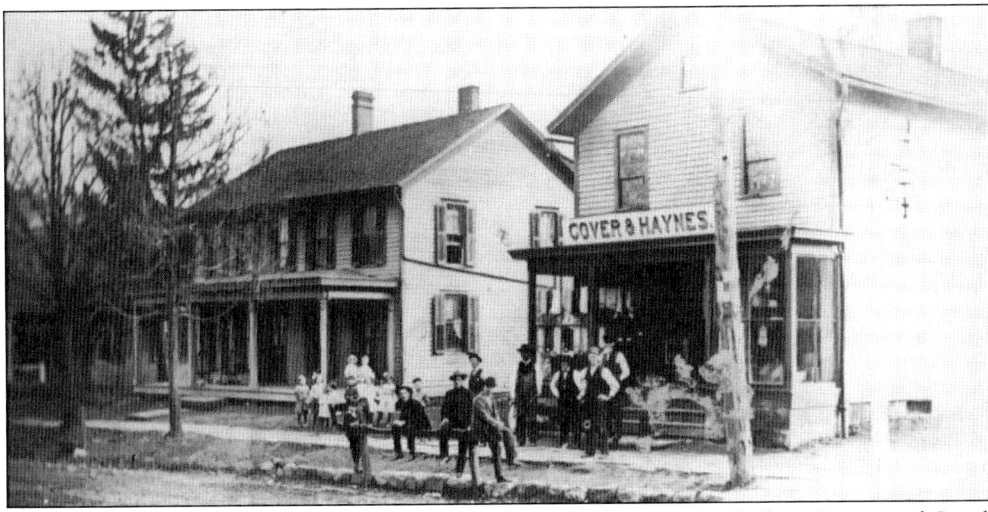

Cover and Haynes General Store was at the corner of what is now College Street and South Main Street, now the site of the current Home Savings Bank, c. 1910. That corner would later become the site of Seidel's Grocery Store, the Isaly's Dairy before recently becoming the Home Savings Bank. Notice Main Street then was still an unpaved muddy road.

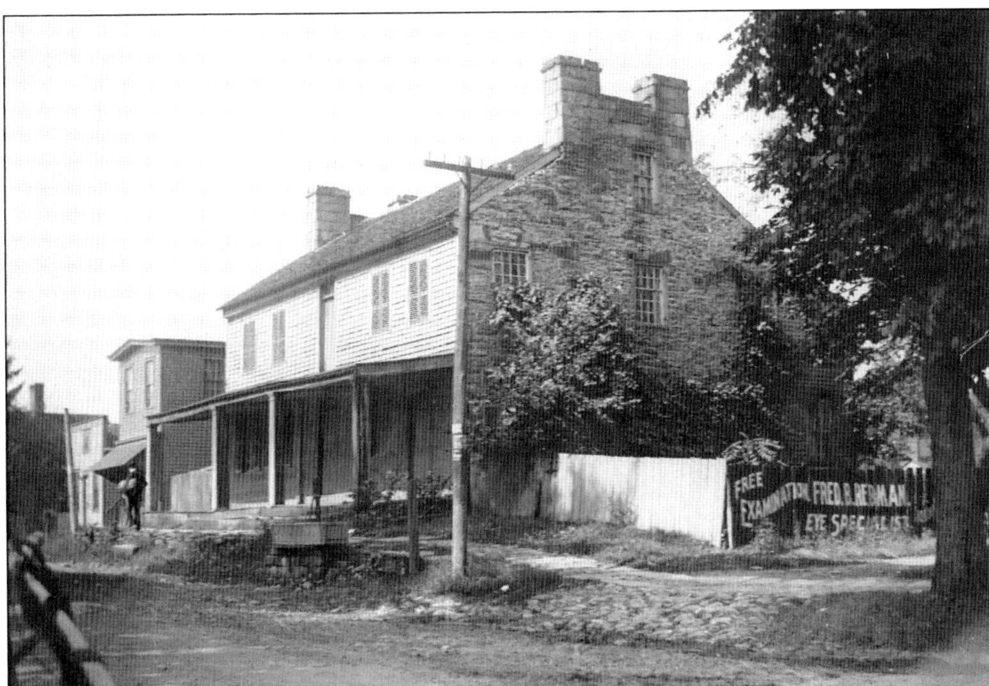

Old Stone Tavern is shown as it appeared on South Main Street in 1910. Note the dirt road, no curbs or wooden sidewalks. A watering trough for horses is visible in the front, as is an advertisement on the fence for free eye examinations. (Courtesy Poland Historical Society.)

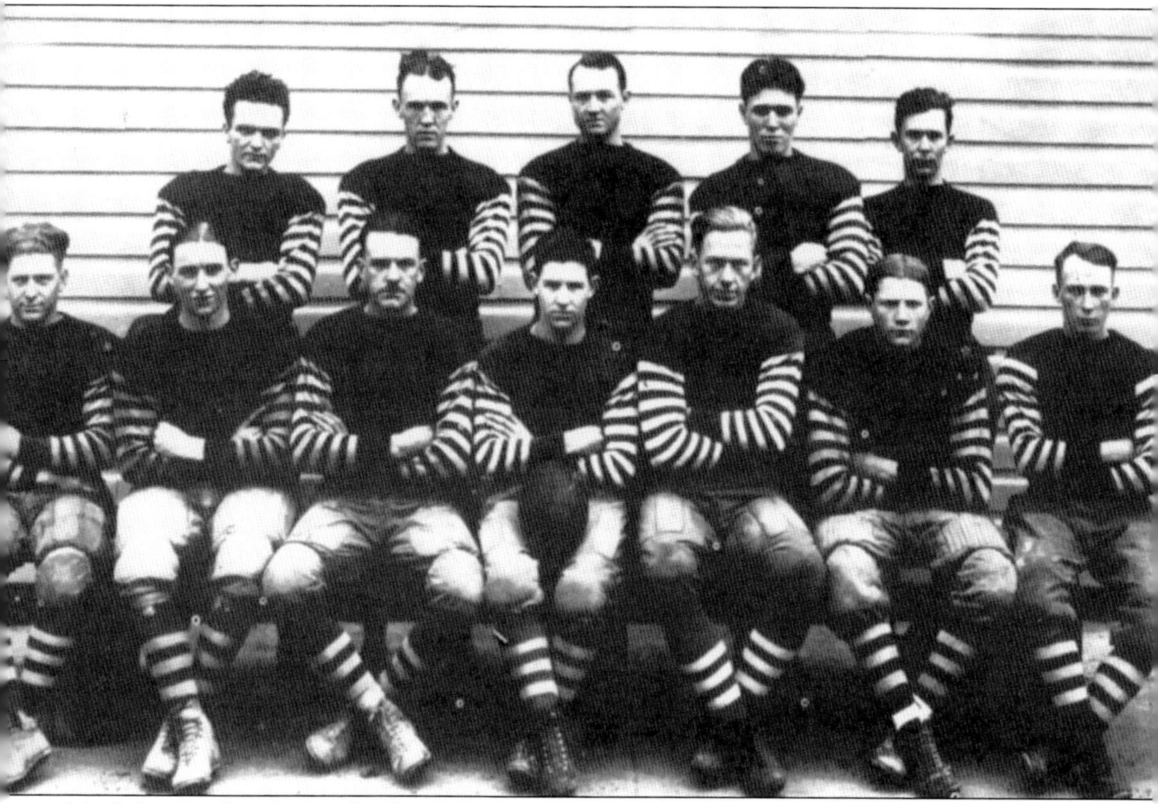

A little-known fact about Poland is its 1927–1929 professional football club that played where the Methodist Church is now on Route 224. (Courtesy of Poland Historical Society.)

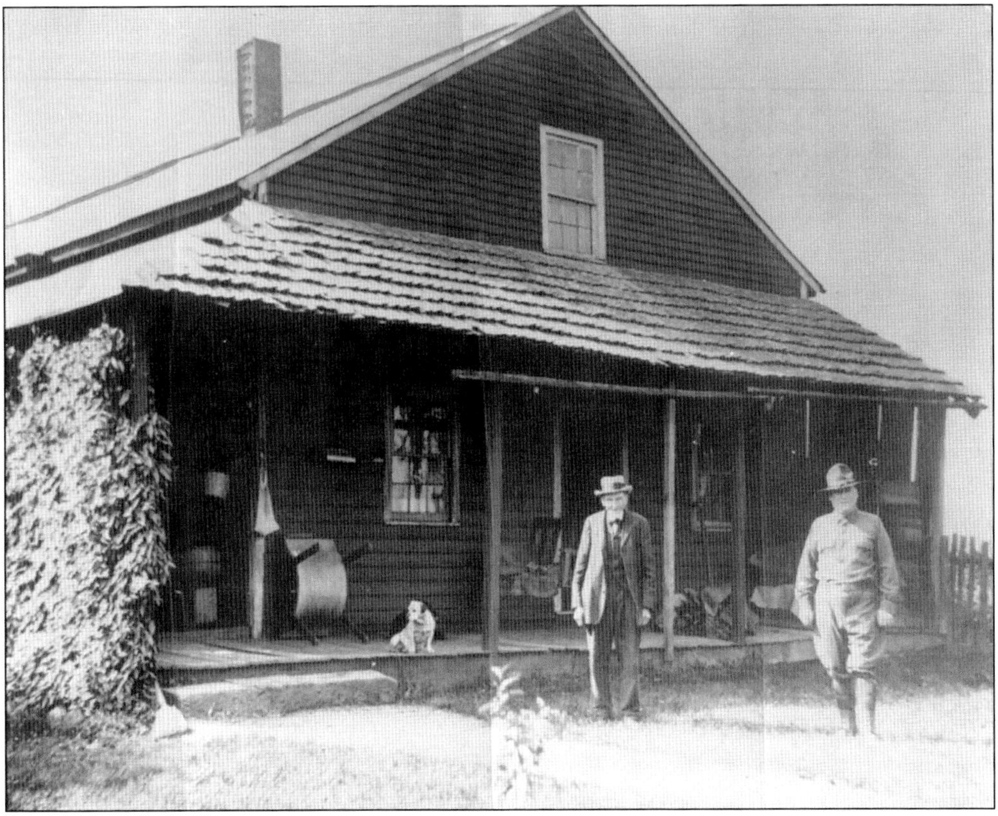

Dr. Raymond Love, left, is shown here with his son in his army uniform on their farm in Poland Township in 1917. It was the day before his son left for World War I training in Alabama in the 10th regiment of Poland boys, which he organized. (Courtesy of Janie Jenkins.)

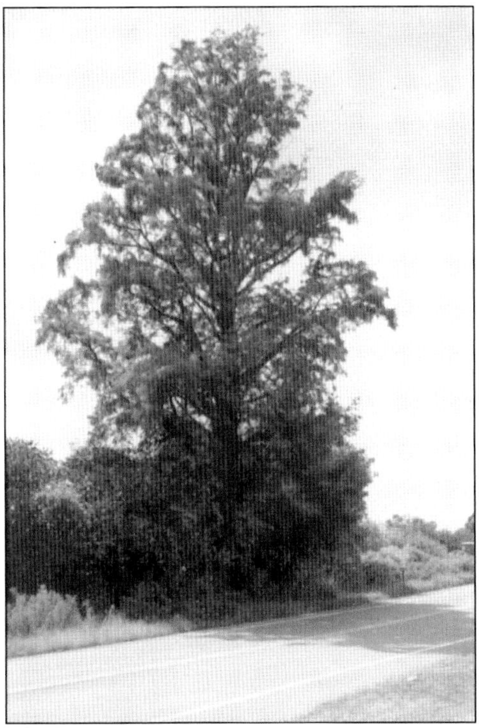

Poland's cypress tree on Route 224, just east of Struthers Road, is the largest of this species to be found in Ohio and is rare to be found in a northern Midwest state, as it is a southern tree. For these reasons, this Poland tree is recognized by the Ohio Forestry Association.

Three

THE WAY WE WERE

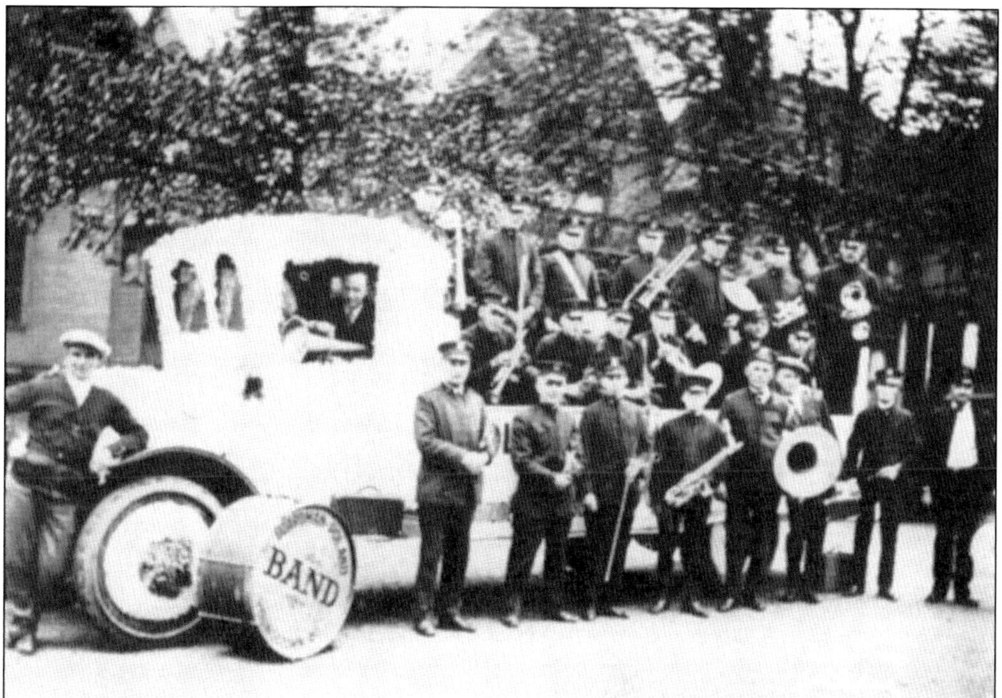

By the late 1930s, Poland was in transition from a small college town in the midst of rural surroundings to the start of suburbia. Shown here is Poland's Fife and Drum Corp that was the hit of Memorial Day parades in Poland in the late 1920s and early 1930s. (Courtesy of Poland Historical Society.)

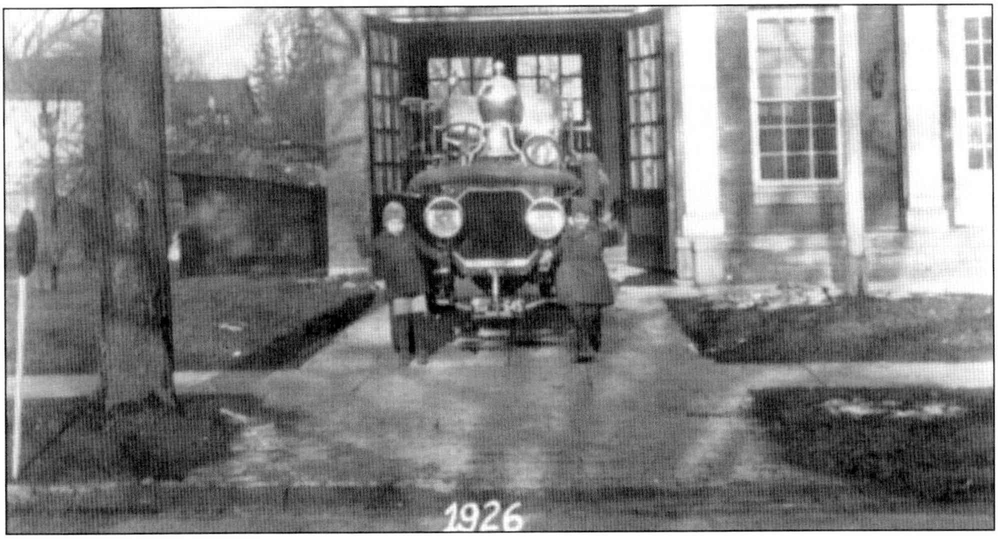

Poland's fire truck was purchased for $150 from the city of Youngstown in 1924. This was the volunteer fire department's only truck. (Courtesy of Poland Historical Society.)

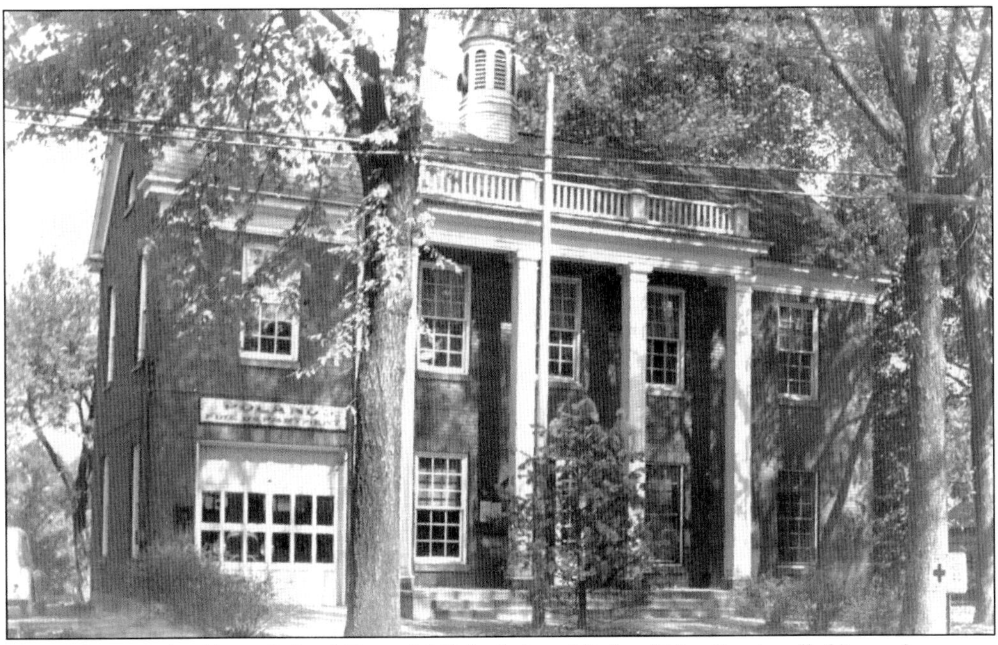

Located in one building, Poland Town Hall (right) and Poland Fire Station (left) are shown on Main Street in the 1930s. (Courtesy of Janie Jenkins.)

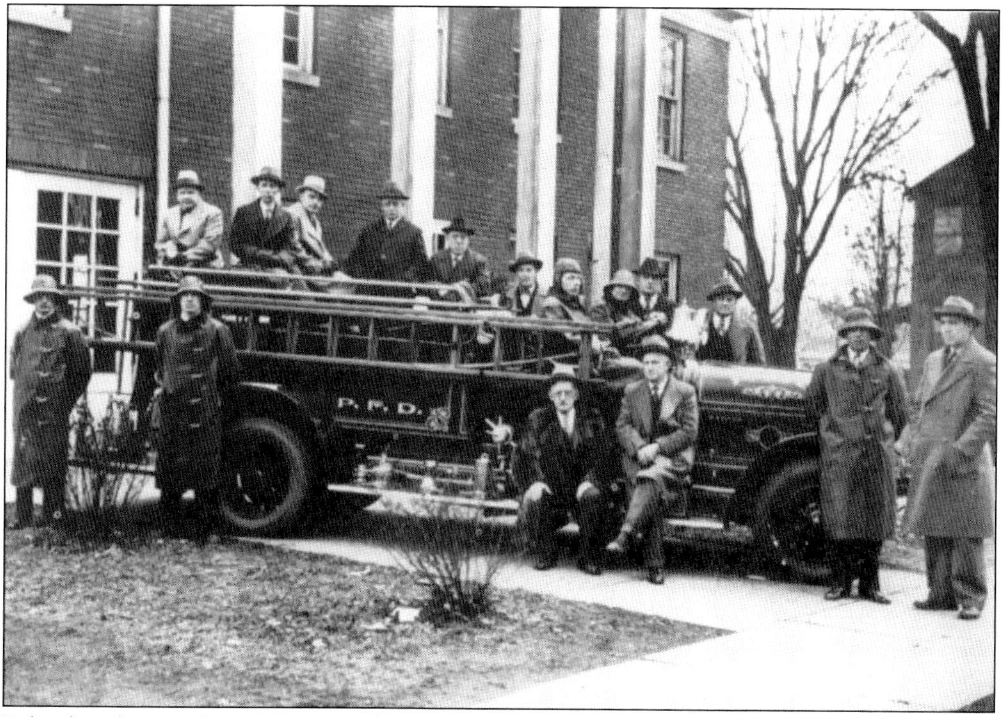

Poland's volunteer firemen pose on their fire truck in 1930, prior to a meeting. They are (first row) Delmar Kerr, Hubert Linden, John Case, William Clark, Ralph McCoy, and Charles Johnston; (second row) Ben Cover, Paul McCreary, Howard Cover, Clark Nesbitt, John McDonald, Julian Johnston, Donald Lewis, Smith McCoy, Clyde Kelly, and Dale Fithian.

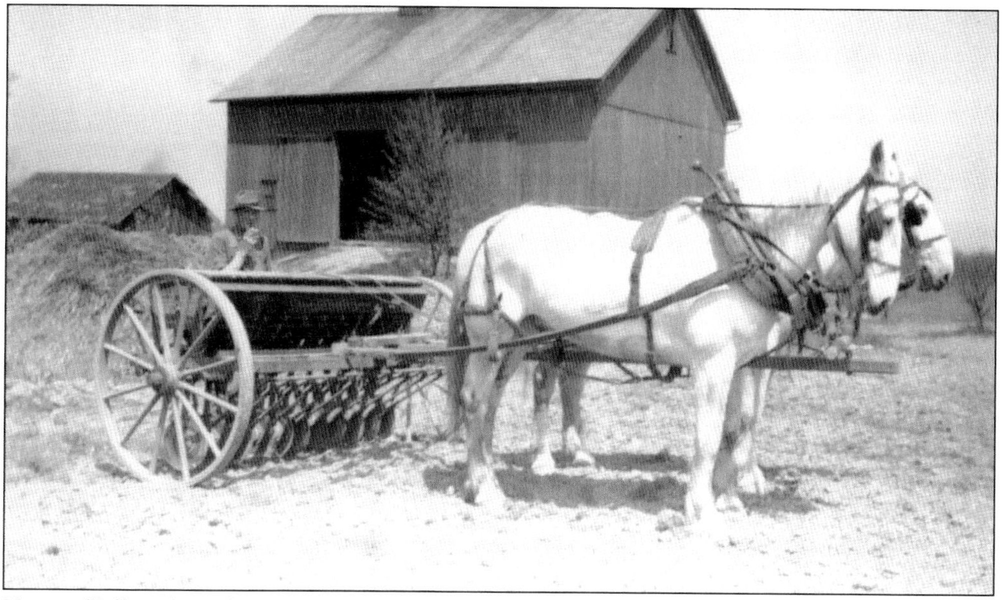

Horses (Bill and Dan), in 1937, are ready to begin sowing oats at the Stacy farm, which is on Kansas Road in the township. The barn in the background was torn down several years ago, and in 2007, the slate from the barn roof was donated by Laura Stacy to repair the Union Elementary slate roof. (Courtesy of Laura Stacy.)

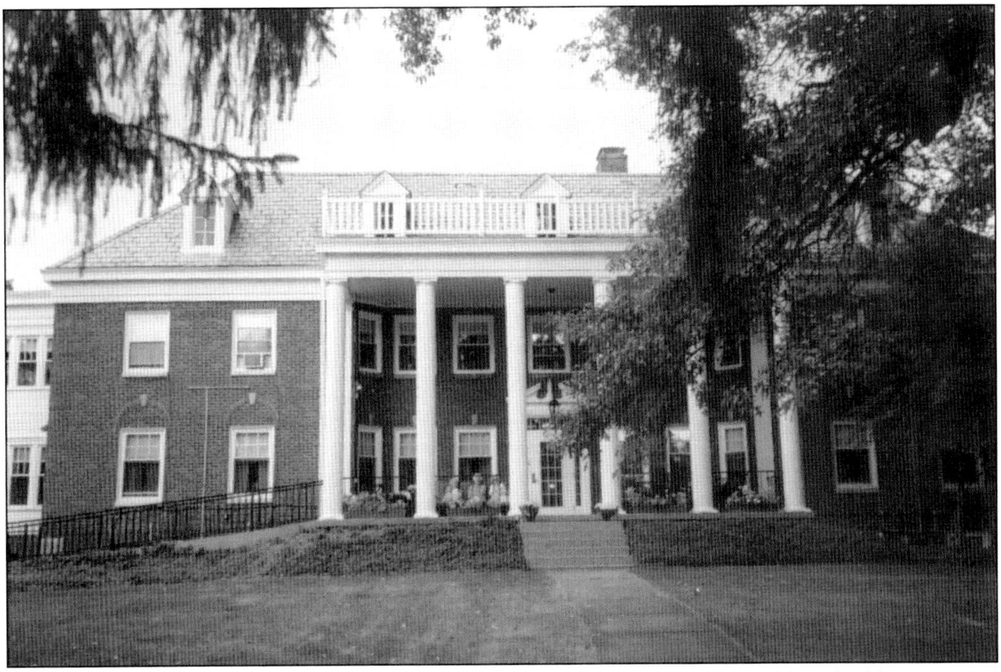

The Blackburn Home for Aged People was built in 1934 on Water Street. The Blackburn Home is still in operation today. Its name comes from Sylvester Blackburn who endowed the home for the elderly. (Courtesy of Poland Historical Society.)

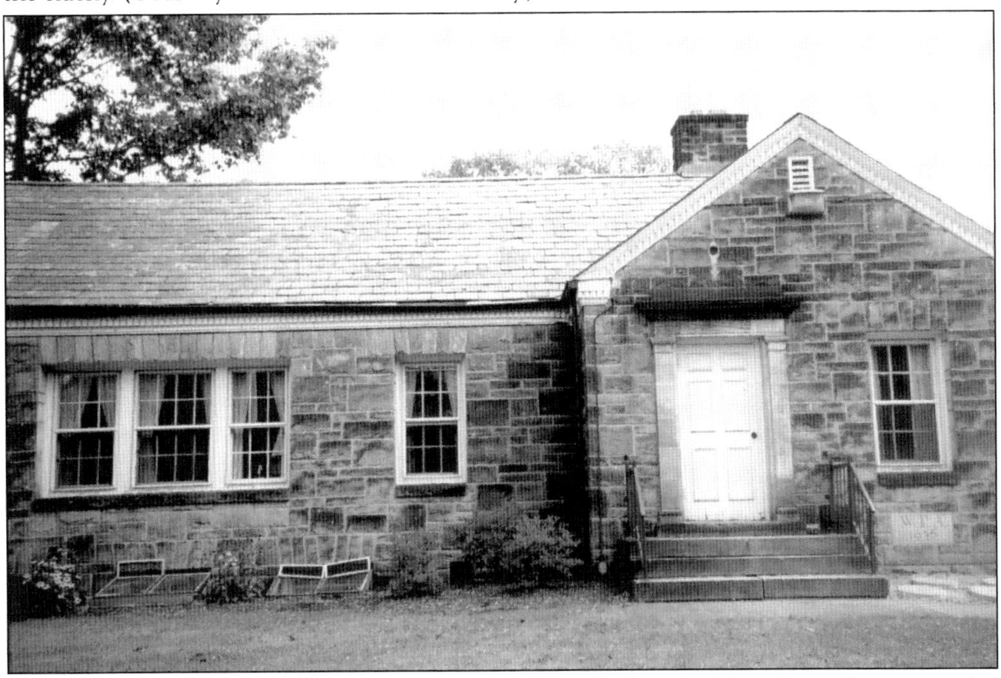

The American Legion Post, on Cortland Street, was built in 1936 and is still in use today by the legion. The legion members assist veterans' families, especially in death, and decorate soldiers' graves with flags in the Poland Cemetery every Memorial Day. (Courtesy of Poland Historical Society.)

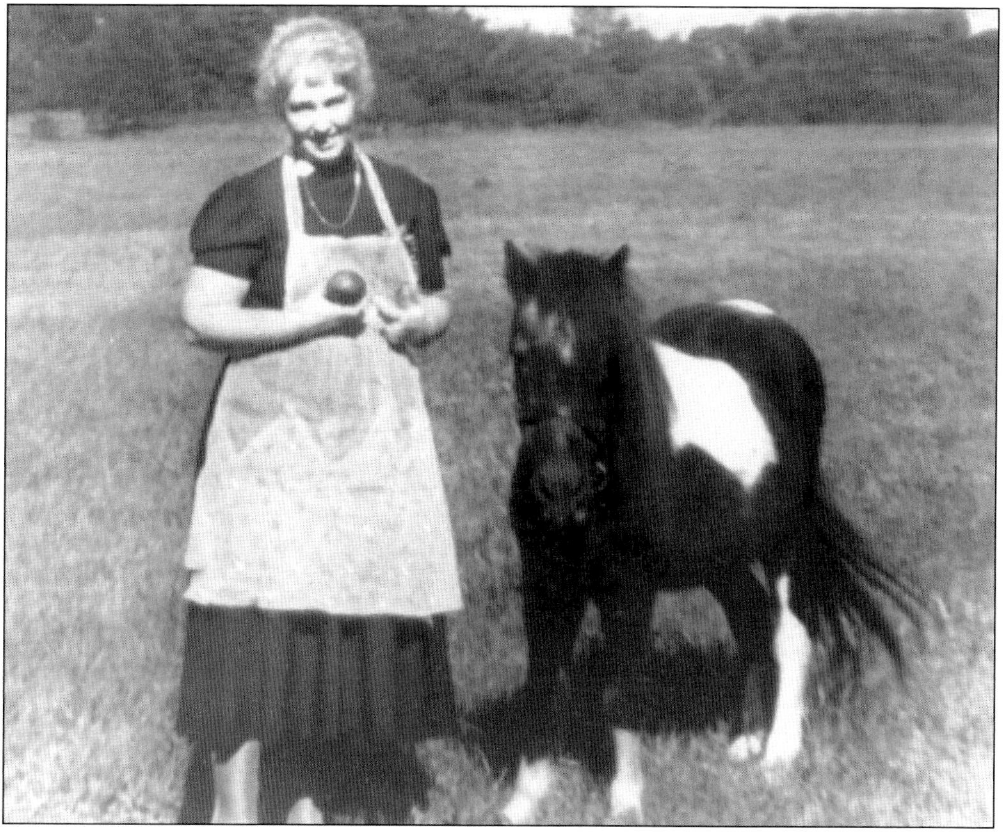

Grace Hull Miller (1889–1962) was the author of many children's books back in the 1930s. Her best-known book was *White Saddle*, a true popular story of a little black pony with white markings. She lived in the log cabin on Clingan Road in Poland. Today one may view White Saddle's tombstone in the front yard of that same cabin. Her books are still in demand at the Poland library. (Both courtesy of Poland Historical Society.)

Grace Hull Miller, author of The Story of Quailwood, The Wayward Schoolmaster, Out of the Roaring Loom, The Fisherman of The Arrowhead Nature, and of course, White Saddle. The author is in this picture, taken in Mill Creek Park, Youngstown,Ohio is feeding her beloved horse, White Saddle, so named because of the white markings on his back and side in the shape of a saddle. White Saddle is buried near a log cabin in Poland Township, OH in a wooded setting. Photo circa 1920's or 1930's

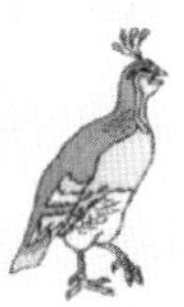
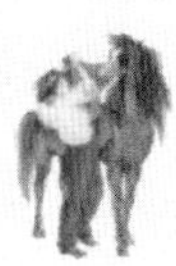
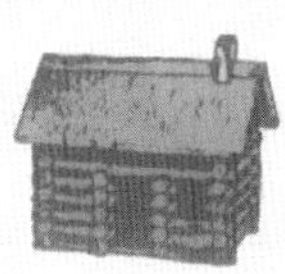

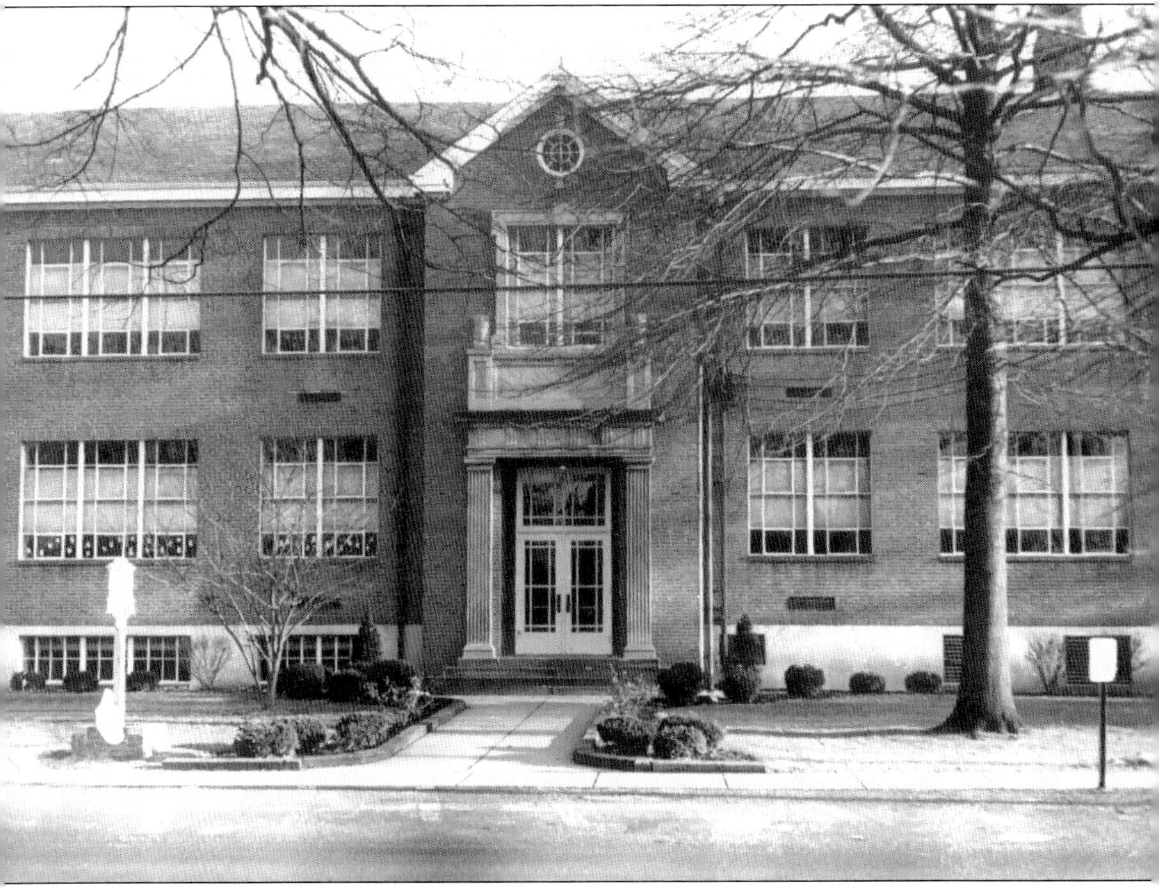

Poland Union Elementary on Riverside Drive is shown here in the late 1960s. There has been a public school on this site since the 1830s. William McKinley attended here before going on to the Poland Academy. At one time, this site housed all grades, from first through twelfth. Later it housed grades nine through twelve. After that, the school housed grades one through six. Today the school houses preschool through fourth grade. (Courtesy of Poland schools' archives)

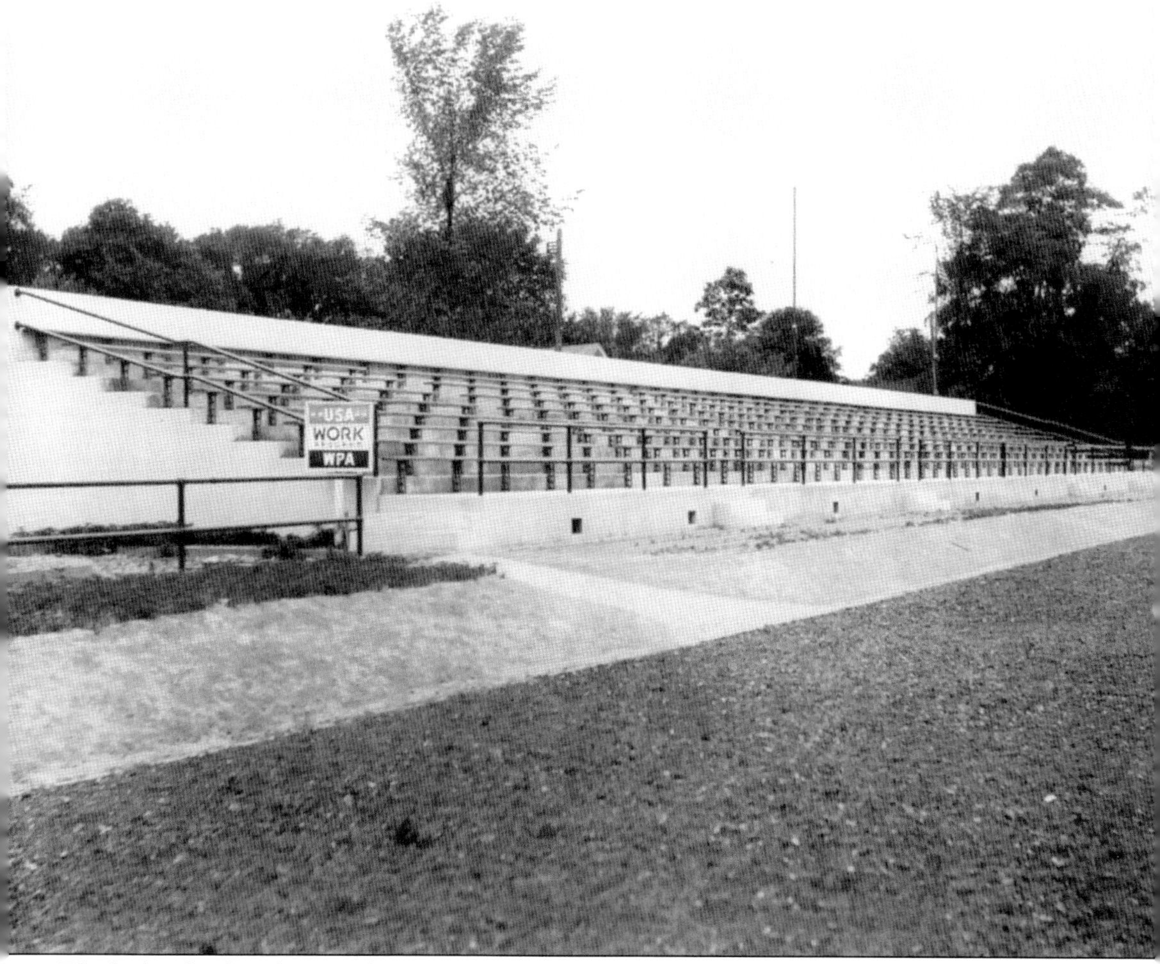

The high school stadium at the corner of Lee and Cortland Streets is shown here when it was completed on May 16, 1936. It was built largely by federal dollars through the government's Work Progress Administration (WPA). Note the WPA sign at the left. The stadium was renamed in 1945 as Baird Mitchell Field, after one of the community's World War II heroes, and would serve at the district's high school field until 1986 when it became the middle school field. This photograph was taken when the facility was brand new. (Courtesy of Poland schools' archives.)

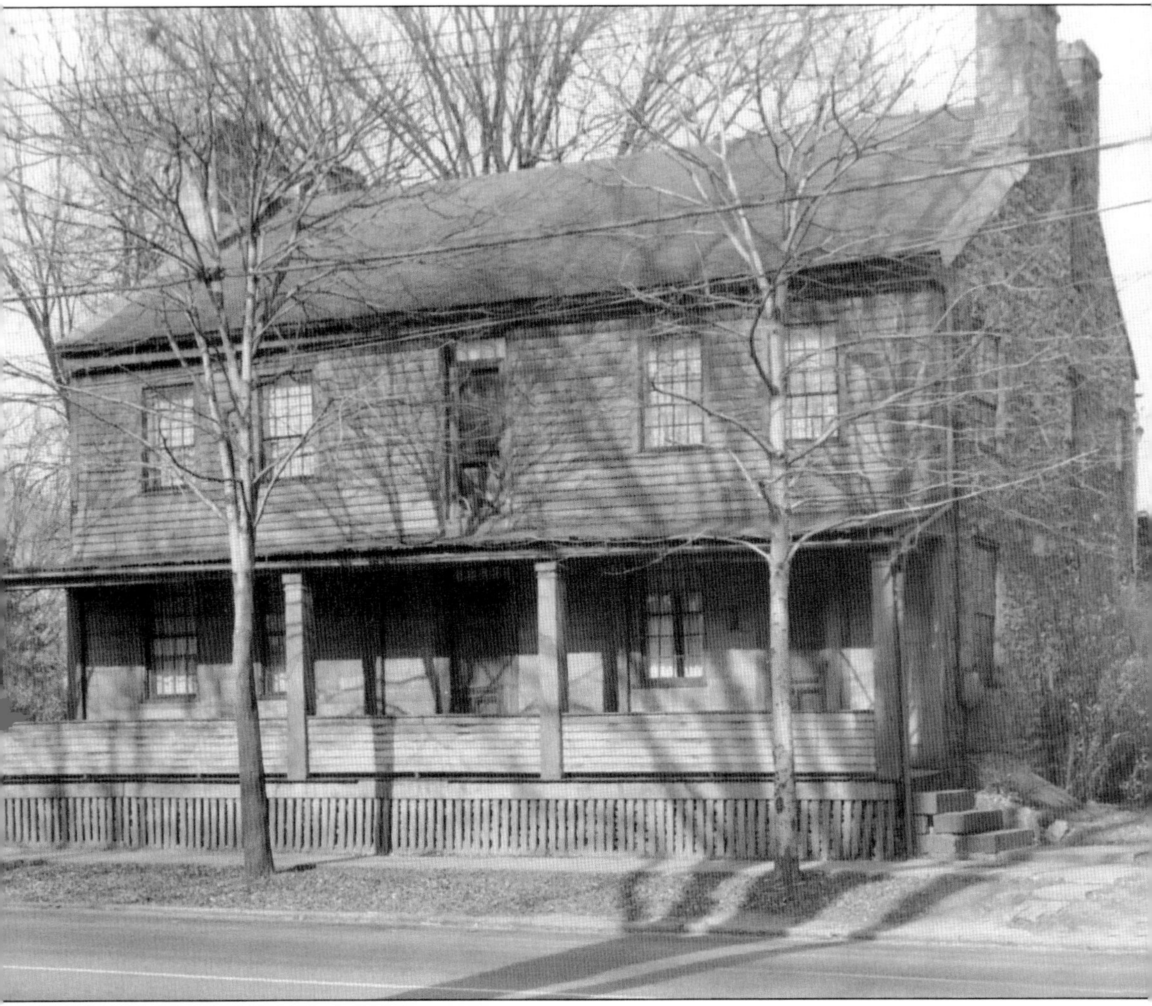

The Old Stone Tavern on South Main Street as it appeared on December 2, 1945. In 1804 this was a tavern opened by Jonathan Fowler. It became a popular stagecoach stop mid-way between Cleveland and Pittsburgh. Stables behind the tavern also housed 50 to 60 horses for quick changes of horses for stagecoaches traveling west. Later during the Civil War days, William McKinley enlisted in the Union Army from the porch of this tavern. (Courtesy of Janie Jenkins.)

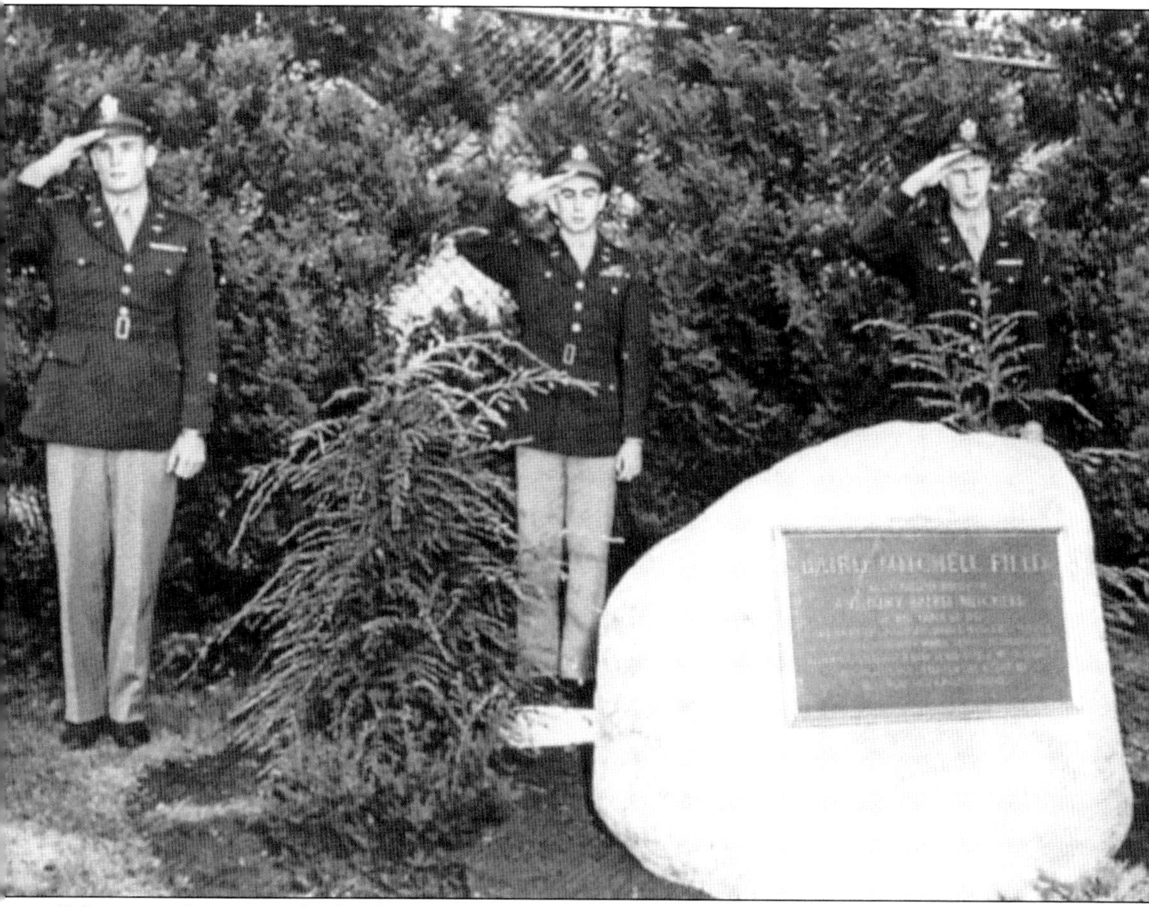

Saluting and paying a final tribute to their fallen team member, friend, and former classmate, Baird Mitchell, are, from left to right, captains Jack Johnson, Robert Barton, and Frank Powers. All were members of the class of 1937. All comprised the four-man relay team that enabled Poland to win the 1937 state track championship. All went off to war to help their country in its time of need. All became captains in the U.S. Army Air Corps, and all returned home to Poland—except Baird Mitchell who returned in memory only. (Courtesy of Poland Schools' archives.)

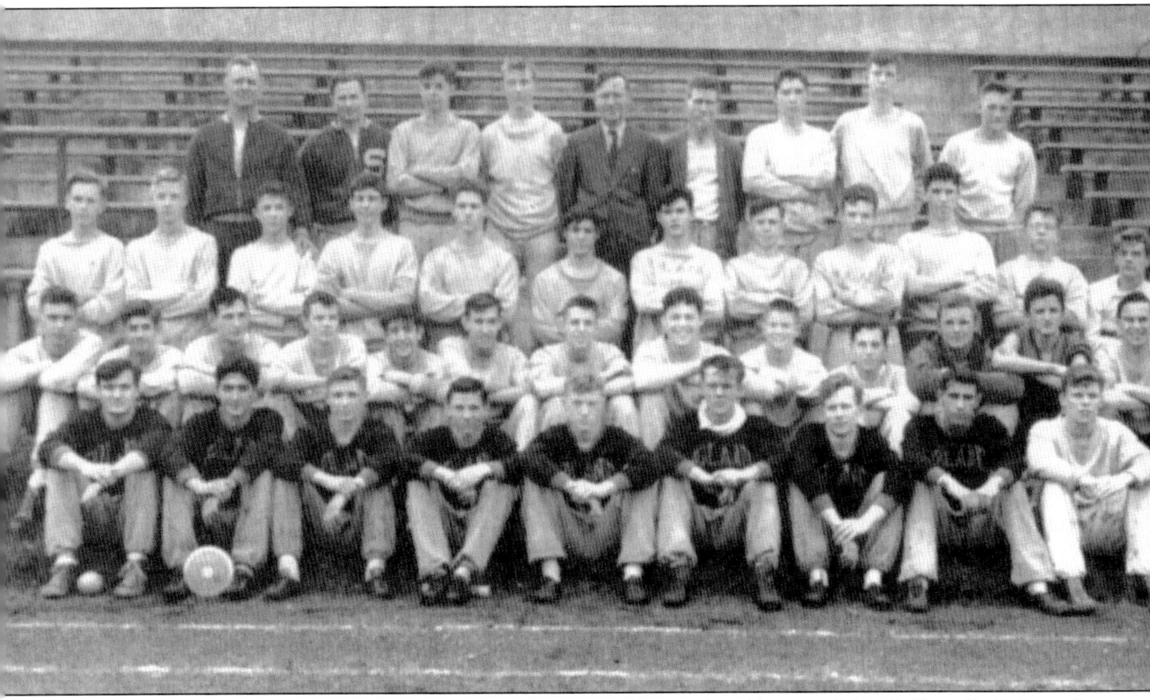

The 1947 state boys track champions were, from left to right, (first row) D. Tullen, D. Polito, B. Kibler, B. Strand, J. Allen, H. Freiheit, W. Kelly, D. Davis, and D. Hill; (second row) P. Good, R. Clapie, J. Shurilla, F. Cockman, R. Clapie, J. King, C. Reichard, G. Jones, E. Meeds, P. Riddle, T. Dale, B. Fauver, and D. Miller; (third row) G. Millard, J. Scholl, J. Schill, D. Lewis, J. Walker, C. Richardson, J. Geddes, G. Watson, R. Howell, D. Renstrom, B. Spanabel, and R. Guterba; (fourth row) coach Charles Stone, coach Ronald Paris, J. Hold, J. Williams, coach Clarence Goterba, coach Lester Hawk, G. Luteran, D. Dearing, and J. Prater. Poland won the class B state boys track championship in the spring of 1947, led by seven returning lettermen. Poland that year beat Austintown 81-37, and they swamped Leavitsburg 93-13. Poland placed second in the Ohio Wesleyan relays. This was the tenth season at Poland's Baird Mitchell track. (Courtesy of Poland schools' archives.)

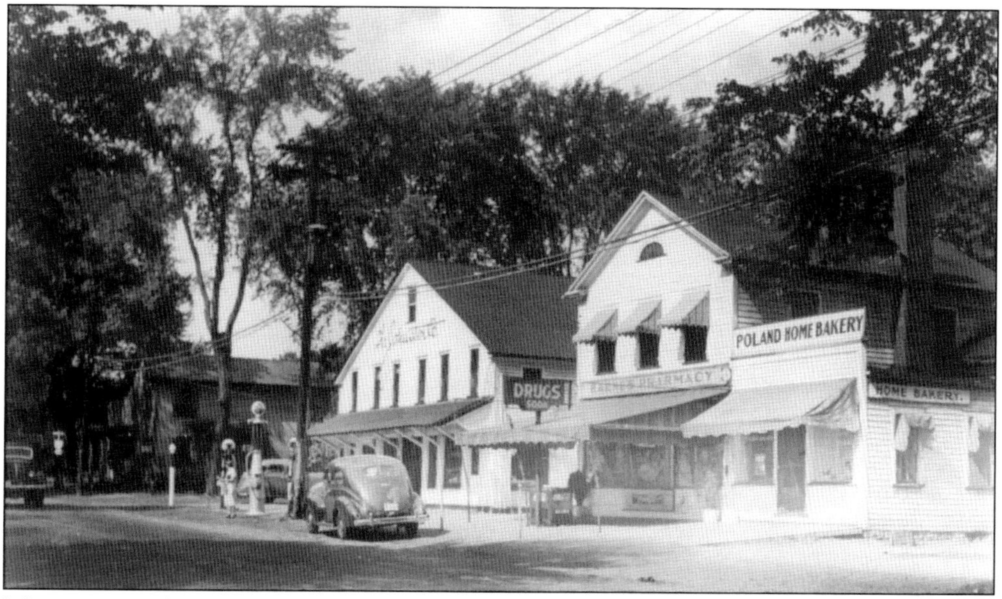

Johnston's Hardware, on the corner of Water Street and South Main Street, is shown here as it looked in the 1940s. Notice the Poland Home Bakery next to the hardware store. The bakery was popular in the 1940s, 1950s, and 1960s. (Courtesy of Poland Historical Society.)

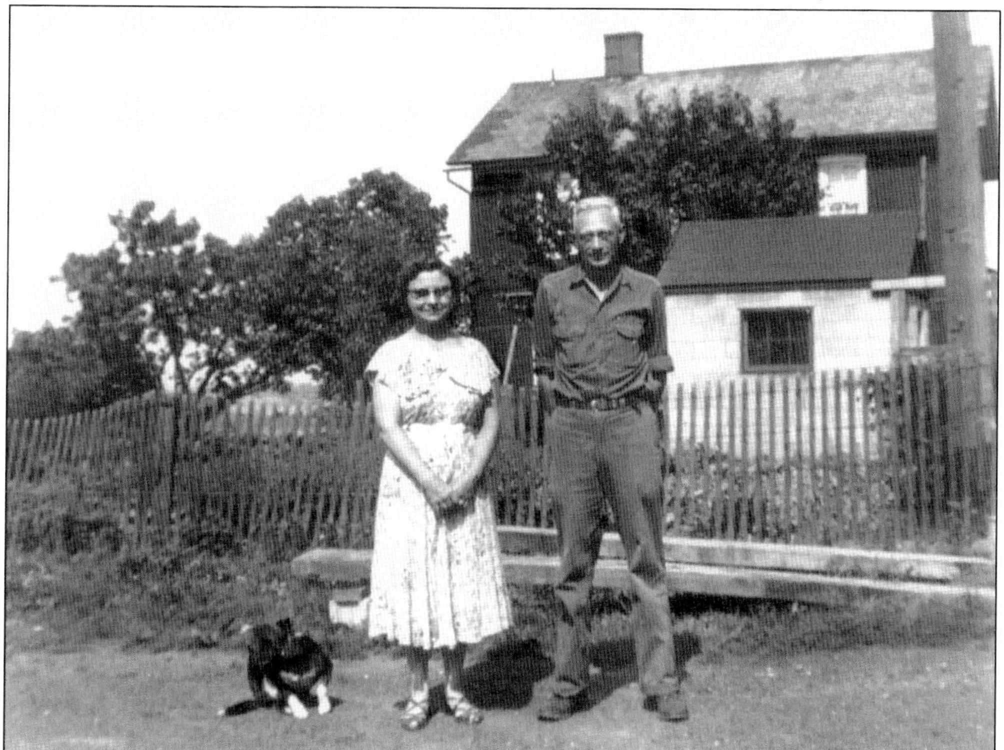

Shown here in 1937 are Hugh Sr. and Helen Stacy at their Kansas Road township farm. Hugh Stacy was a direct descendent of Mathew and Jane Stacy, who settled this same farm site in 1806. This farm today in 2009 is still owned by the Stacy family. (Courtesy of Laura Stacy.)

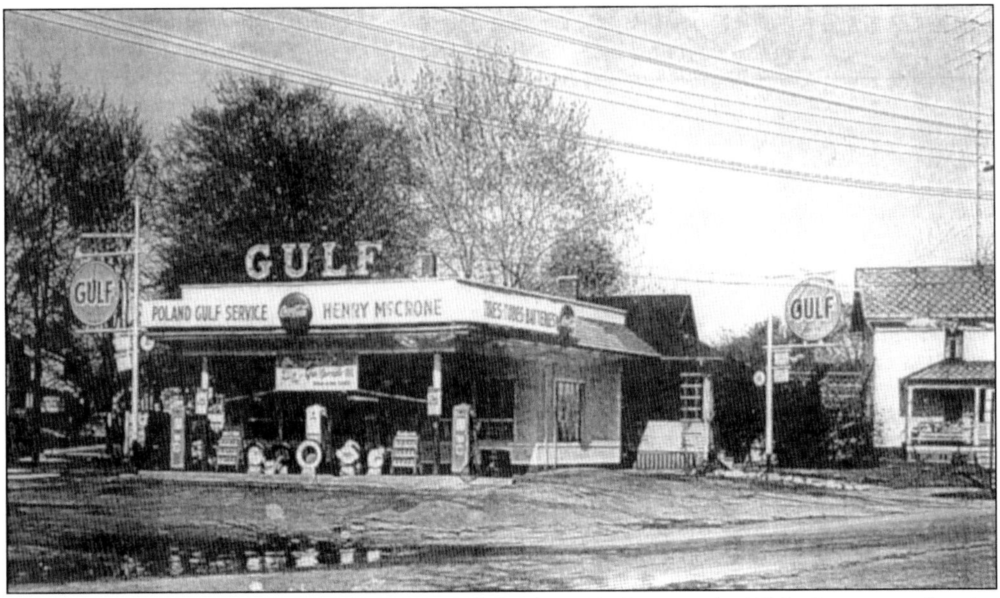

McCrone's gas station is shown here around the late 1940s to early 1950s. It is now the site of Walgreens.

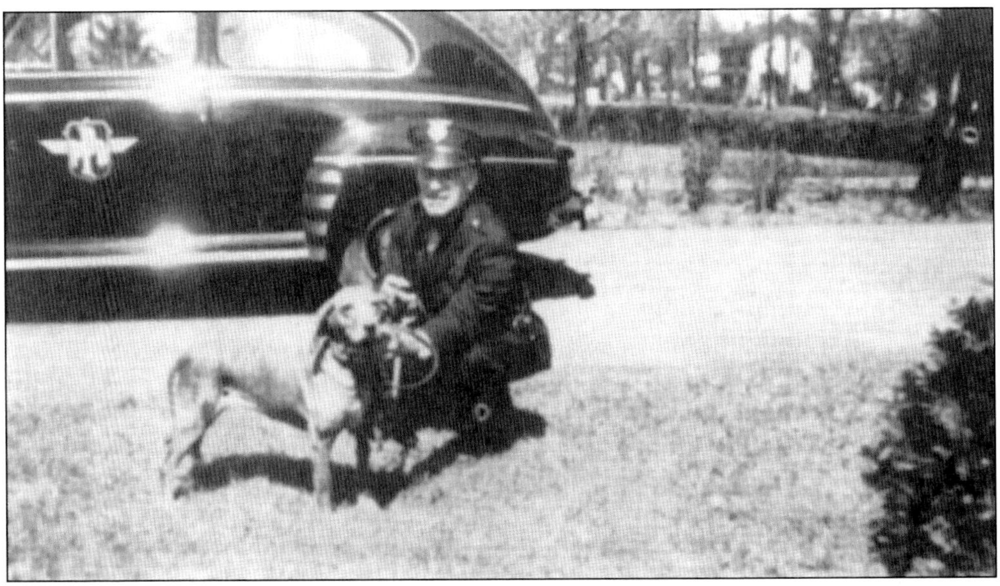

Clark Wagner, Poland's marshall, was the village police chief in the 1930s, 1940s, and 1950s. Marshall Wagner is shown here with the village's only police car, a 1948 Ford, at his home on North Main Street. (Courtesy of Poland Historical Society.)

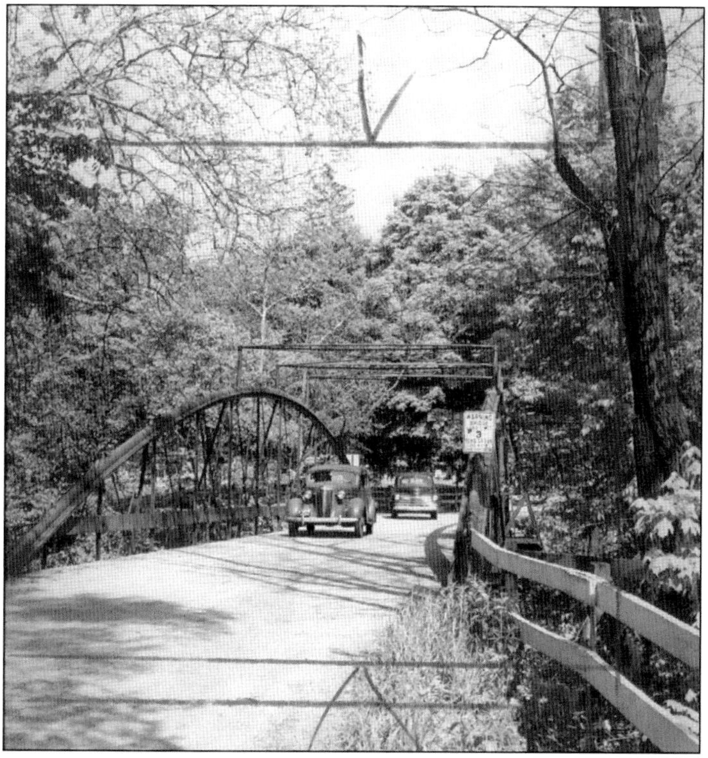

The Cemetery Bridge, as it appeared in 1947 off Water Street, is still standing today but is used now only as a bike path and footpath for hikers and joggers. Shown crossing the bridge are 1938 and 1946 Chevrolets. (Courtesy of Janie Jenkins.)

Poland's American Legion honor guard, in 1949, commemorates Memorial Day and those who have died in the armed forces serving their country. This is still a Poland tradition to this day. (Courtesy of Poland Historical Society.)

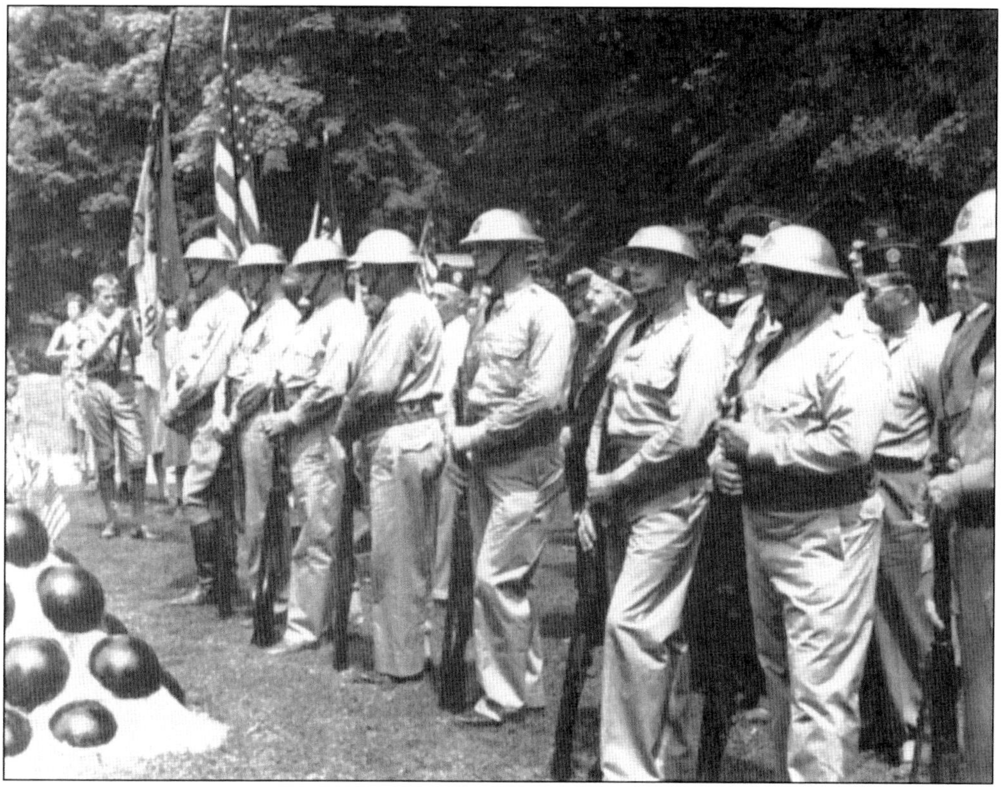

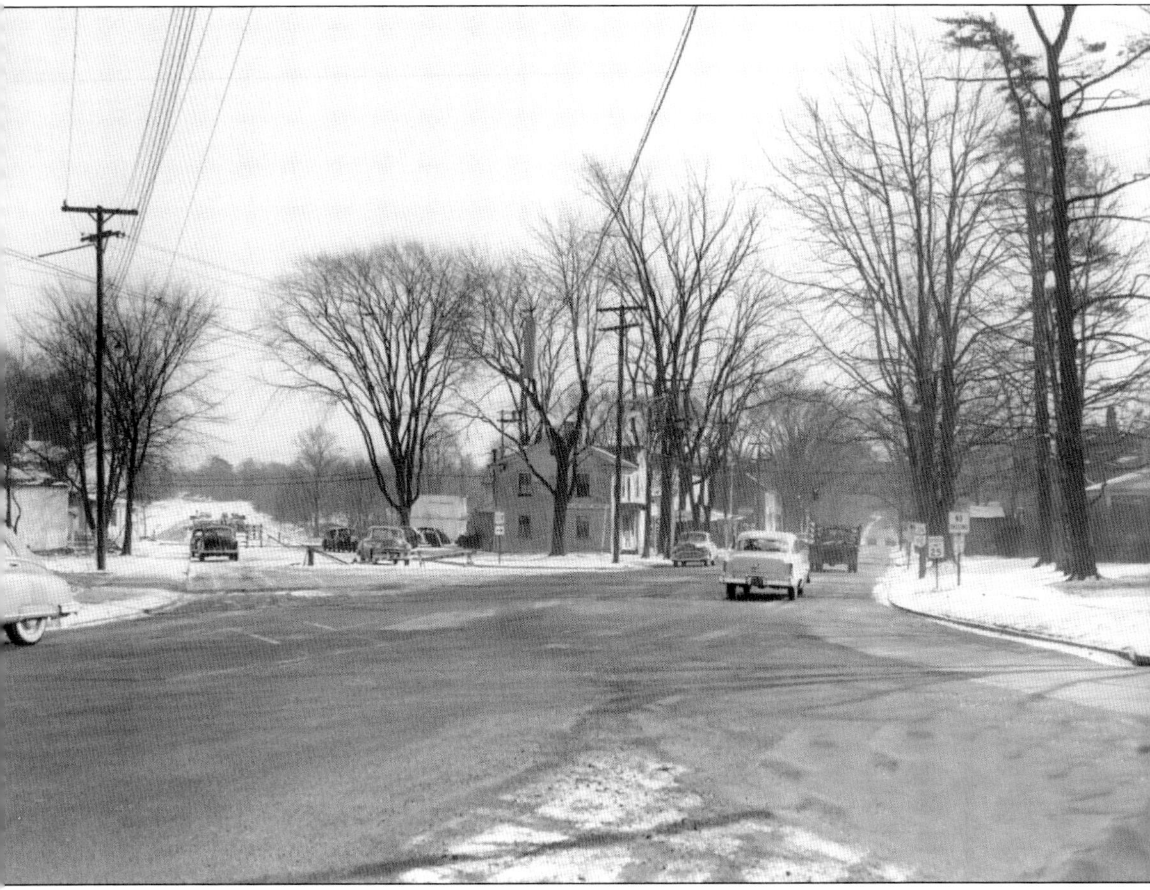

Poland had a new look in 1952, as Route 224 was being cut through the heart of town. Left of center in the photograph you can see the new road under construction, which would cross Main Street.

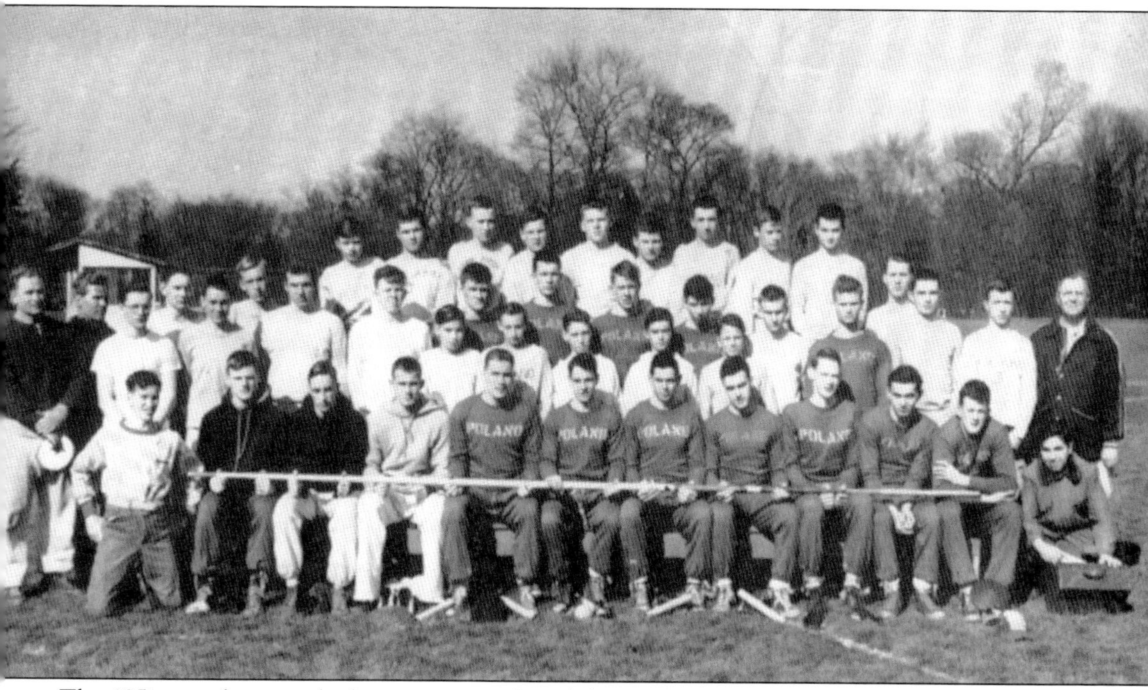

The 1951 state boys track champions are, from left to right (first row) E. Crites, D. Olson, A. Webber, D. Kelly, D. Stone, R. Richardson, J. Shurilla, P. Johnson, R. Tredwell, C. Smith, D. Gettig, and R. DiBlasio, the manager; (second row) J. Bordenkircher, J. Bolander, K. Saunders, R. Sarkies, and R. Walker; (third row) coach Ronald Paris, J. Diamond, R. Taaffe, D. Smolanovich, J. Klinke, J. Murine, J. Chambers, W. Seidner, W. Luteran, J. Kummer, W. Simon, E. Geddes, T. Smolanovich, and coach Charles Stone; (fourth row) coach Lester Hawke; W. Reese, W. Worsencroft, D. Peacock, R. Miller, A. Chinowth, W. Eich, D. Worsencroft, B. Kagarise, J. Bishop, R. Moore, and F. Conzett. The Bulldogs started the 1951 season by capturing two dual meets, then winning the Ohio Wesleyan College relays the third straight year, and then winning the Mentor, Ohio, relays for the third straight year. The Bulldogs also won the county championship for the eighth consecutive year. The team finished the year winning the state boys track class B championship. (Courtesy of Poland schools' archives.)

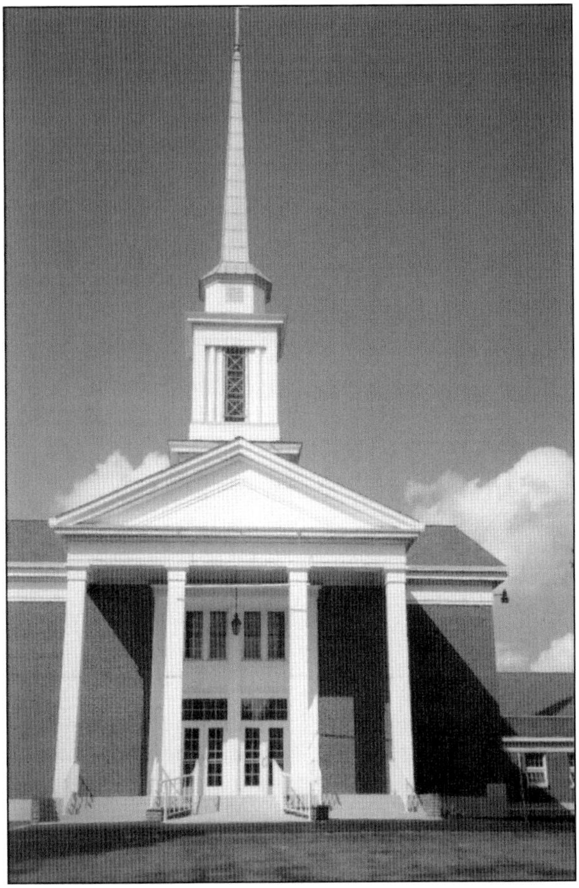

Poland Methodist Church on Route 224, Boardman Poland Road, was built in 1957 after the church on North Main Street burned.

Wittenauer Drug Store, on South Main Street, was originally constructed in the 1950s as a one-floor building with the post office on the left side, as seen by the doors in the photograph below. The left door led to the post office and the right to the drugstore. The difference in brick between the second floor addition and the first floor can be seen. Wittenauer's closed in 2010.

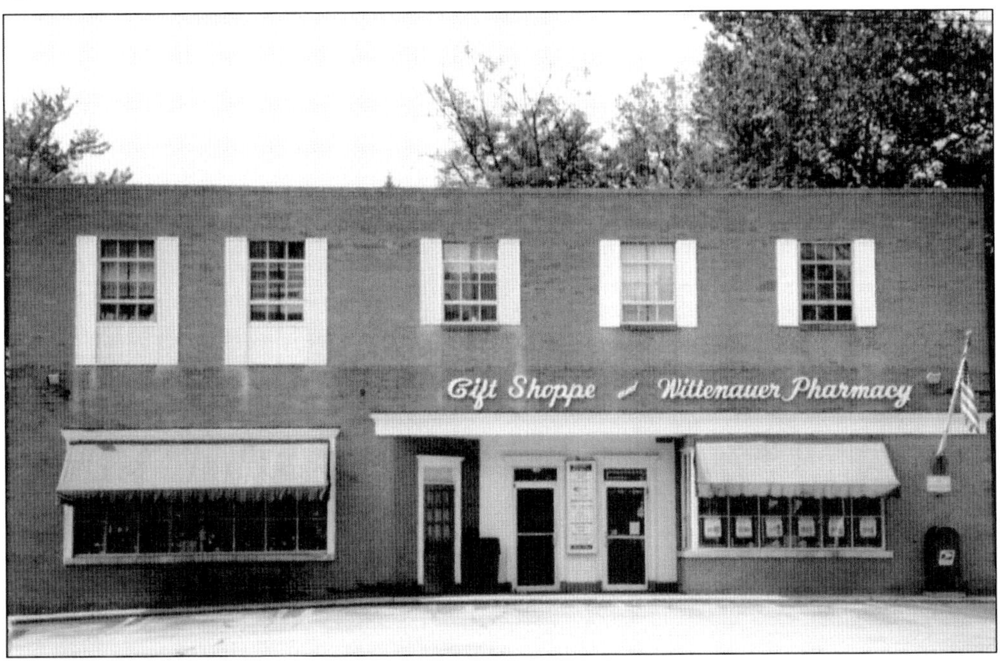

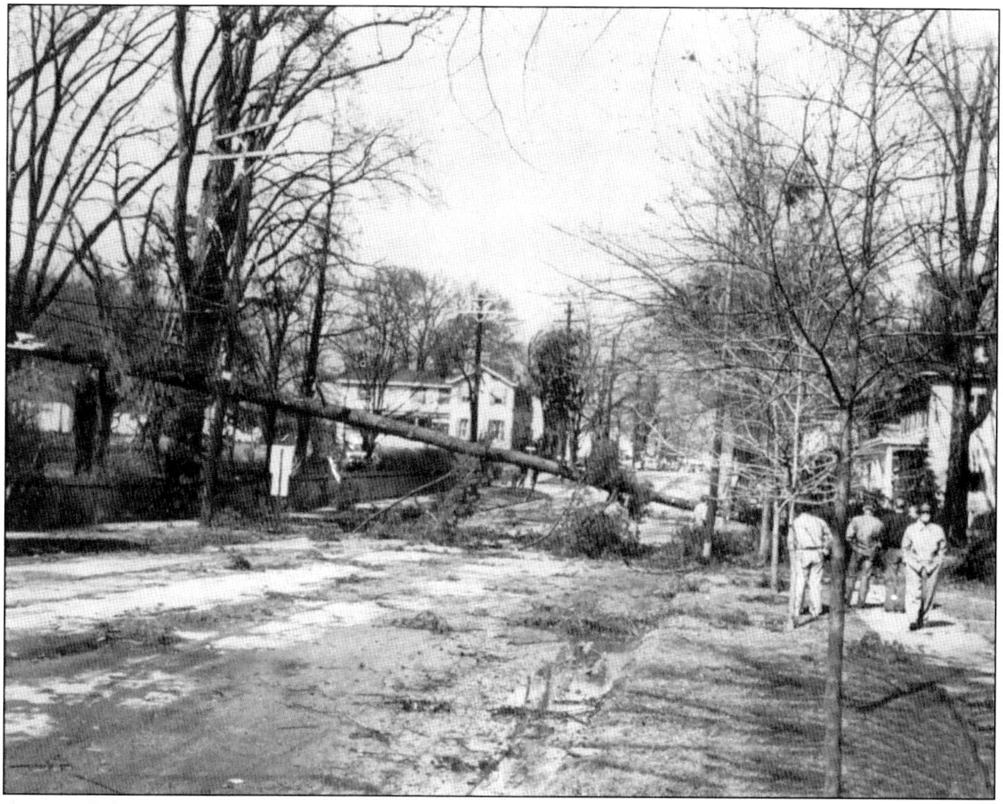

A tornado hit Main Street, Poland, on March 22, 1955, and looking west from the Yellow Creek bridge toward the center of town, the damage can be seen. (Courtesy of Poland Historical Society.)

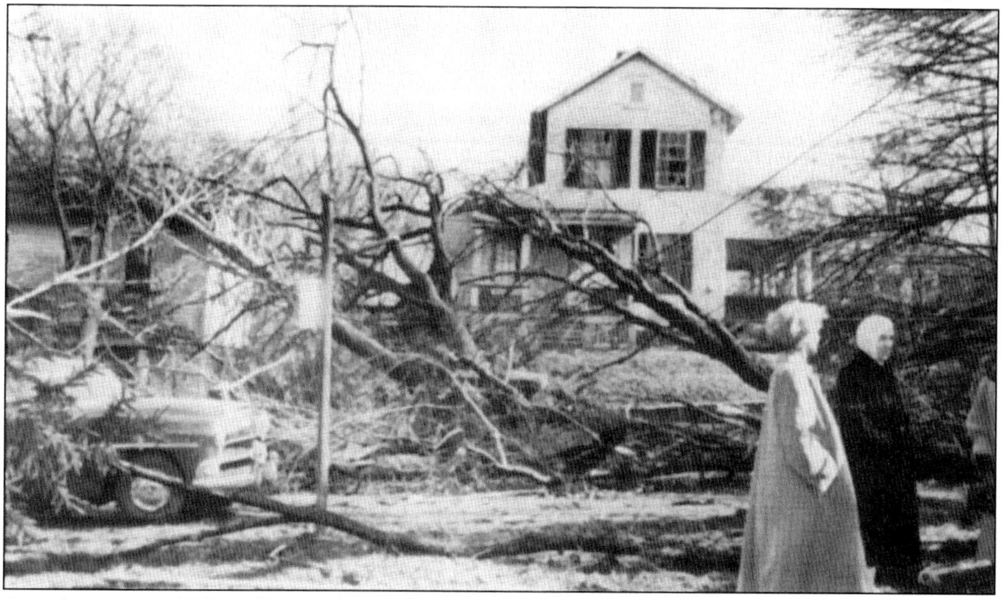

Another view of Main Street shows the tornado damage Poland suffered in spring 1955. For several days, the town was without power and some of the streets were impassable by automobile. (Courtesy of Poland Historical Society.)

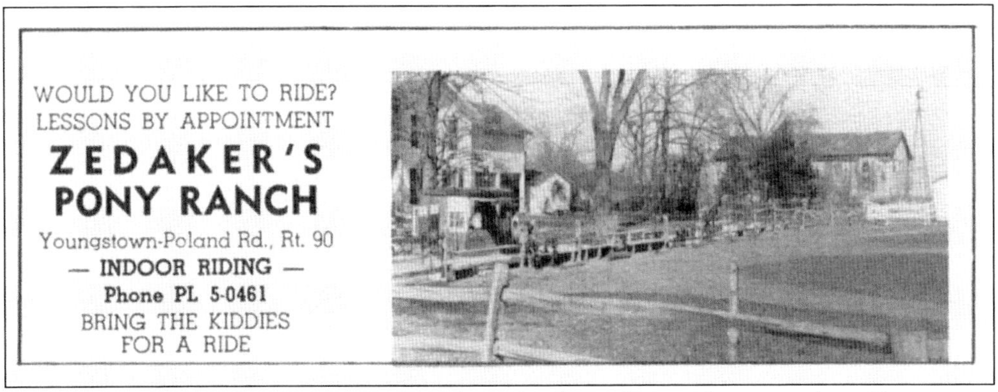

A Zedaker's pony ranch advertisement from the 1950s shows the popular pony ride on Youngstown Poland Road. The barn, horses, and pasture are still there today and still look as they do in this picture. (Courtesy of Robert and Elinor Zedaker.)

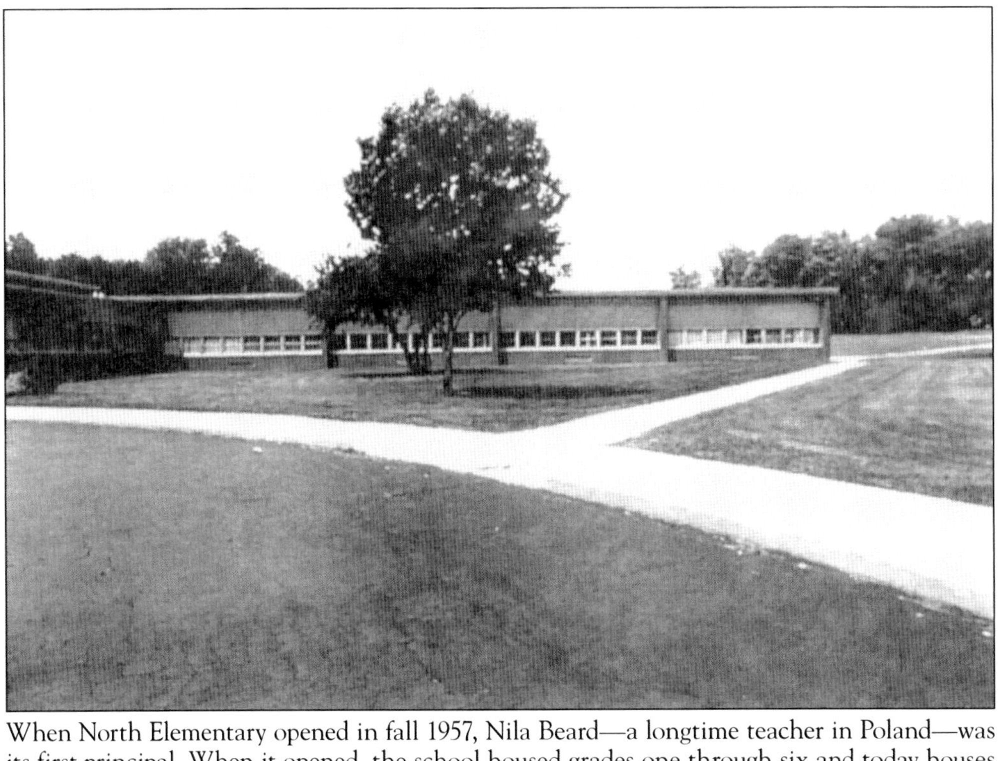

When North Elementary opened in fall 1957, Nila Beard—a longtime teacher in Poland—was its first principal. When it opened, the school housed grades one through six and today houses grades kindergarten through fourth. (Courtesy of Poland schools' archives.)

Four

Small Town Americana

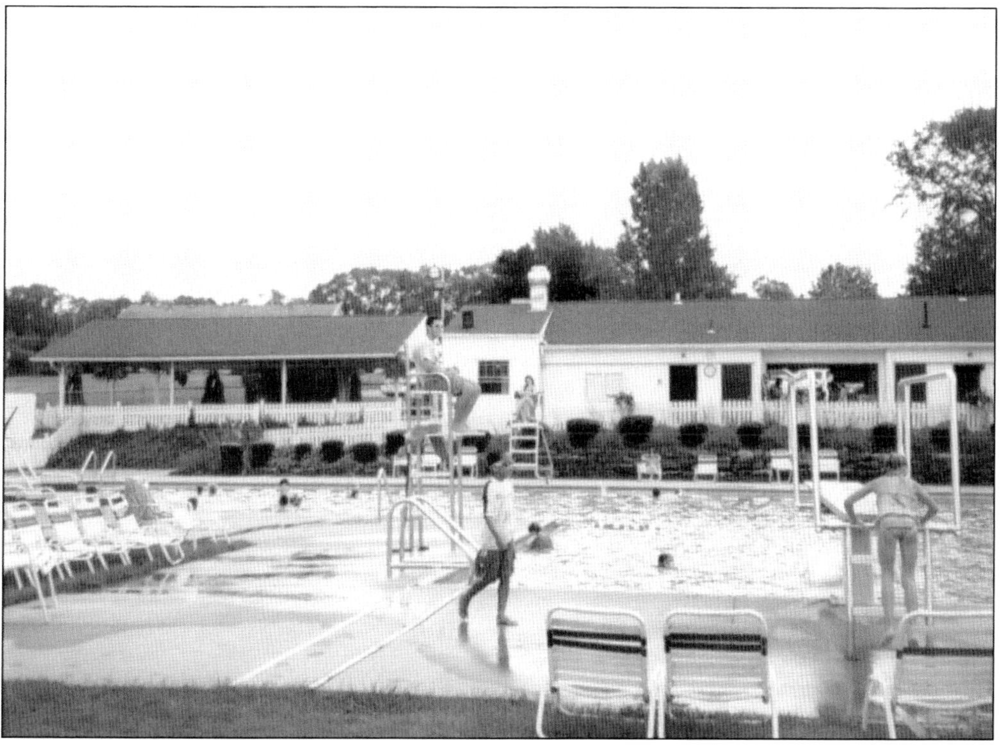

Poland, since the 1860s, has typified suburban living. Shown here is the Poland Swim Club, built in the 1950s, on Clingan Road. It is a favorite summer recreation spot for many Poland youth.

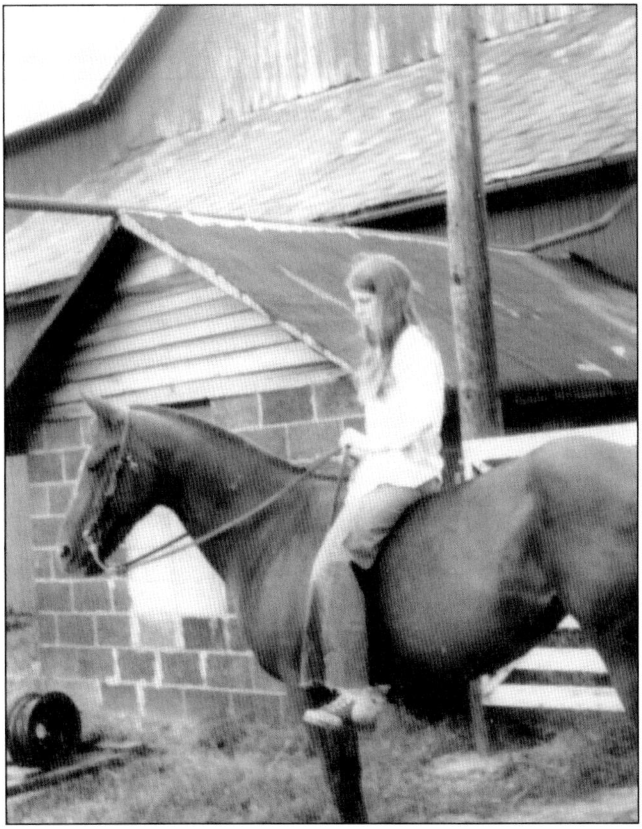

The 4-H organization was popular in Poland in the 1960s and 1970s with many suburban youngsters having ponies and horses at barns on the outskirts of Poland. Shown here is one of the young 4-H members at McCullough's Barn on North Lima Road.

McCullough's farm on North Lima Road was a popular spot for horseback riding until just a few years ago. The original 300 acres were gradually sold off, and the 1877 farmhouse was torn down in 1996. Today condos are being built where 4-H children once romped and played. This 1969 photograph shows one of the McCullough barns.

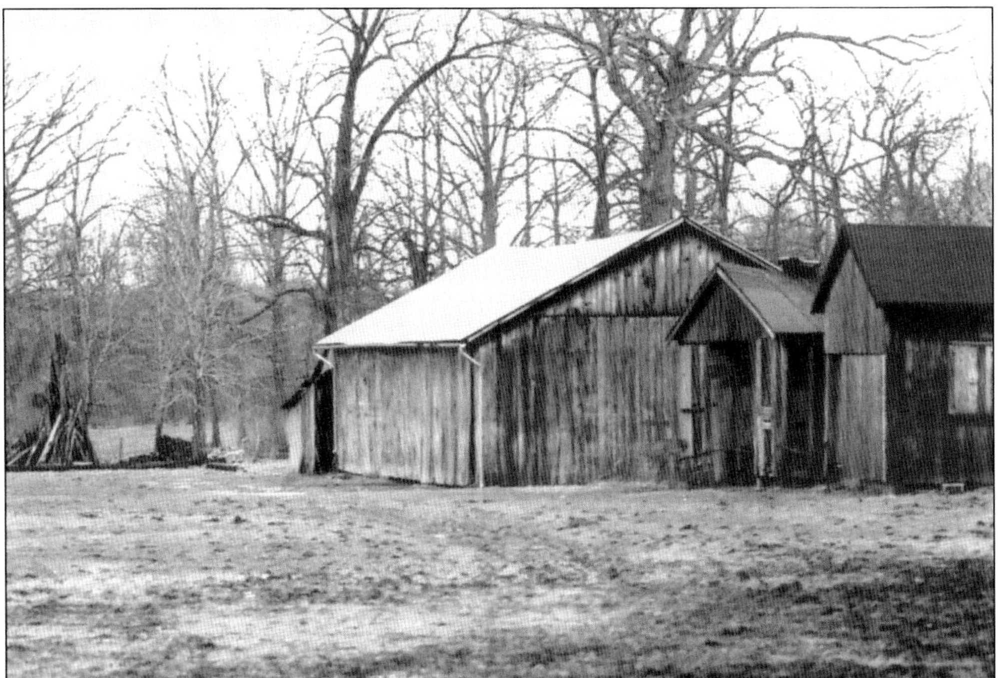

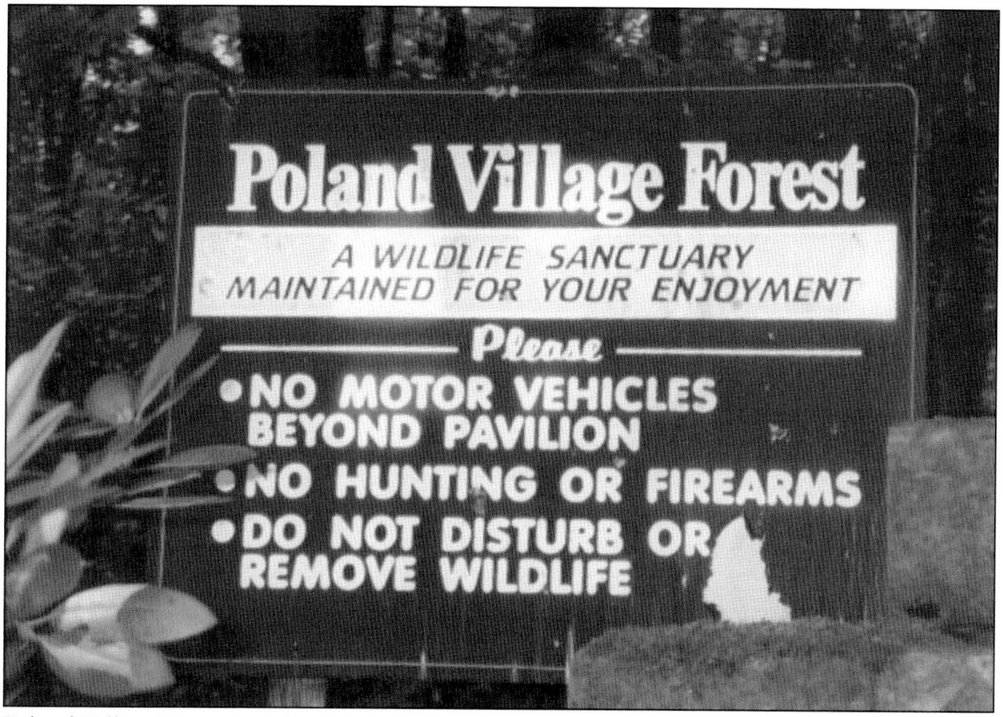

Poland Village Forest was the first municipal forest in Ohio and is still a natural forest setting today. With the main entrance at the end of College Street, the forest trails wind alongside Yellow Creek. The Poland Woods are perhaps best known for the bluebells that bloom every spring, which bring many visitors.

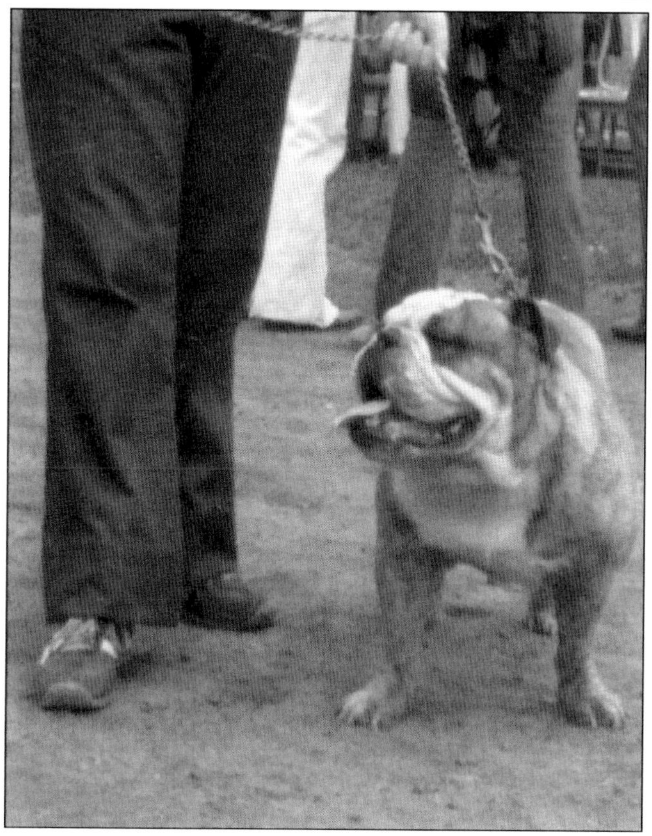

Poland had a bulldog mascot. Anyone attending Poland School football games in the 1960s and 1970s would remember Don Courter's bulldog on the sidelines. He was a crowd pleaser who became excited with every Poland touchdown.

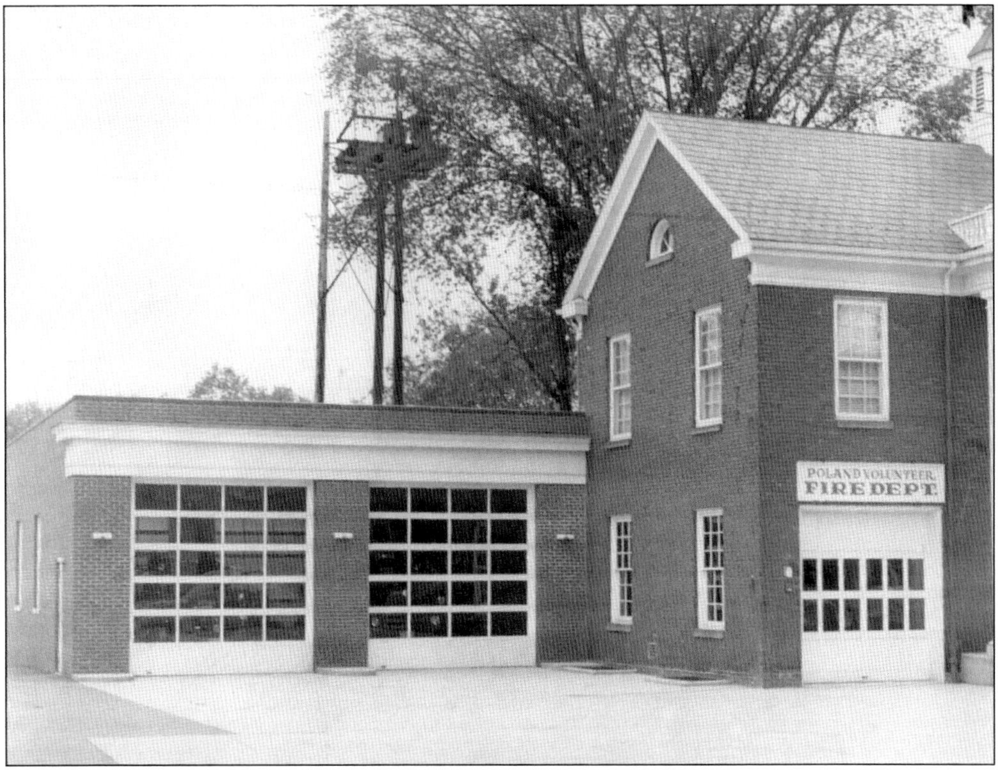

The addition in the mid-1960s to the Main Street fire station was made possible through a federal grant.

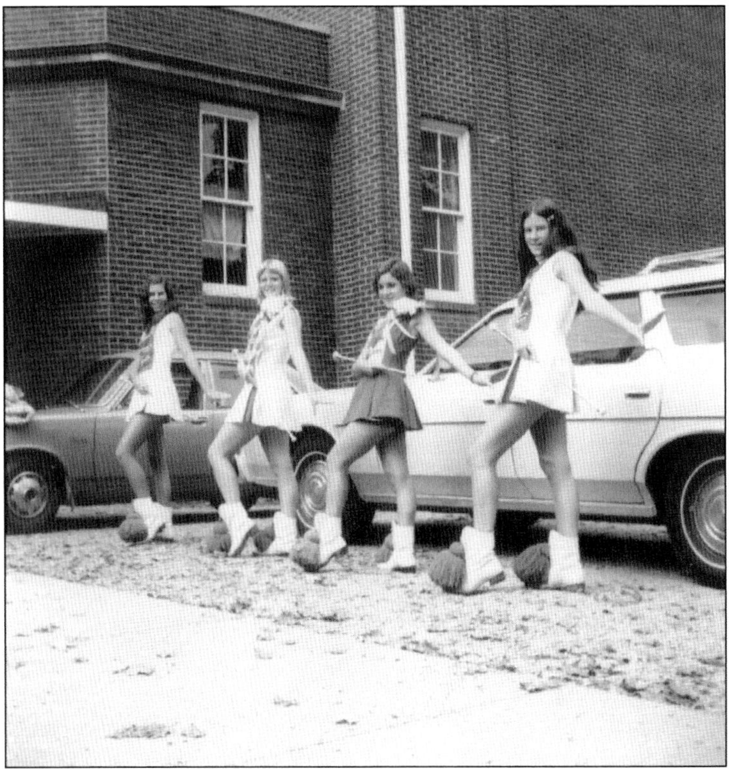

Majorettes of the Poland Seminary High School marching band are still a tradition. Shown here are the majorettes from the mid-1970s when varsity football games were still played at Baird Mitchell Stadium on Cortland Street.

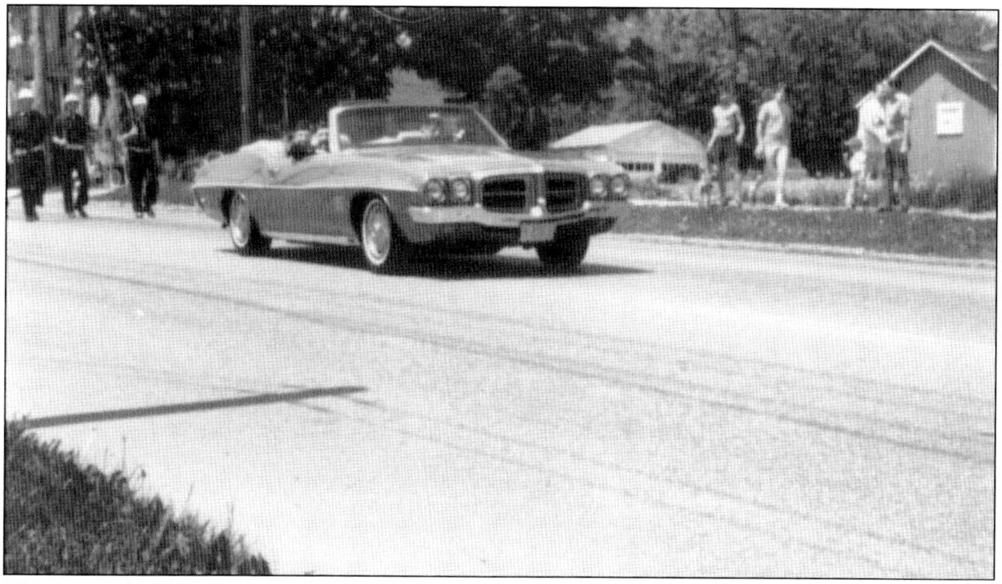

This 1970 photograph shows one of the convertibles that are always a part of Poland's Memorial Day parade.

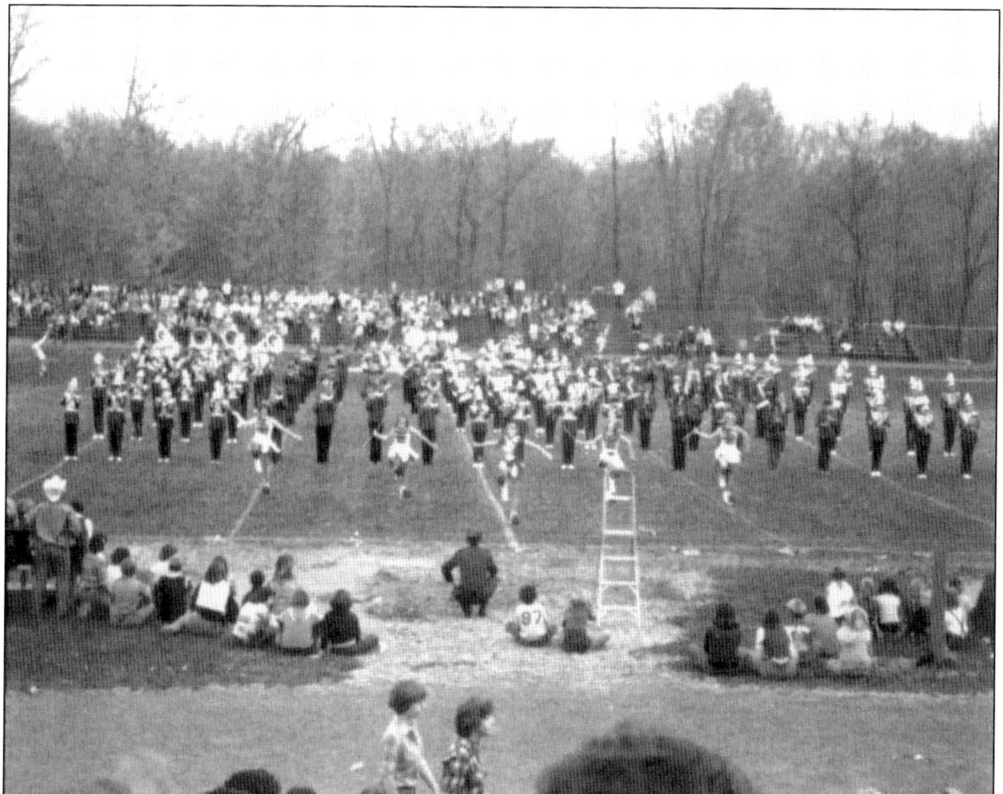

Poland played Saturday afternoon football until the mid-1980s. Shown in this 1976 photograph is the halftime band show at Baird Mitchell Field as seen from atop the press box. The Poland Woods can be seen across from the home side.

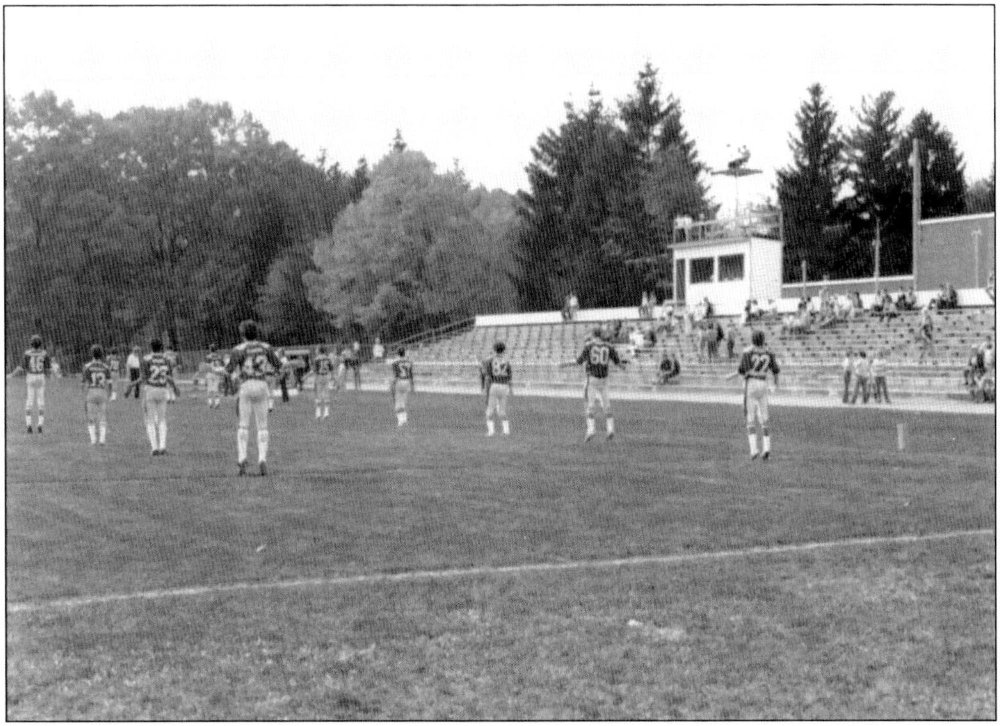

Shown here around 1973 is a varsity football pregame warm-up at Baird Mitchell Field on Cortland Street.

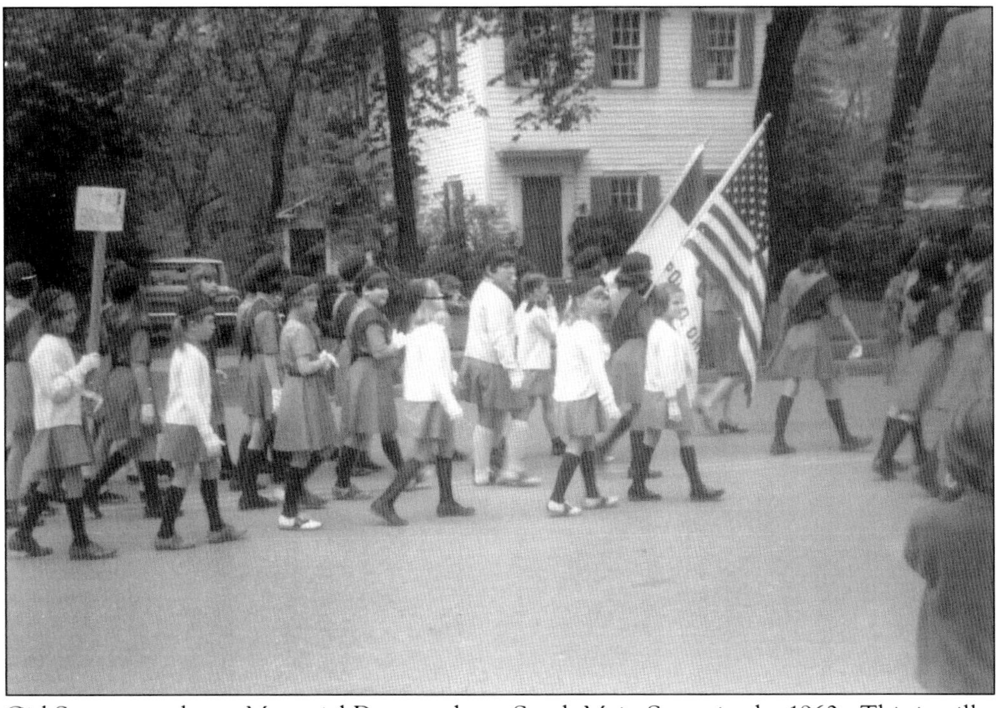

Girl Scouts march at a Memorial Day parade on South Main Street in the 1960s. This is still a tradition today in Poland.

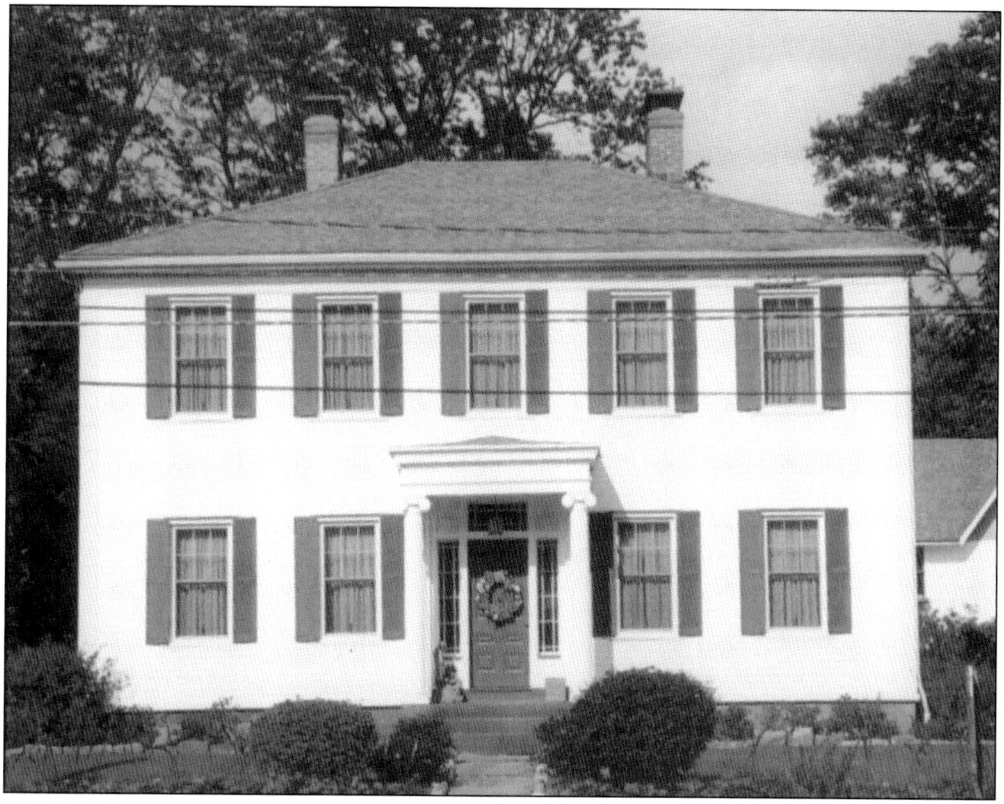

The Hine house, as it was commonly known, was immediately across from the Poland Presbyterian Church on South Main Street that was built in 1845 by George Kirtland. It was occupied by Turhand's son and later by his niece, Emma Kirtland-Hine. Nell Hine's playhouse (below) was built near the house in 1899 and is still there today. A little bear stands near the playhouse on South Main Street in the lot next to the Hine house in this 1960 photograph. The little bear is no longer there. It was sold when the house changed hands several years ago.

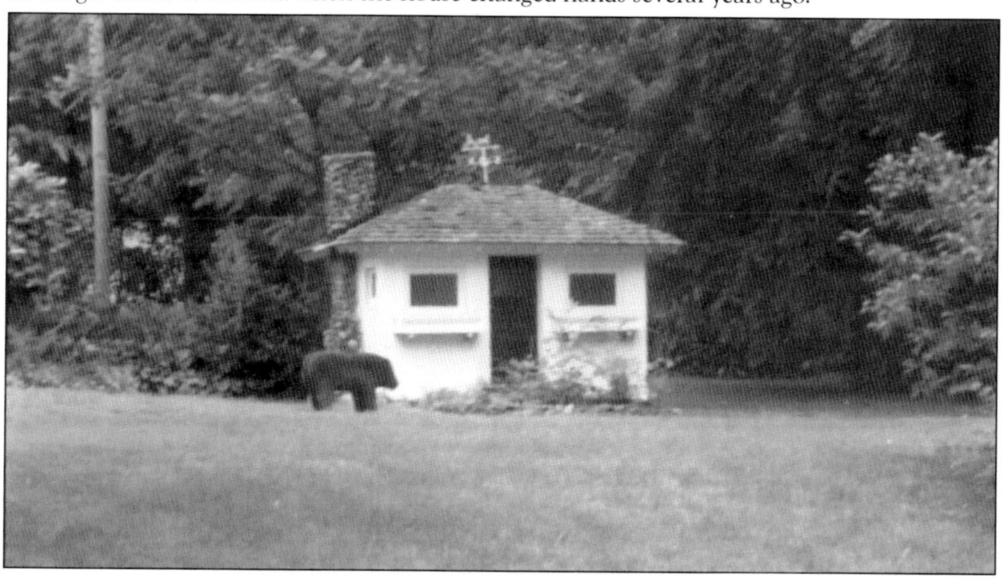

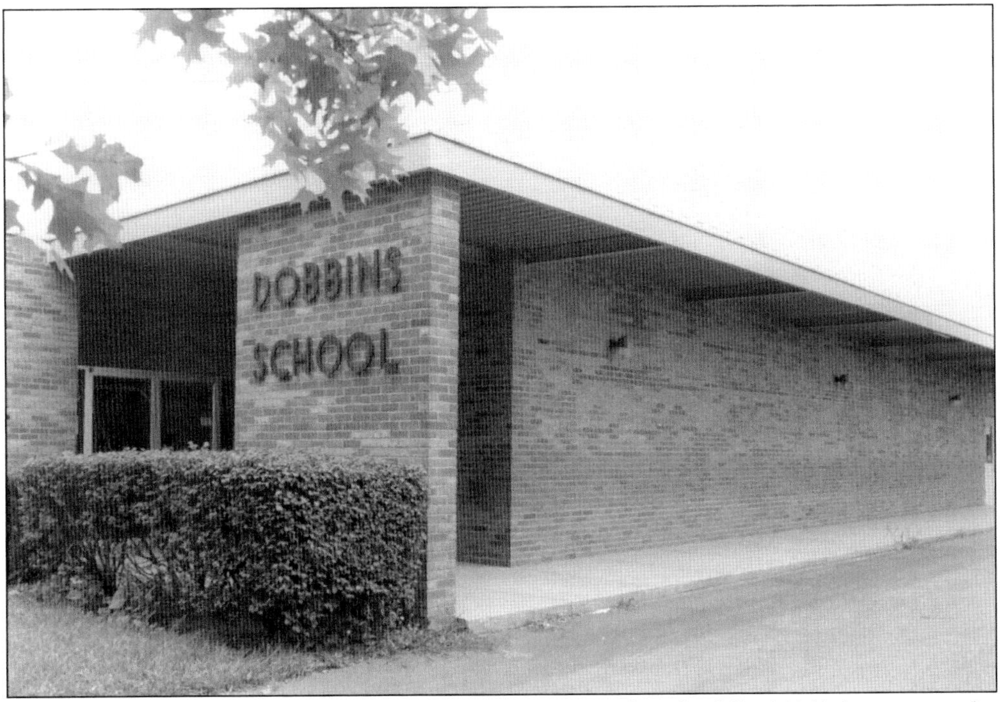

Dobbins Elementary is shown as it appeared when it opened in the fall of 1963, housing grades one through six. Today it houses grades kindergarten through fourth and has been renovated to its present colonial appearance. (Courtesy of Poland schools' Archives.)

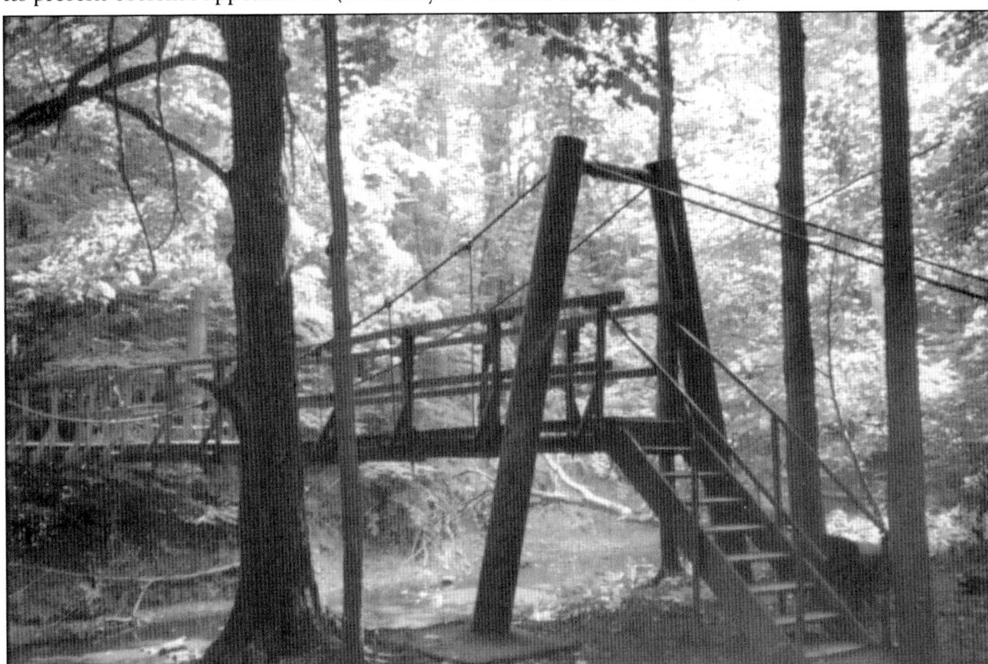

The Mauthe footbridge, built in 1956 over Yellow Creek in the Poland Woods, is a familiar site to joggers, walkers, and those visiting Poland's bluebells.

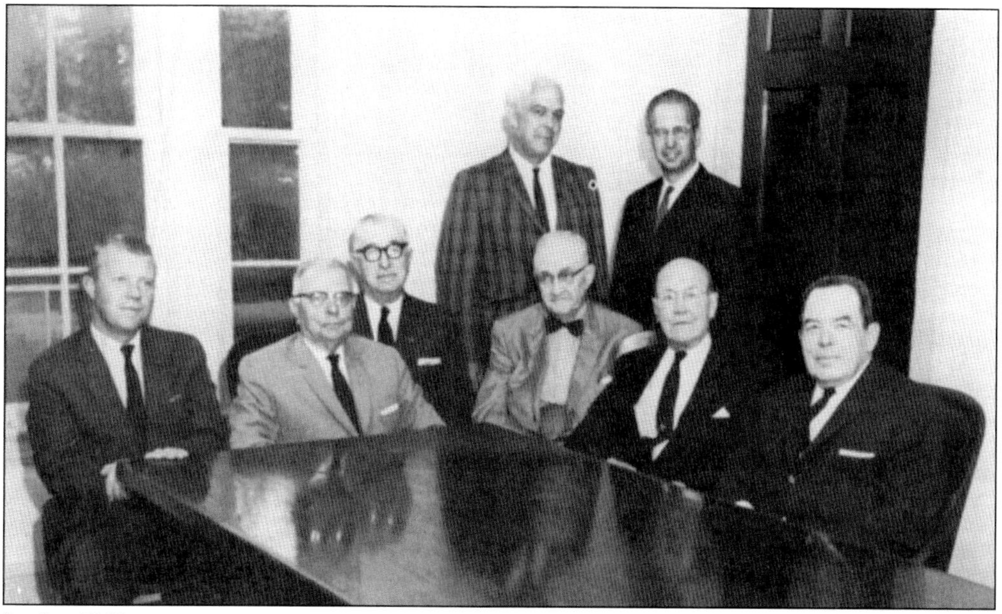

In this 1960 photograph, the Poland Municipal Forest Board is shown. From left to right are (first row) George McNab Jr., Philip Heim, Frank Thacher, Osborne Mitchell, J. L. Mauthe, and James B. Thompson; (second row) Robert Zedaker and T. Evan Brett. (Courtesy of Poland Historical Society.)

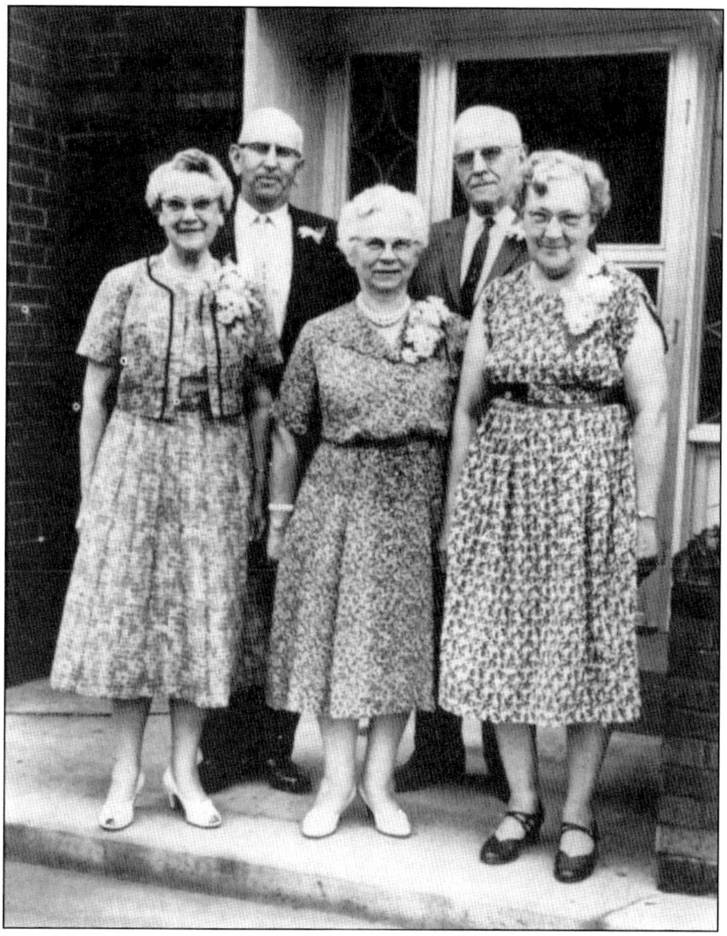

The PSHS class of 1912 held its 50th reunion in 1962, as shown here. From left to right are (first row) Blanche Cover, Ada Martin (née Holler), and Hannah Guterba (née Basler); (second row) Guy Sitler and Levi Good. (Courtesy of Poland schools' archives.)

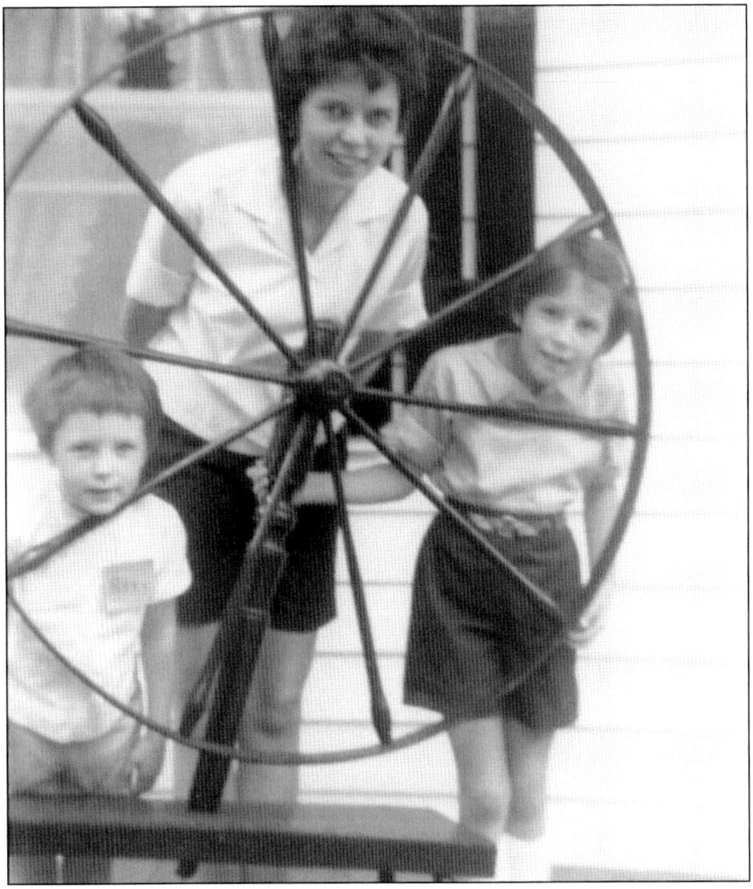

In the early 1800s, this spinning wheel was brought over the Allegheny Mountains to Poland in a covered wagon and is still owned by the family descendants. This photograph was taken in the 1960s.

The Susany farm on Route 224 is a popular place to buy flowers, vegetables, and fruit—all homegrown in Poland, Ohio.

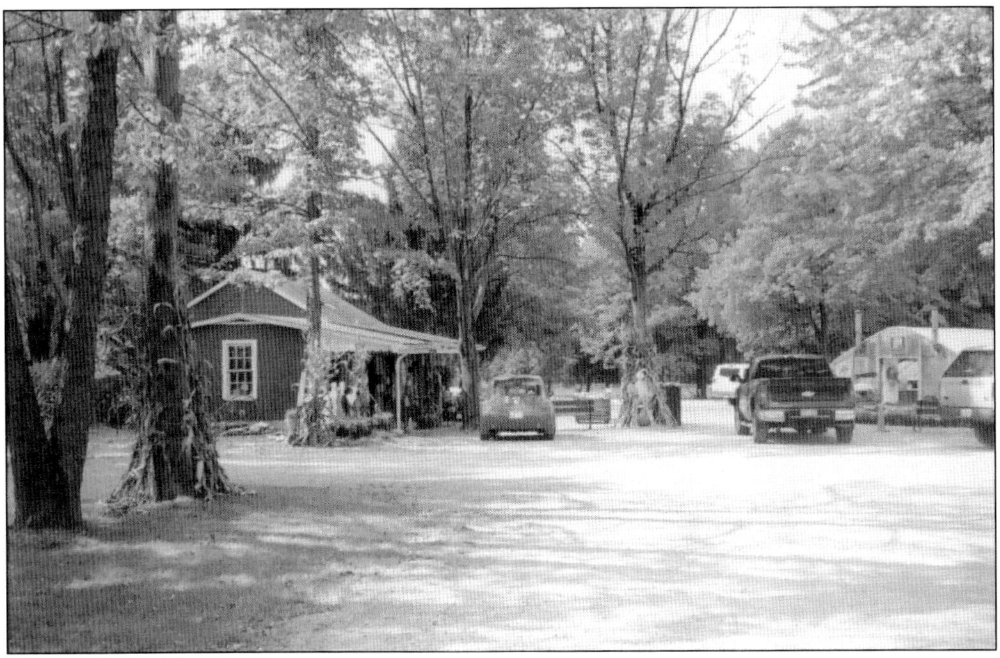

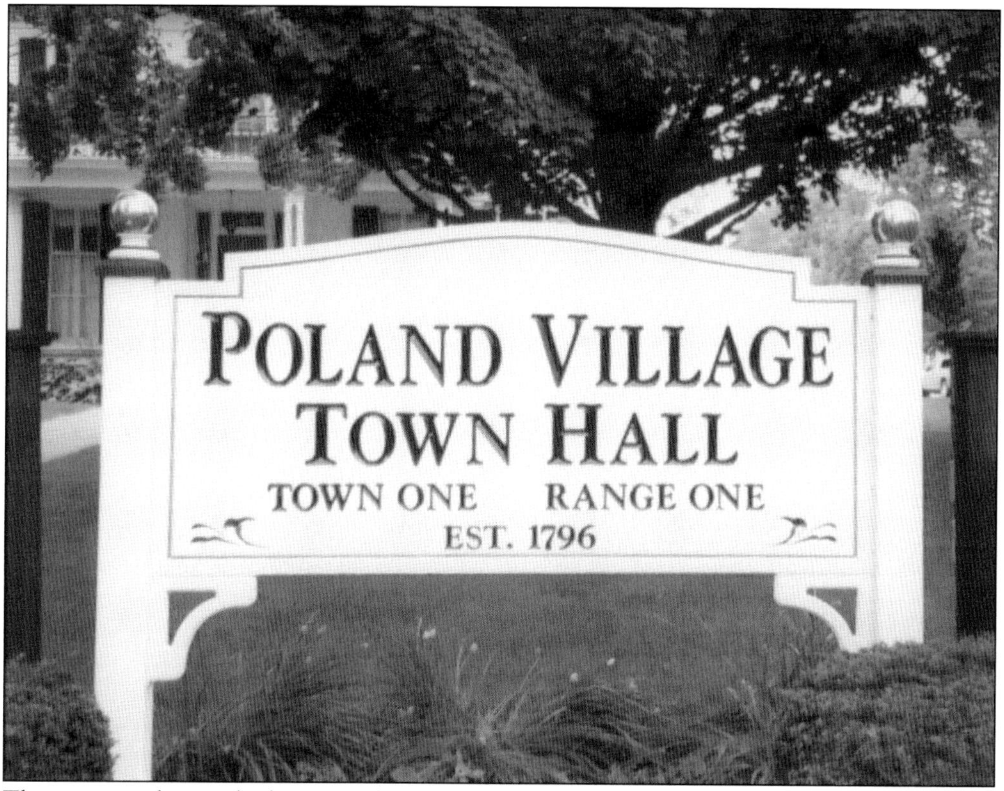

This sign stands outside the Kennedy-Stoddard House at 308 South Main Street. Built in 1845, it was a private residence until 1960, when it was acquired from the estate of Judge Kennedy for use as Village Hall.

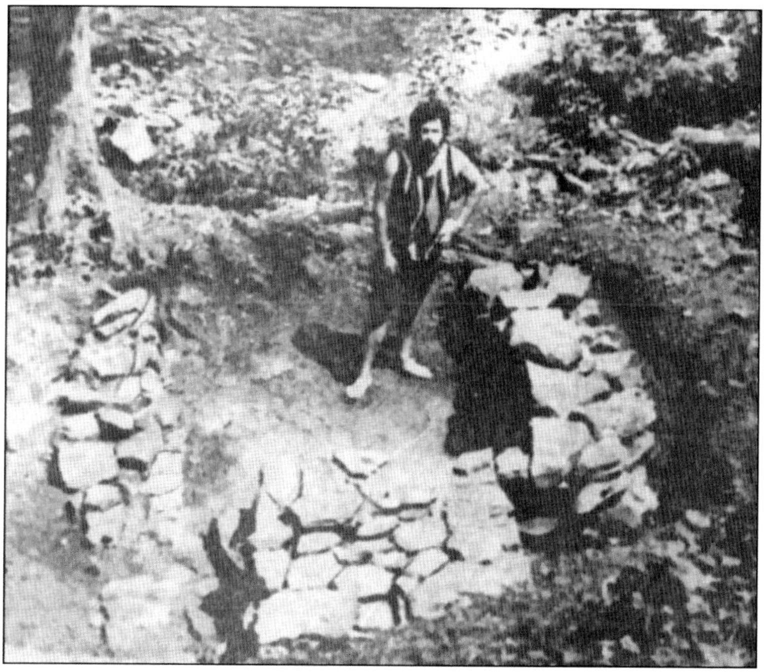

In this 1970 picture, one can see all that is left of Poland's famous Hopewell Blast Furnace from the early 1800s on the bank of Yellow Creek, just past Hamilton Dam. (Courtesy of Poland Historical Society.)

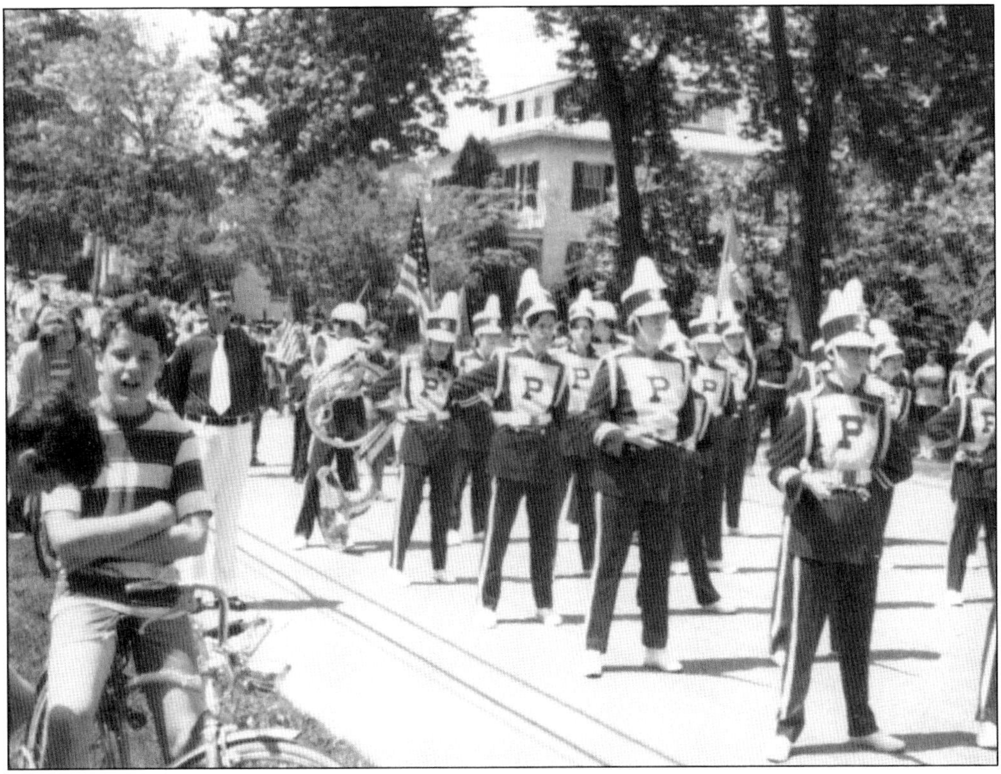

Poland Seminary High School marching band comes down Main Street on Memorial Day in the 1970s.

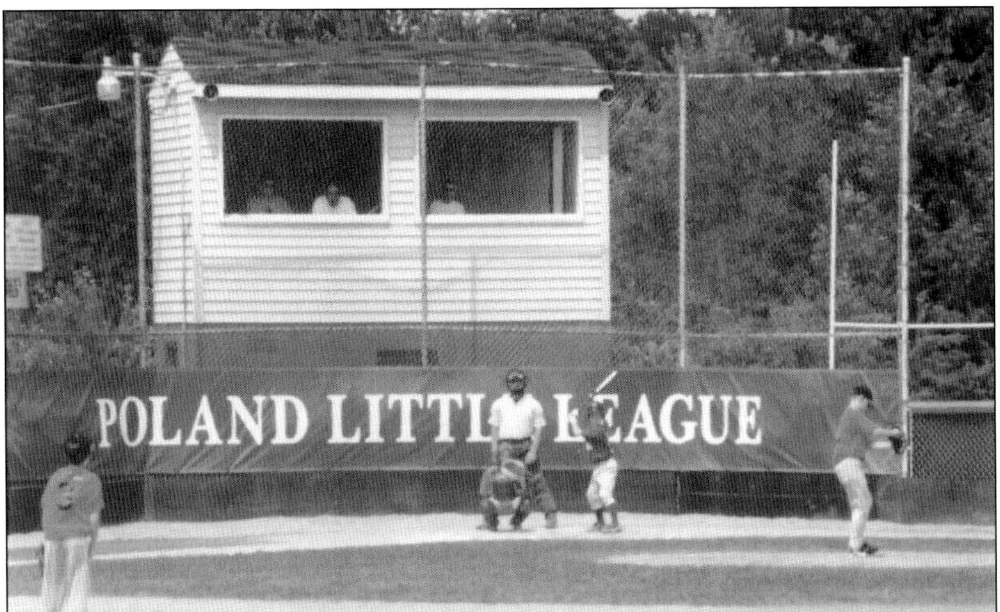

Little League became a key part of Poland's little boys' and girls' summer fun. Shown here is the Poland Community Baseball Association (PCBA) field at North Elementary.

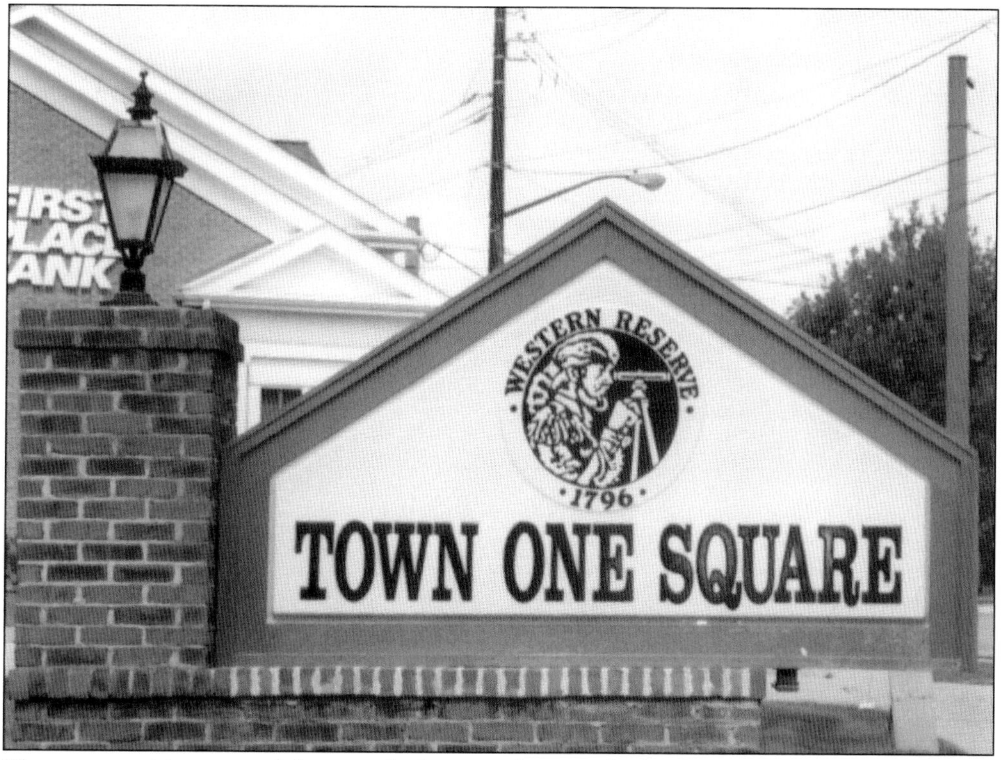

The commercial stores and shops in the business district of Poland on Main Street in Town One Square, built in early 1970s, carried on the tradition of Poland's "Town One" colonial appearance. Notice even the sign refers to the 1796 Western Reserve Heritage.

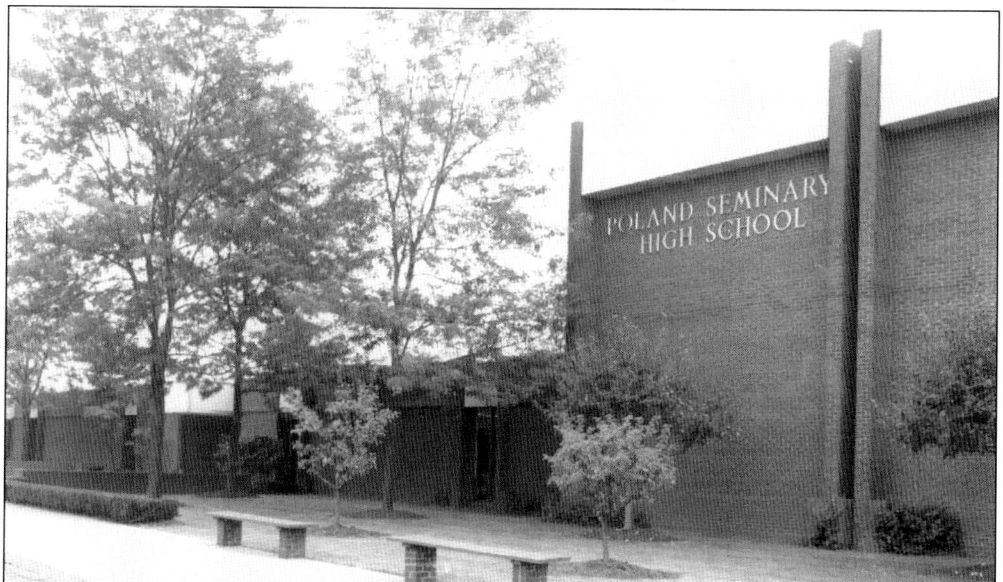

Poland Seminary High School moved from its College Street home to its present location on Dobbins Road in the fall 1971. At that time, the school housed grades 10 through 12. In 1985, the school housed grades 9 through 12. (Courtesy of Poland schools' archives.)

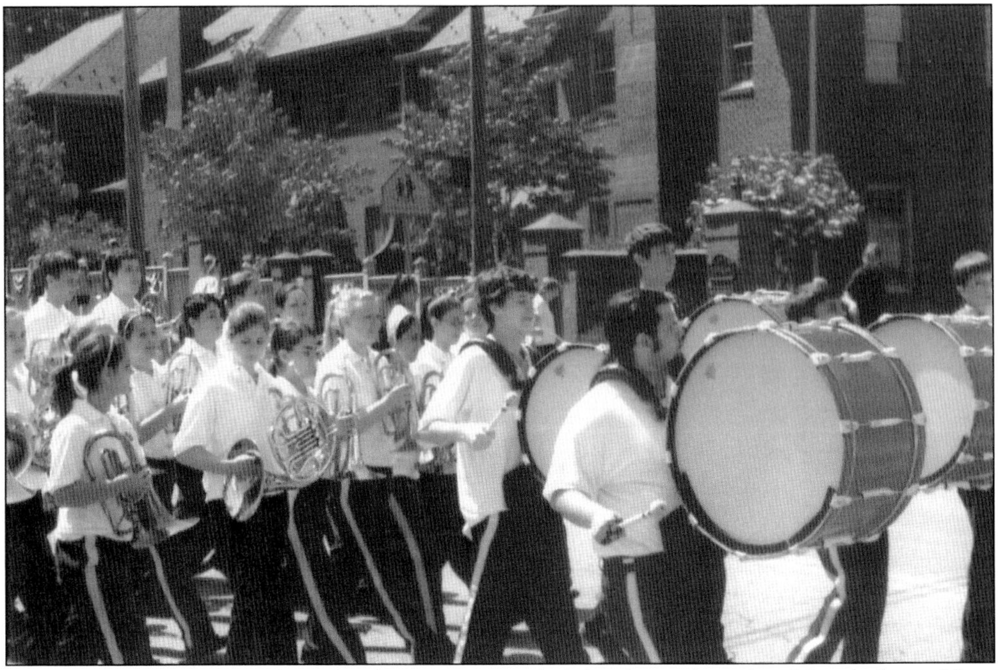

On Memorial Day 2005, the Poland Seminary High School marching band heads down Main Street in summer dress on the way to Poland's Riverside Cemetery to hear the traditional veterans' Memorial Day speech.

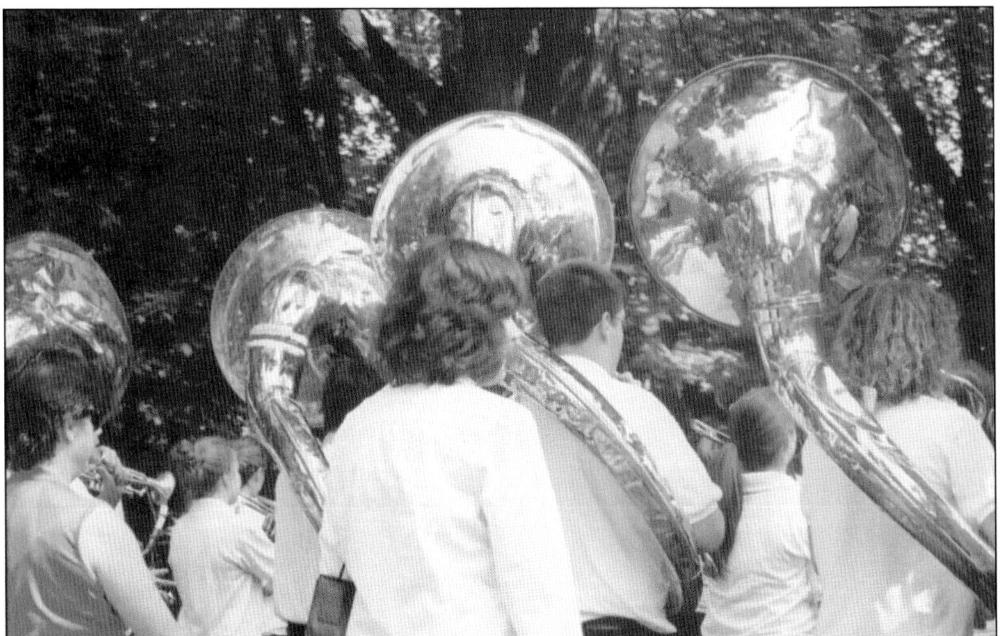

Band parents often walk along the sidelines to support the band in the Memorial Day parade—another tradition.

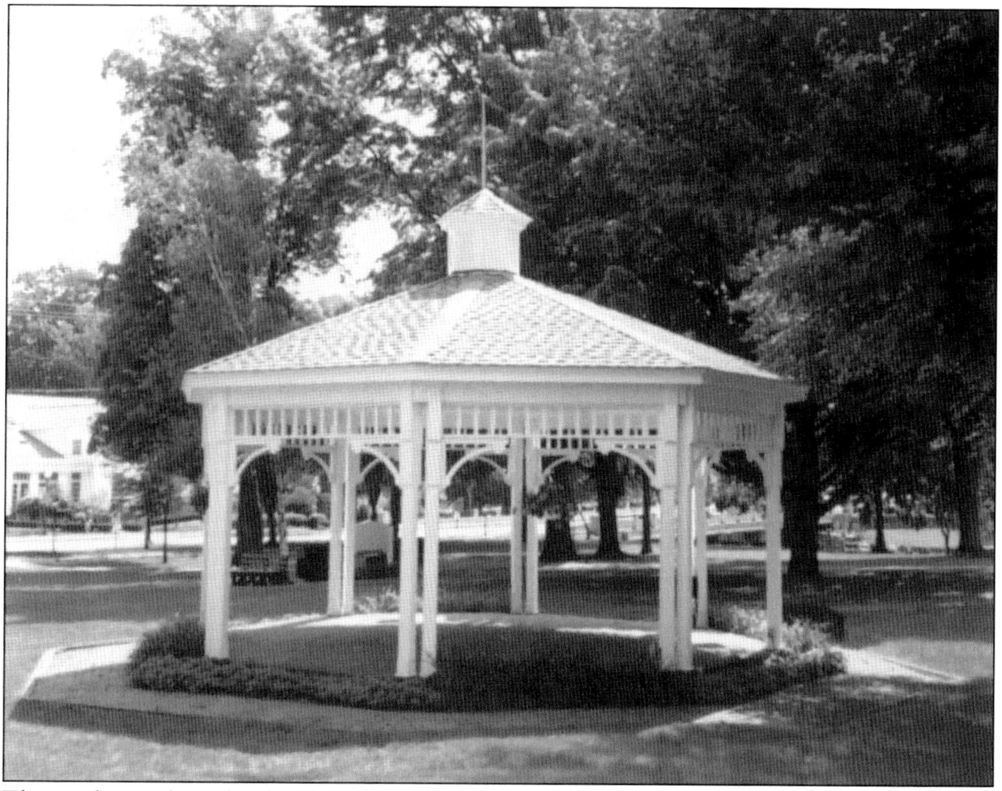

The gazebo on the Poland Village Hall front lawn is a favorite spot for summer band concerts on Monday evenings. Music fills the air as friends and neighbors sit on lawn chairs listening.

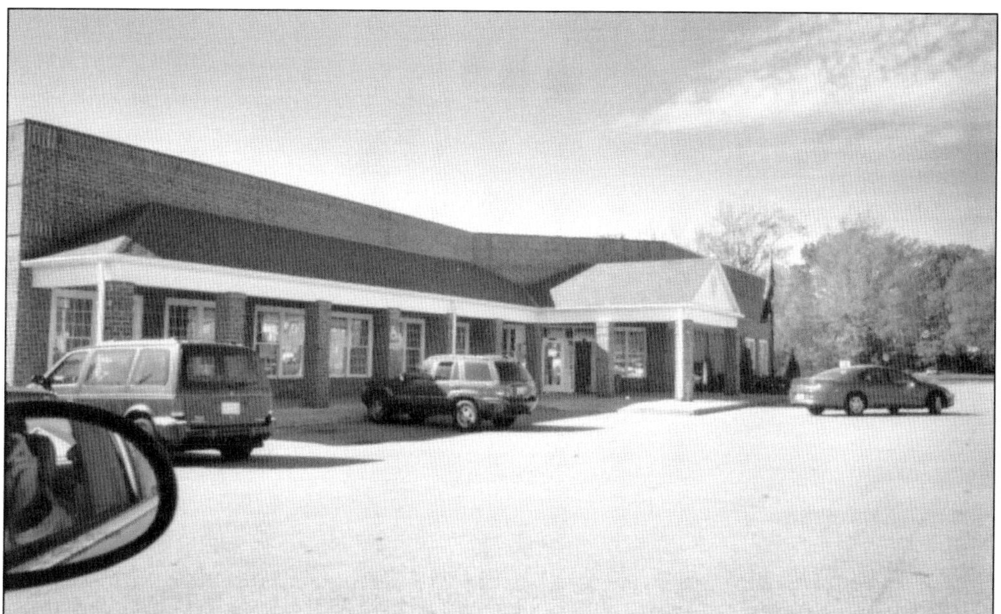

Poland's new post office on Route 224, replacing the former one on Sheridan Road, maintains the tradition of colonial architecture.

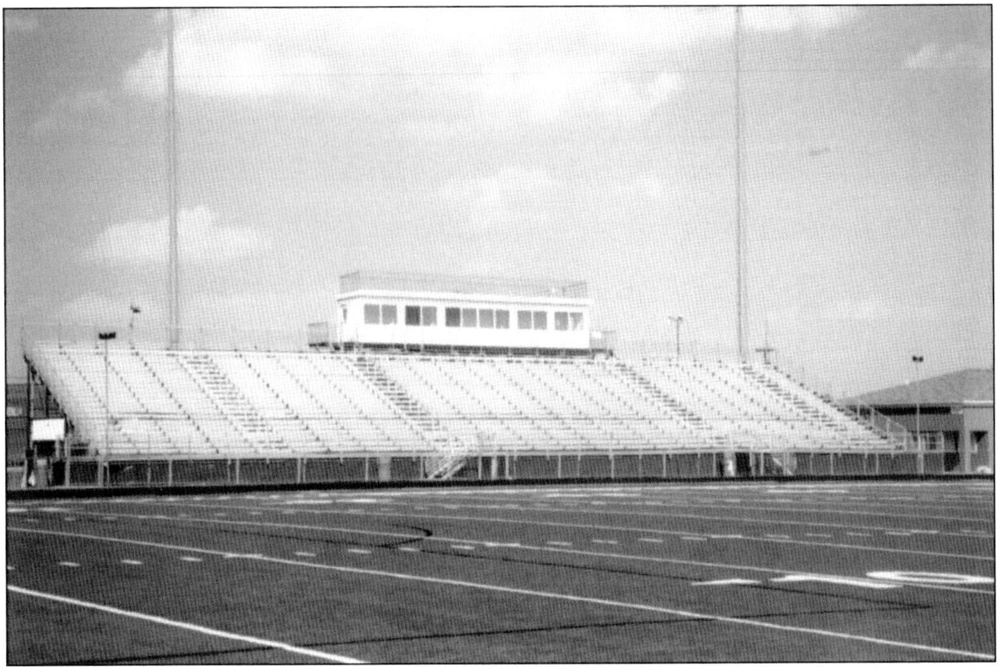

Poland Seminary High School stadium on Dobbins Road is shown at its opening in 1986 at the high school site, moving from Baird Mitchell stadium at Cortland Street. (Courtesy of Poland schools' archives.)

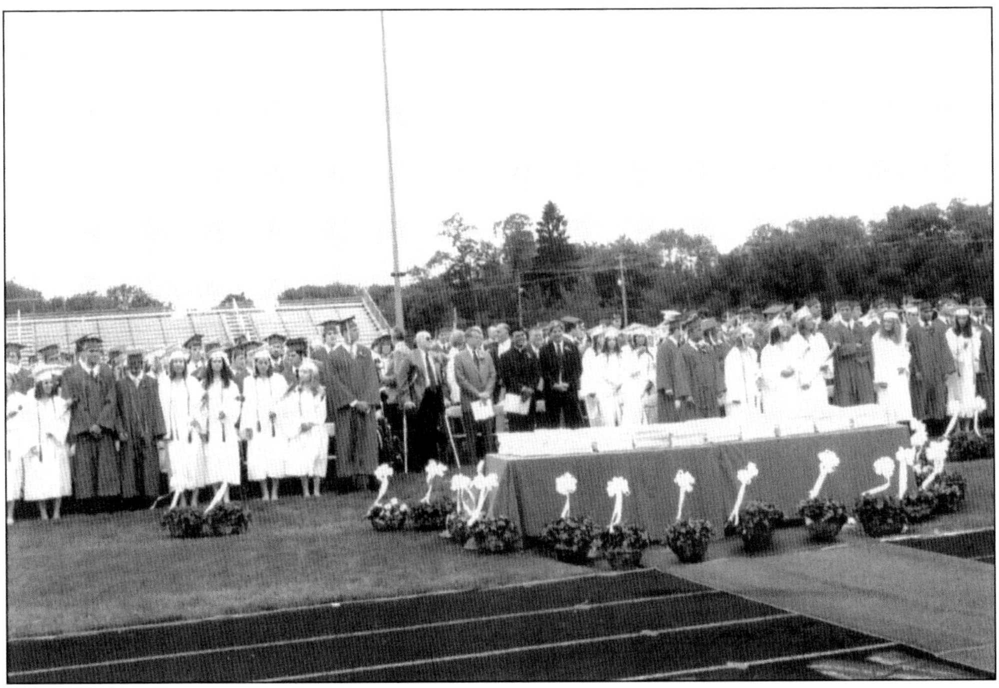

PSHS graduates on the school's field in 2006 are about to throw their hats in the air, continuing another tradition observed in Poland.

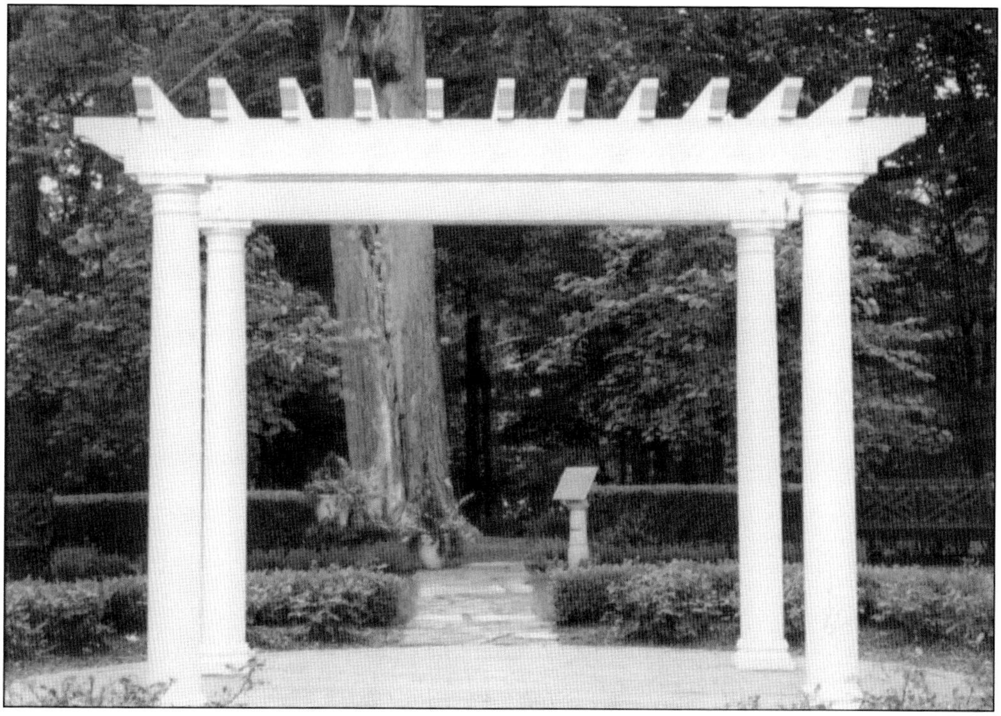

Poland Centennial Gardens, behind Village Hall, was built in 1966 to reestablish the Kennedy Gardens, which were long a focal point in years gone by. The entrance is shown here with the trellis (above) and the entrance sign (below).

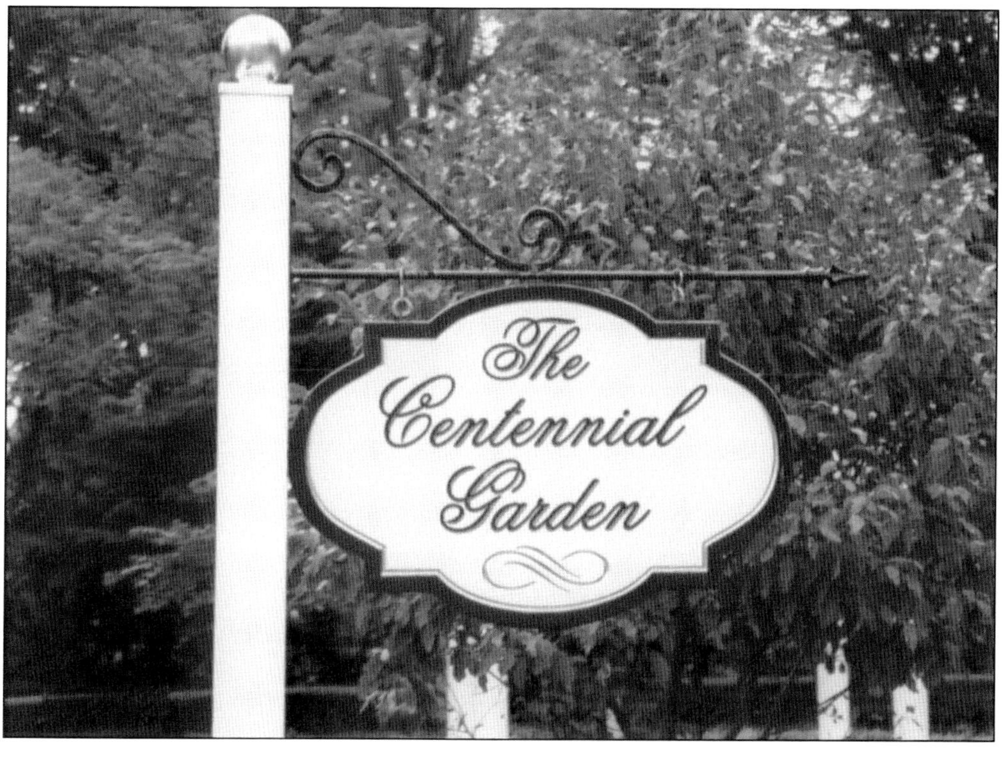

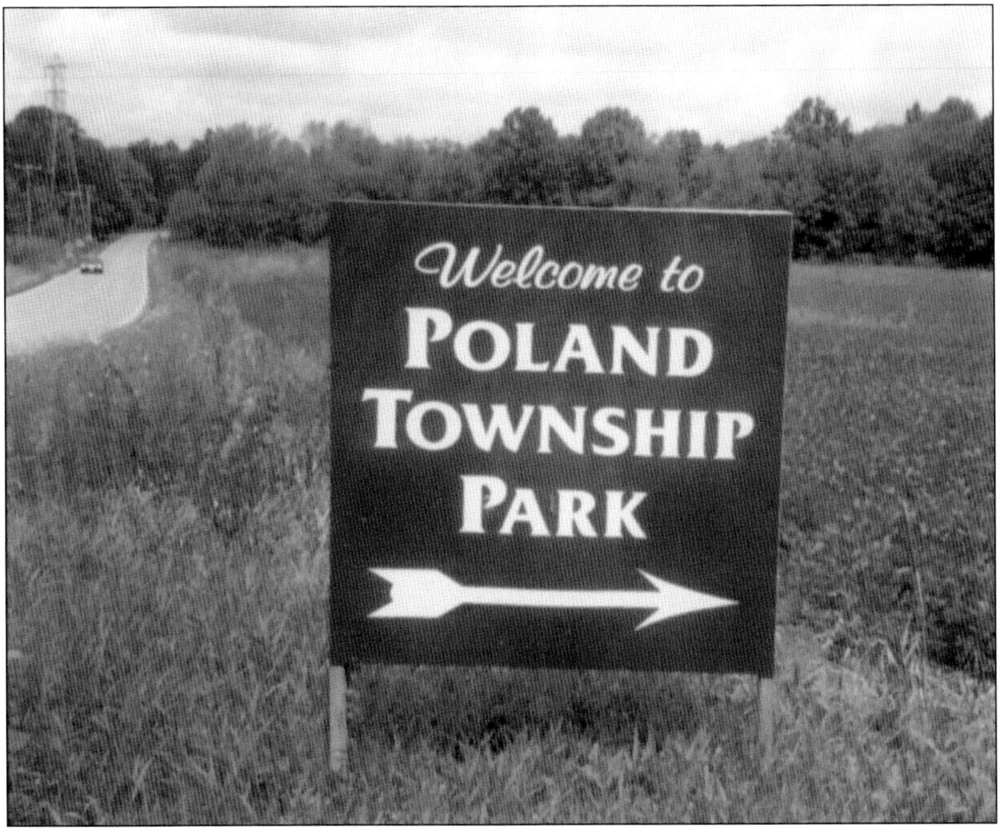

Poland Township Park, opened in 2008, is located between Cowden, Moore, and Miller Roads, is home to the Poland Youth Soccer Association, and has 1.25 miles of nature trails.

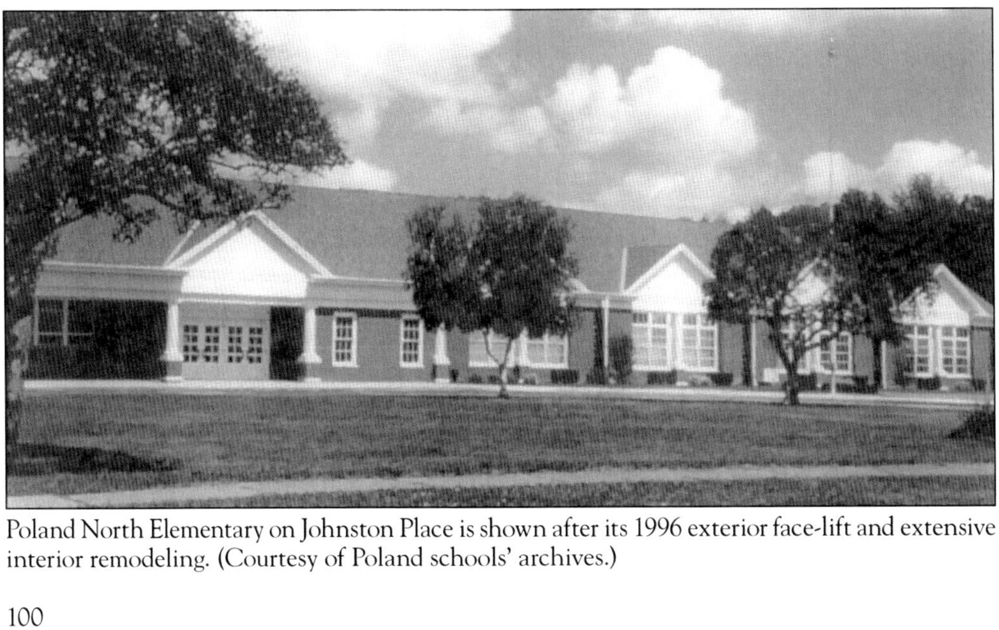

Poland North Elementary on Johnston Place is shown after its 1996 exterior face-lift and extensive interior remodeling. (Courtesy of Poland schools' archives.)

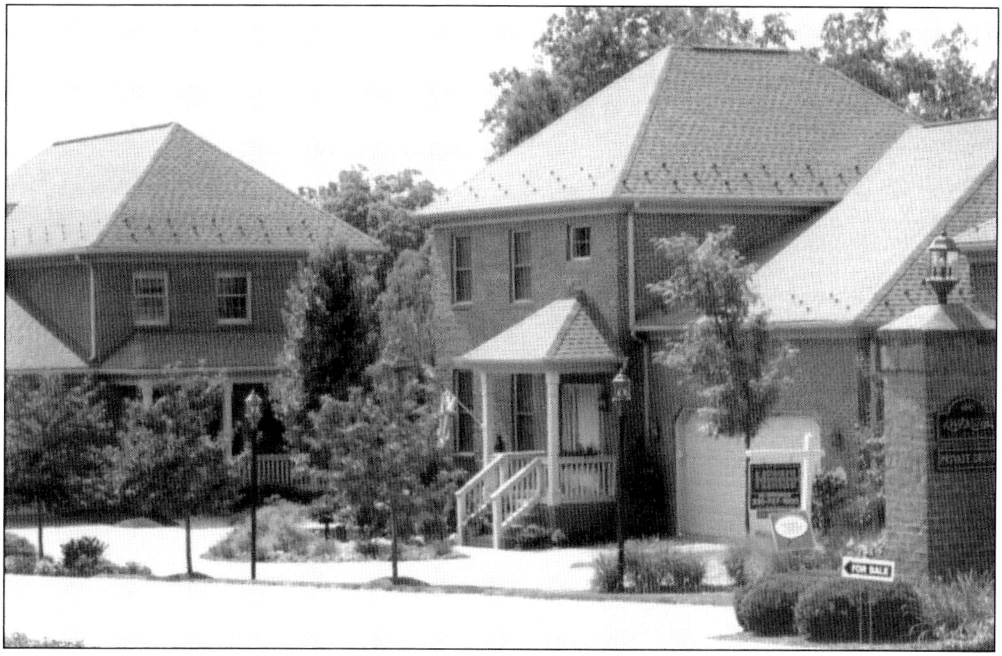

Riverside Court condominiums, at the intersection of Riverside Drive and South Main Street, were at the site of a former business district that started after the civil war.

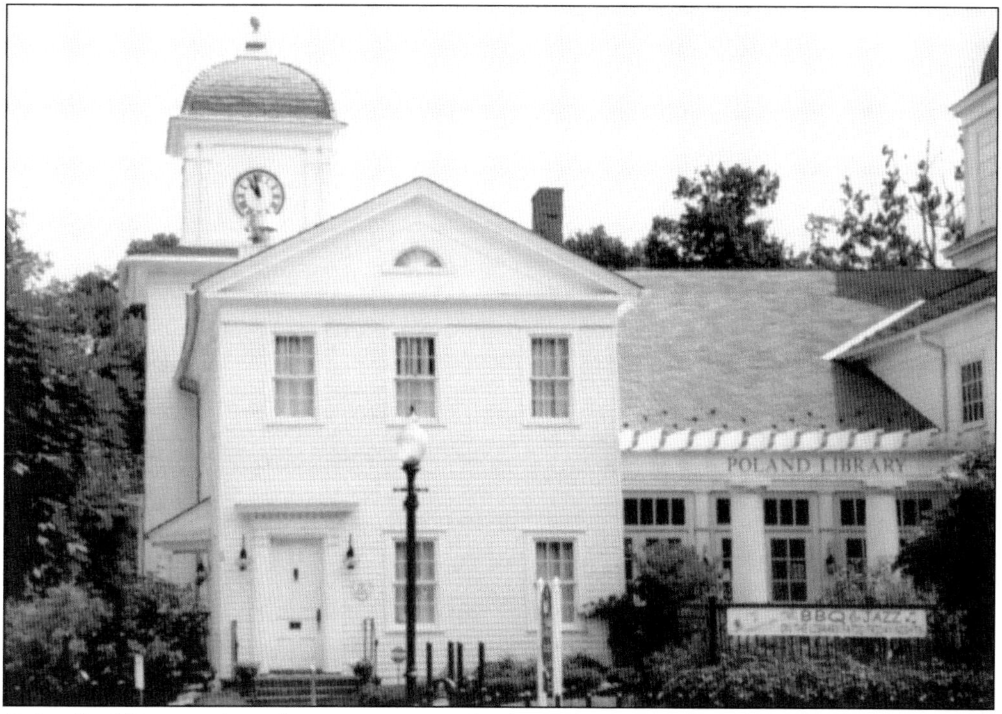

Poland's old historic boys dormitory was used to house boys attending the Poland Academy and then the Poland Seminary on College Street. It is the structure in the far left of this recent photo of the new library on South Main Street. When the new library was built in 2001, the new library incorporated the old dormitory on that site as part of the new library building.

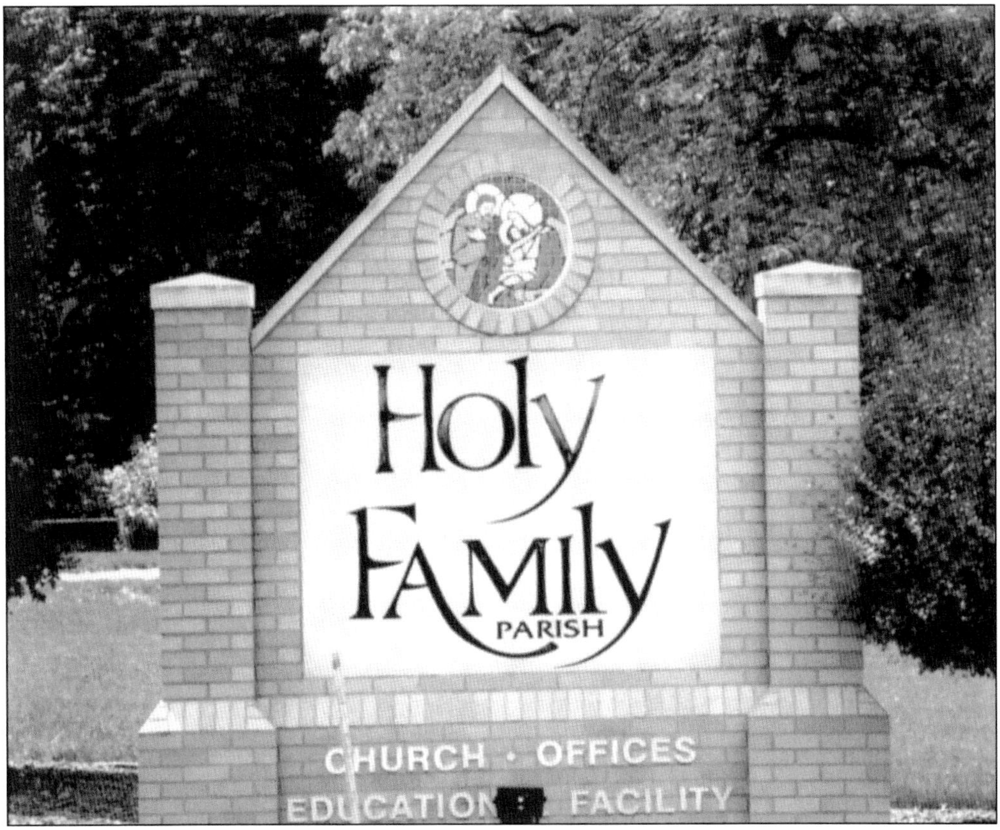

Holy Family became part of the Poland community in 1956 with ground breaking for a church. Shown below is Holy Family's new church built in 1997.

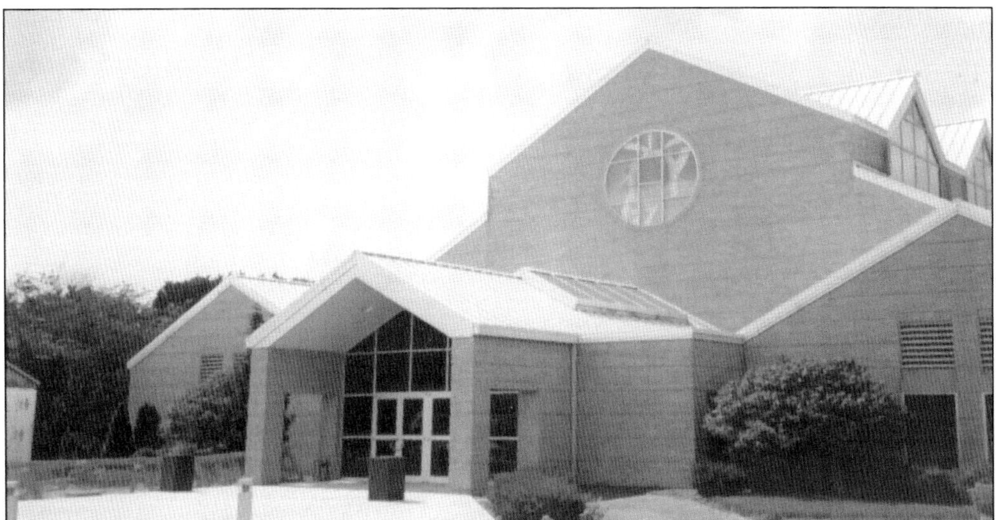

Holy Family's new church is shown as it looks today in 2009. Holy Family's first Poland church was completed in 1957 and served until this new church opened.

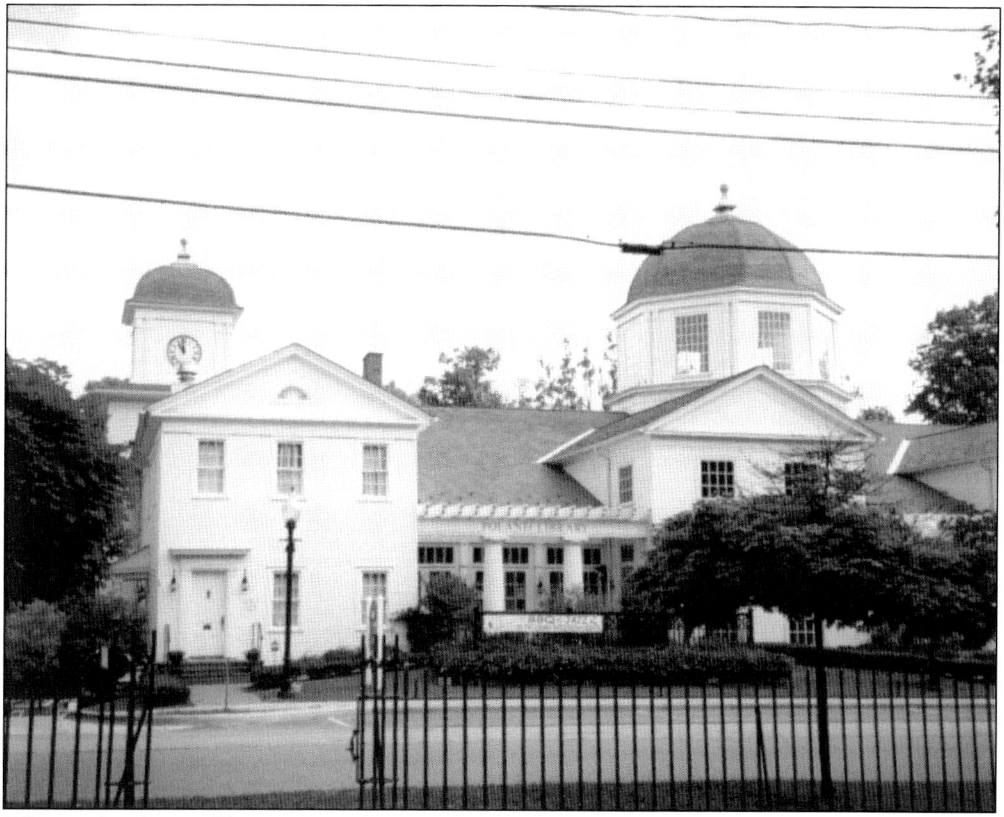

When Poland's new library opened in 2001 on South Main Street, it was an impressive colonial structure. It is Poland's third library and is built on the site of the 1965 library.

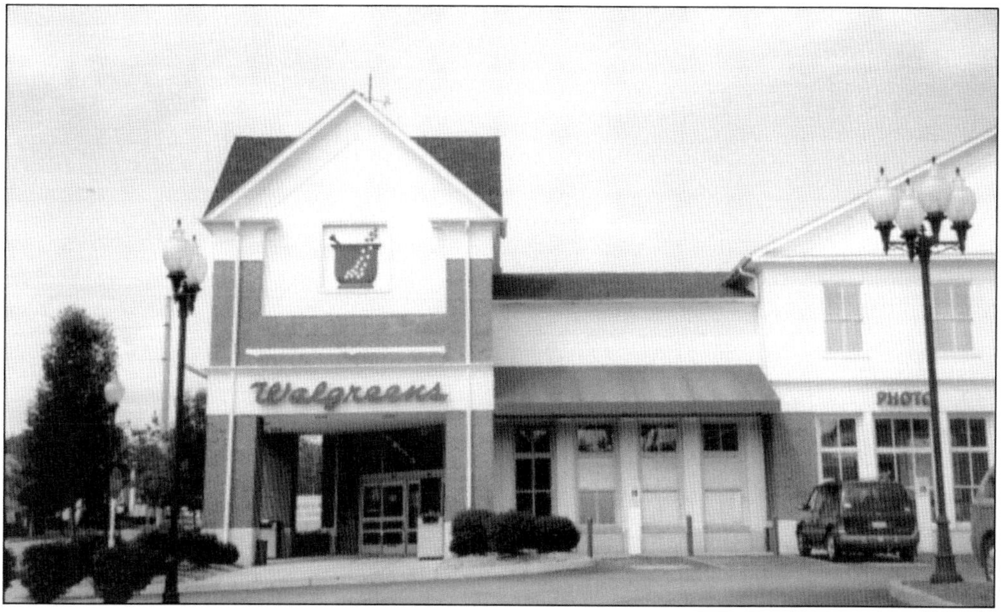

The Walgreens pharmacy in Poland is said to be the chain's most colonial drug store in the nation. The architecture is in keeping with Poland tradition.

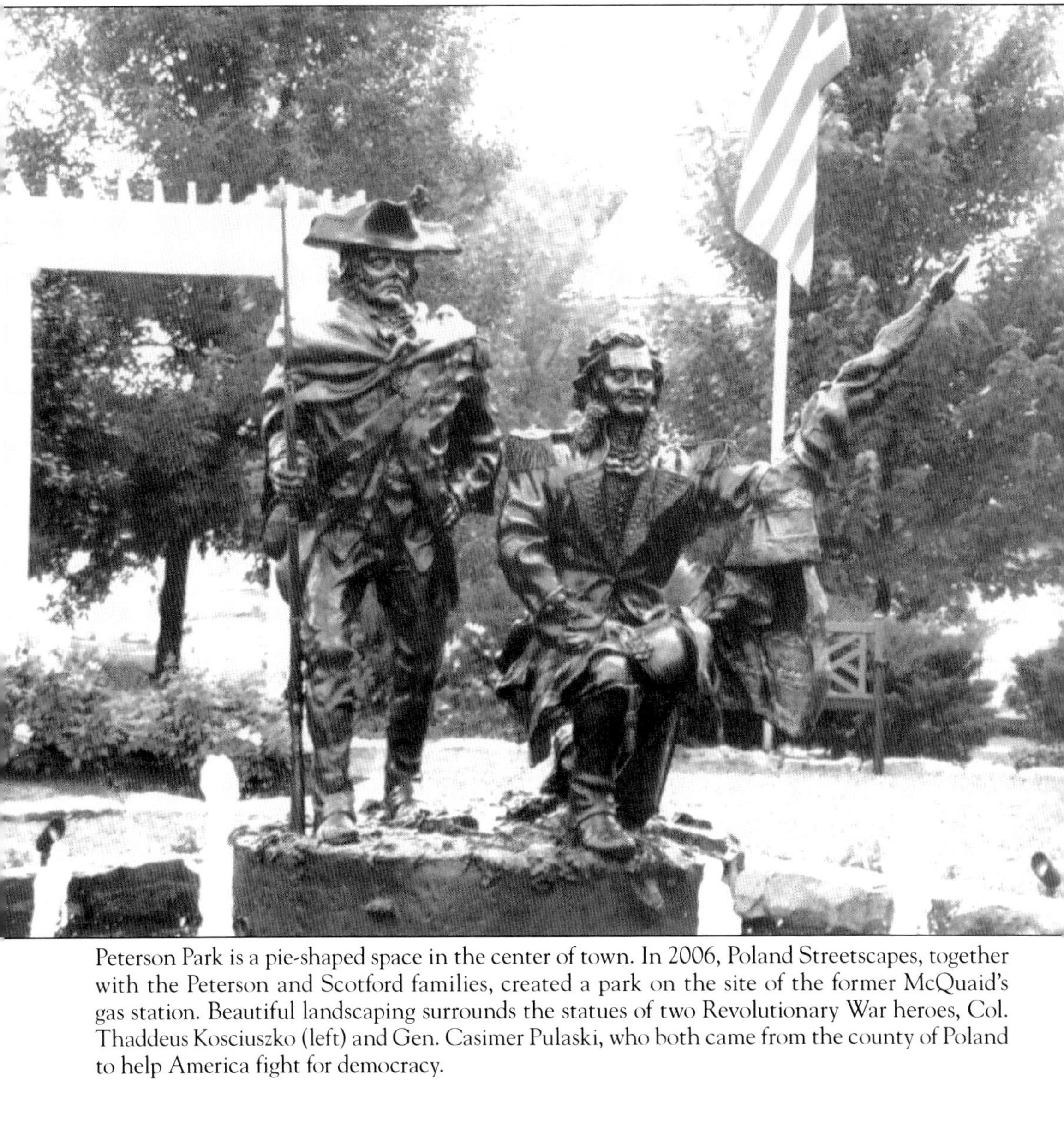

Peterson Park is a pie-shaped space in the center of town. In 2006, Poland Streetscapes, together with the Peterson and Scotford families, created a park on the site of the former McQuaid's gas station. Beautiful landscaping surrounds the statues of two Revolutionary War heroes, Col. Thaddeus Kosciuszko (left) and Gen. Casimer Pulaski, who both came from the county of Poland to help America fight for democracy.

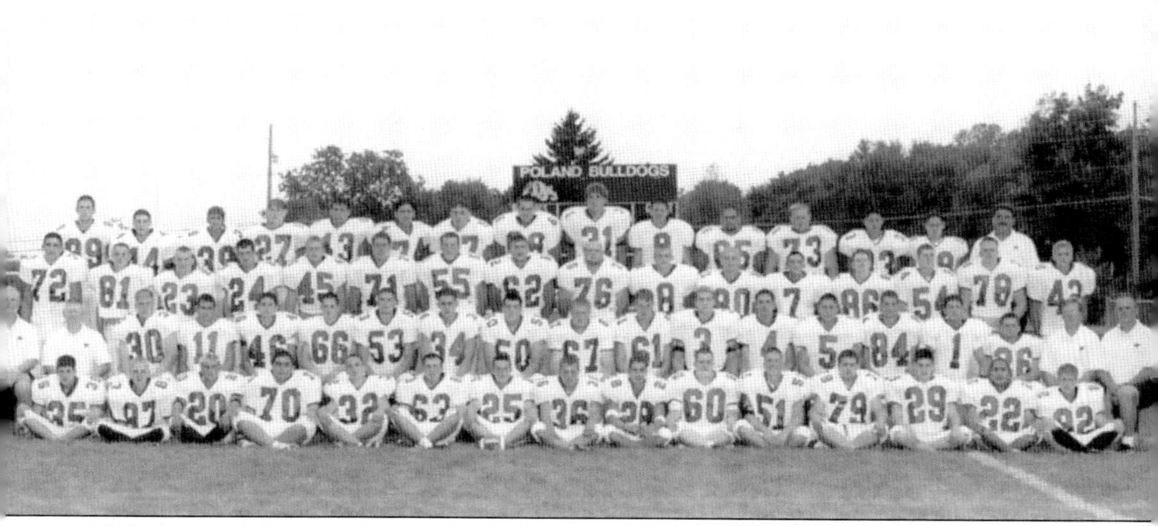

In 1999, the state's division II varsity football team ended with a perfect undefeated 16-0 season, winning the state championship. Members of that year's varsity team are, from left to right, (first row) J. Bajerski, G. Angelo, V. Antonucci, G. Dibo, B. Hallas, B. Moran, S. Davis, J. Mitolo, T. Carline, B. Kolat, C. Holtzman, B. McMahon, B. Dalesandro, L. Zamudio, and K. O'Hallaron; (second row) Coach Rowe, Coach Covell, J. Resch, N. Dalesandro, J. Larouere, M. Antonas, M. Zembower, B. Chipps, C. Smith, J. Shaver, J. Wiery, B. Bair, S. Saad, J. Westrem, D. Colella, P. Day, Coach Hulea, and Coach Brungard; (third row) J. Marchese, R. Marsico, A. Colella, M. Yost, T. Clayton, P. Stanich, J. Bishop, P. Gallo, A. Detwiler, D. Bole, P. Modelski, M. Daprile, J. Douds, R. Chance, J. Strudwick, and J. Courtney; (fourth row) J. Bero, J. Stroh, P. Perry, T. DiNunzio, L. Davanzo, D. Burnett, C. Ratliff, D. Coutris, M. Harris, J. Simko, J. Antonucci, A. Perry, P. Brine, J. Modelski, and Coach Gallo.

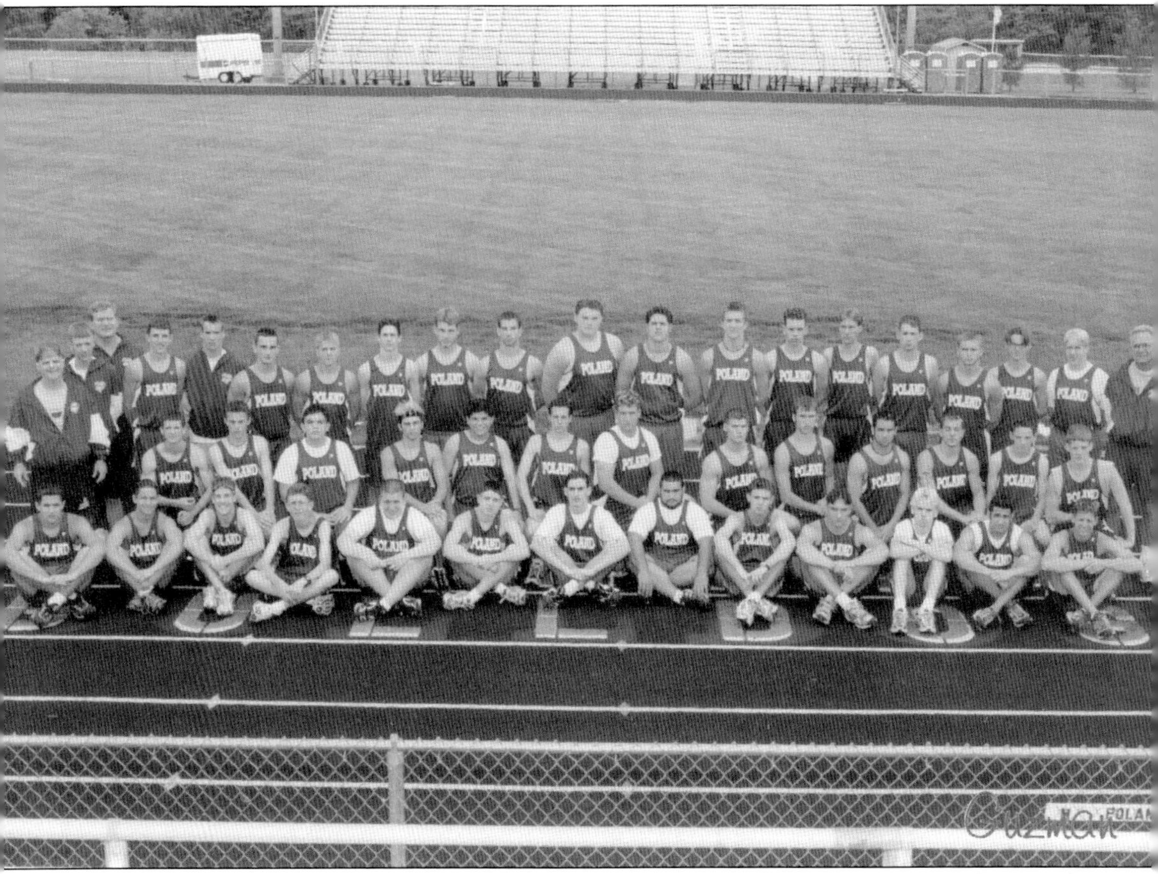

Poland's high school track team won the 2000 state championship for division II. This was the first year Poland brought home a state track title since 1951, making PSHS the home of two state titles in one school year, 1999–2000—a rare occurrence in any school. Pictured from left to right are (front row) Dave Burnett, Jack Modelski, Tony Dinunzio, Keith Young, Luke Skinner, Mike Stoll, John Grahovac, Joe Antonucci, Andy Fusselman, Chris Ratliff, Bob Decapua, Pete Perry, and Joe Simko; (second row) Steve Hruby, Mark Carbon, Mike Crnarich, Vince Antonucci, Chris Patrick, Julian Malizia, Jason Resch, Kevin Jennings, Beau Tiger, Nick Dalesandro, Tony Villanueva, John Ramson, and Jim Zembower; (third row) coach Don Smaltz, Brandon Buxman, coach Michael Simington, Drew Frum, Andy Colella, Robert Virostek, John Jeren, Liam Malone, Jordan Shaver, Jason Westrem, Chuck Hayes, Pete Stanich, Jeff Wiery, Ryan McCarthy, Griffin Wesler, Chris Wheatley, Pete Modelski, Jeremy Mount, Pat Rigney, and coach David DiRienzo. (Courtesy of Poland schools' archives.)

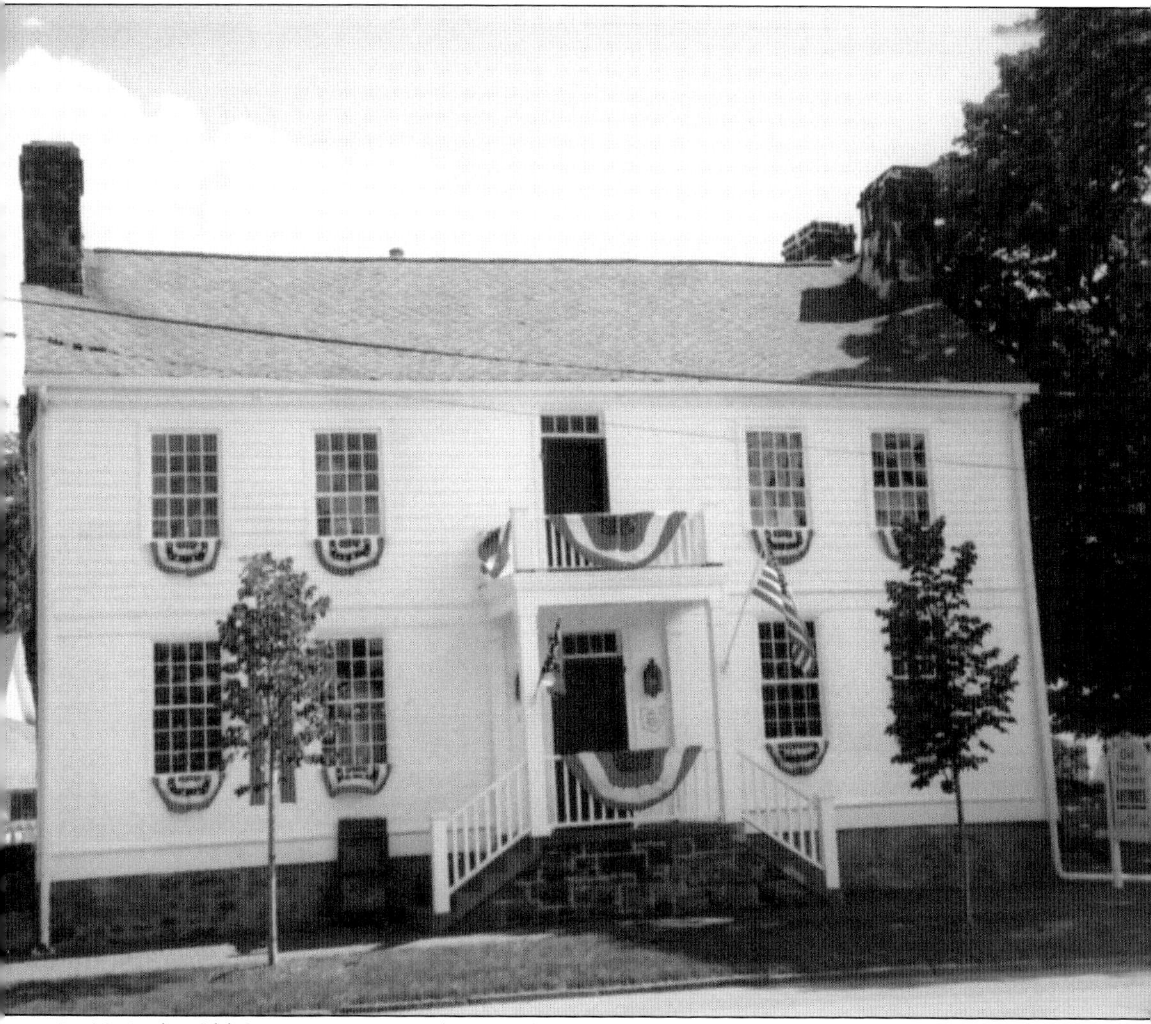

In 2009, the Old Stone Tavern was decorated for the July 4 celebration. The tavern is Poland's oldest building and is also the largest, oldest building still standing in the Connecticut Western Reserve.

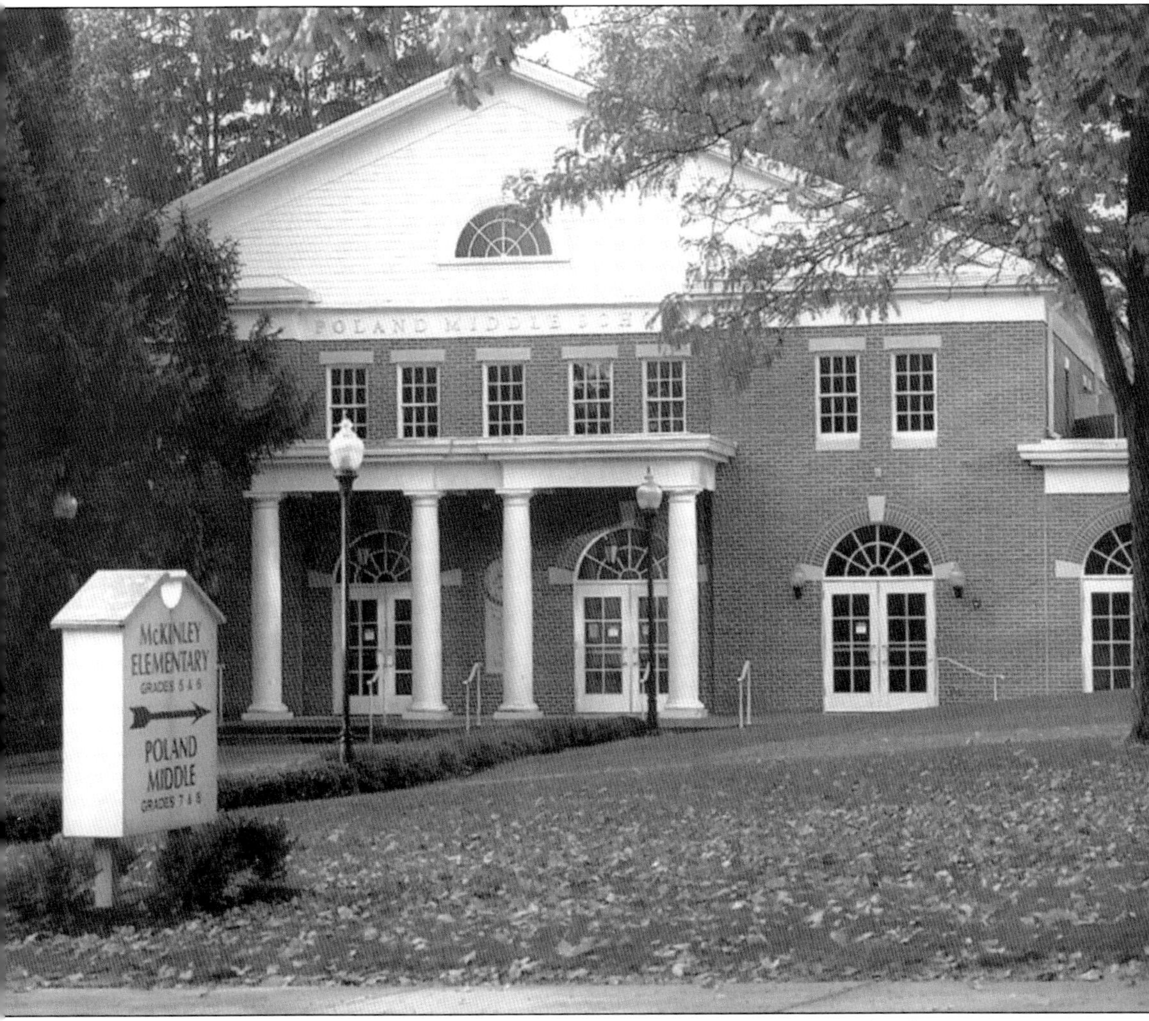

The Poland connector brought McKinley Elementary and Poland Middle School into one campus. Shown here, the connector was built in 2004–2005 over what was Elm Street, which once ran between the two schools. (Courtesy of Poland schools' archives.)

The bell tower in Peterson Park, in the heart of Poland, is another streetscapes project that enhances and beautifies Poland. The chimes can be heard through much of Poland and add a distinctive air.

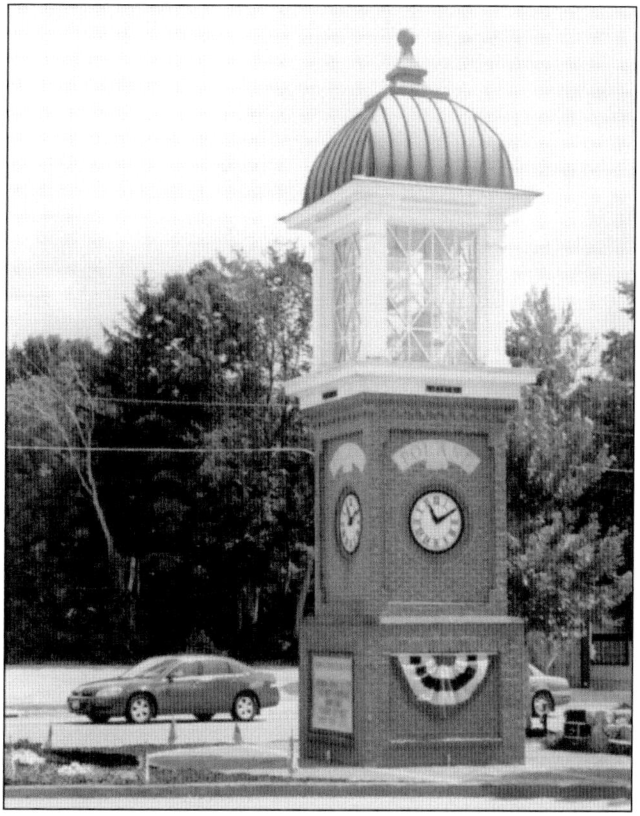

Until 2008, junior varsity football was played at Baird Mitchell Field on Saturday mornings. The new artificial turf at the high school stadium now enables all the high school football games to be played there.

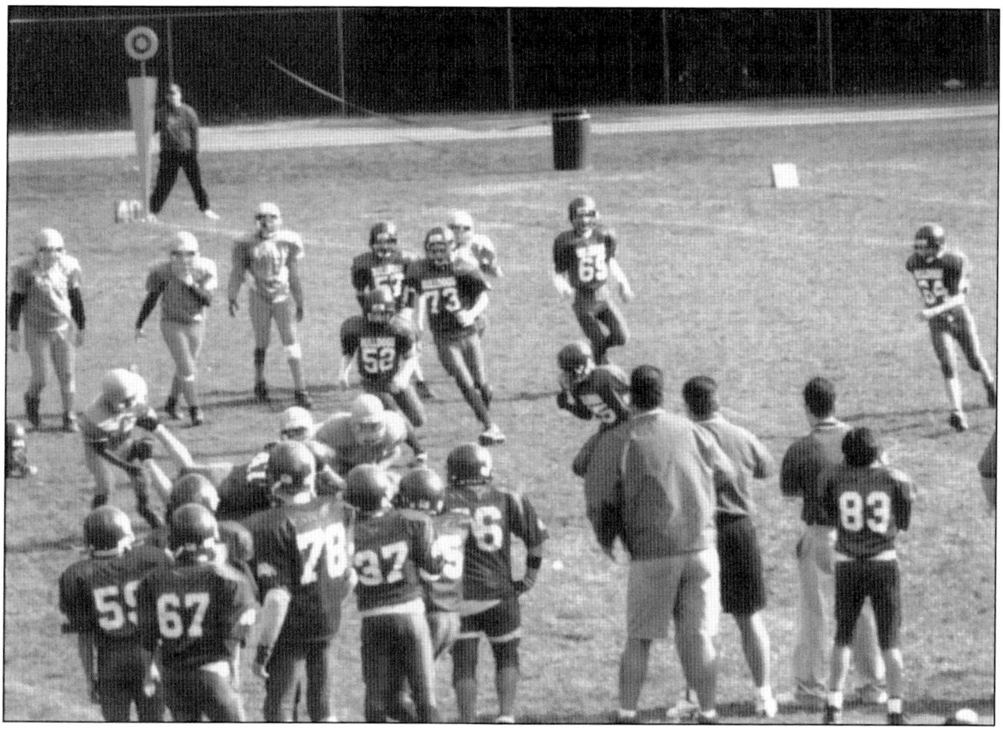

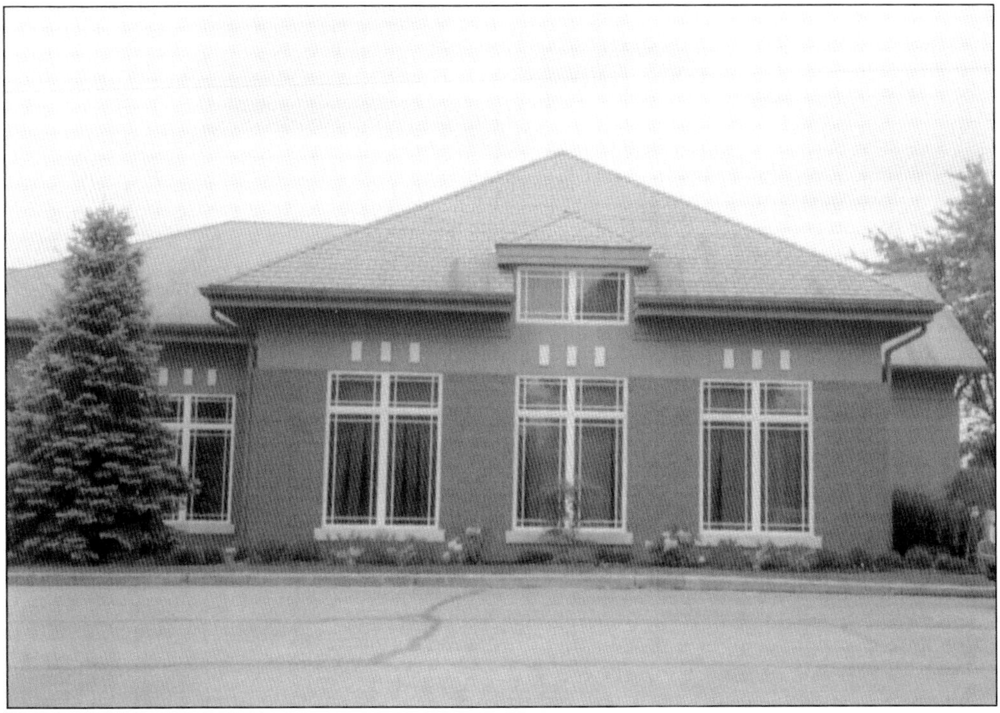

Poland Township's new government building on Dobbins Road also houses the township police department.

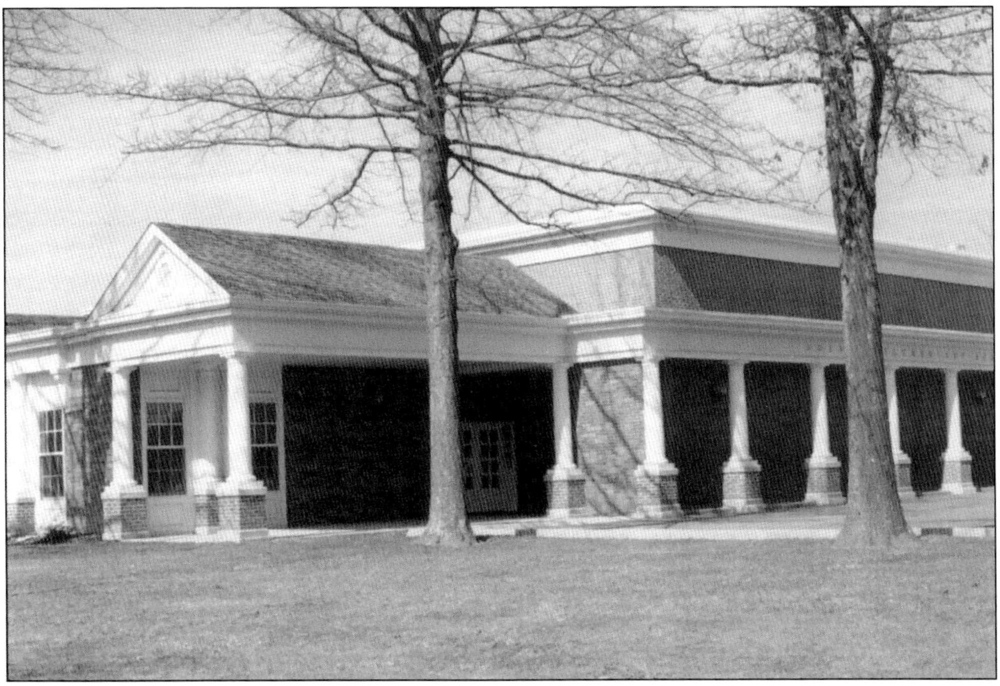

Dobbins Elementary is shown here after its extensive interior and exterior renovation in 1996, converting the school from a 1960s building into a beautiful colonial setting. (Courtesy of Poland schools' archives.)

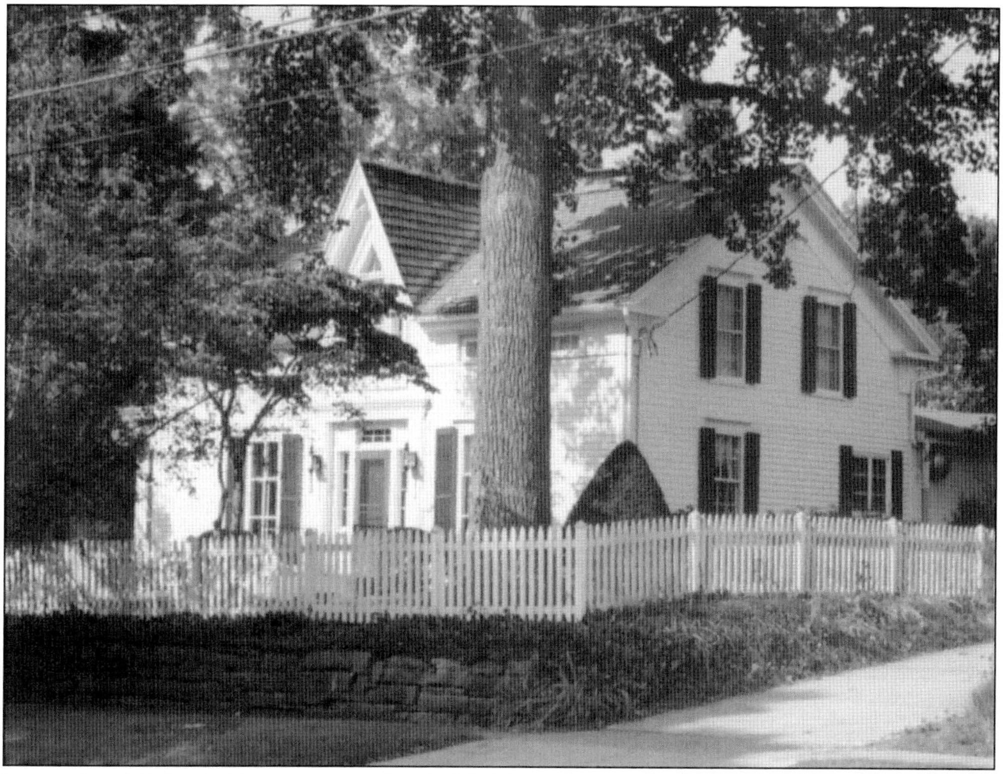

Located at 433 South Main Street is the Dr. Eli Mygatt house, constructed about 1831. This home was built by Dr. Mygatt at the time of his marriage to Lois Yale Kirtland, and this is the structure as it looks today in 2009.

This structure is commonly known as the Sweeney House today. Located on South Main Street across from the Presbyterian church, the center section is the original home built by William Augden, a cabinetmaker, in 1850. The center section of this residence was moved in 2005 from its original location near the Yellow Creek Bridge and South Main Street as part of the Sweeney residence.

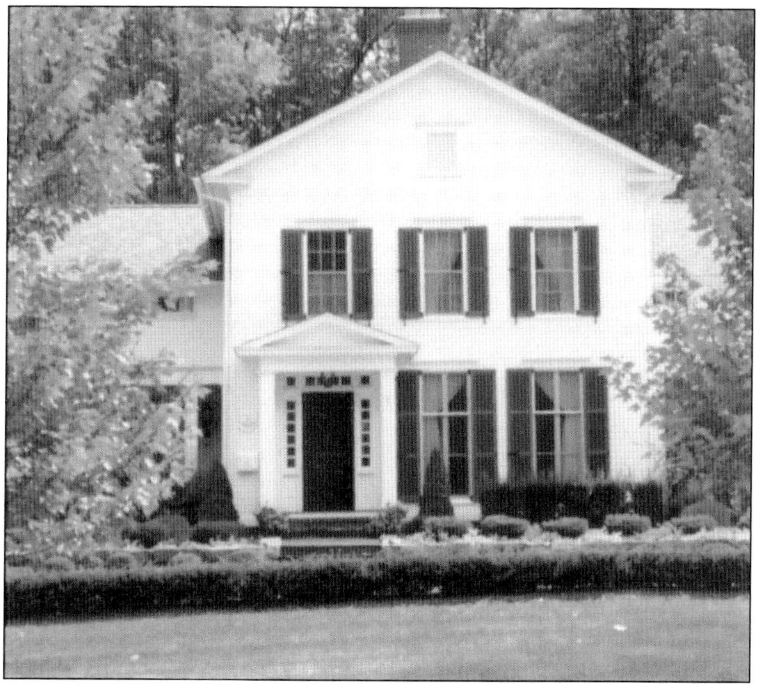

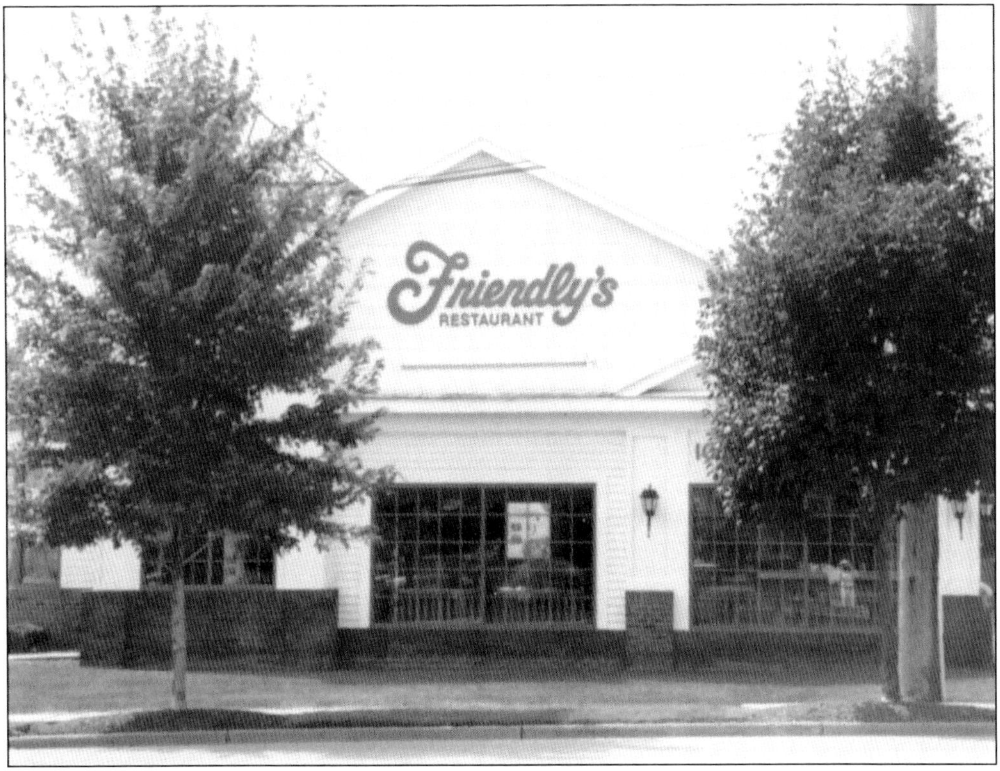

Friendly's Restaurant in the heart of Poland is the site of a Friday after-school tradition, where middle school students gather with their friends, packing the place to enjoy after-school snacks.

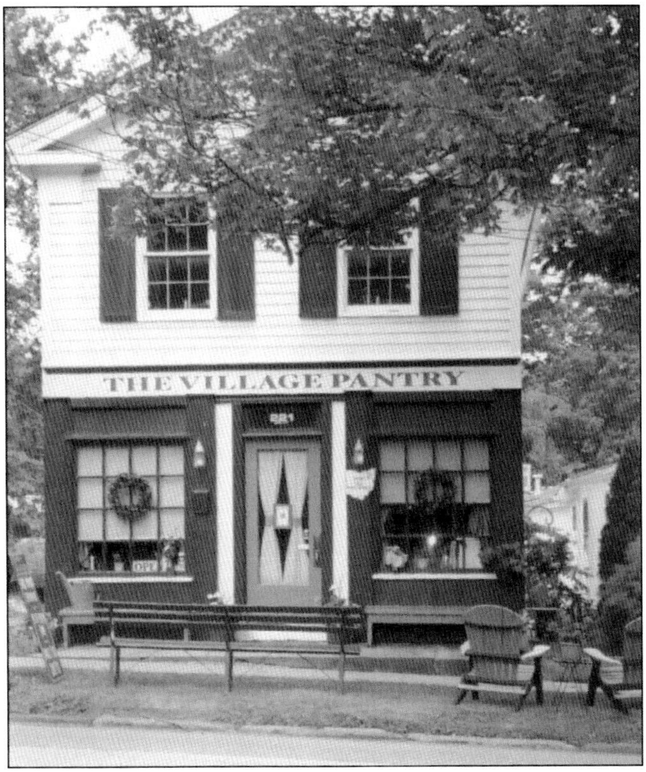

The old Poland Post Office on South Main Street, built in 1850, served as such until 1927. The second floor was once the residence of Daniel May and his wife, Mary, who was William McKinley's sister. This building has been a confectionary, shoe shop, grocery store, floor tile store, and today is home to the Village Pantry.

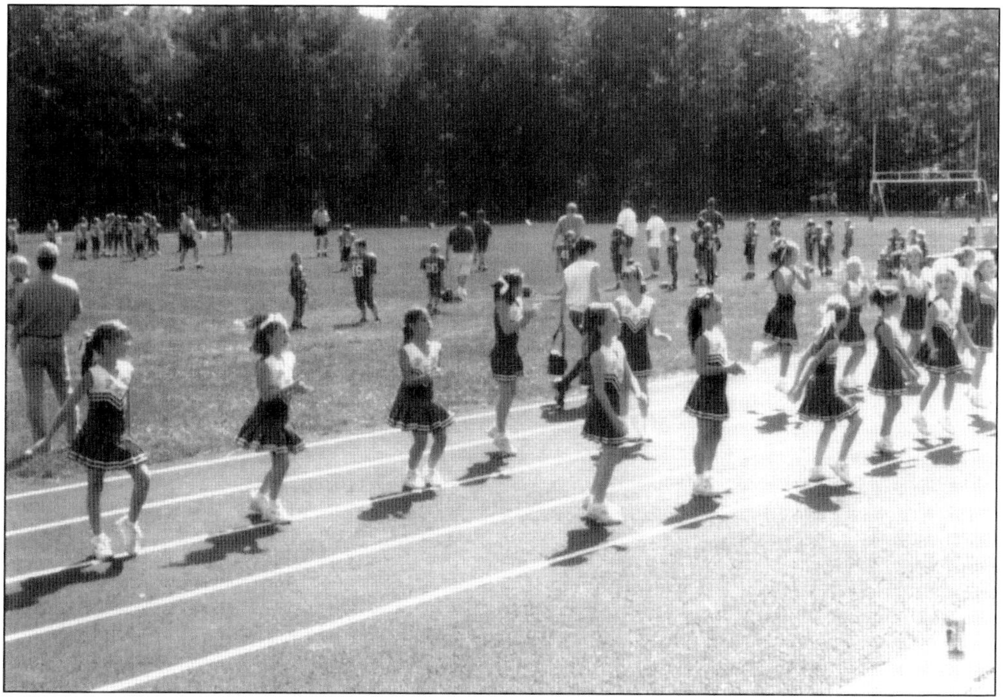

Shown here are Poland Little Bulldog cheerleaders on a Sunday afternoon at Baird Mitchell Field in the early 2000s, cheering their team on to victory.

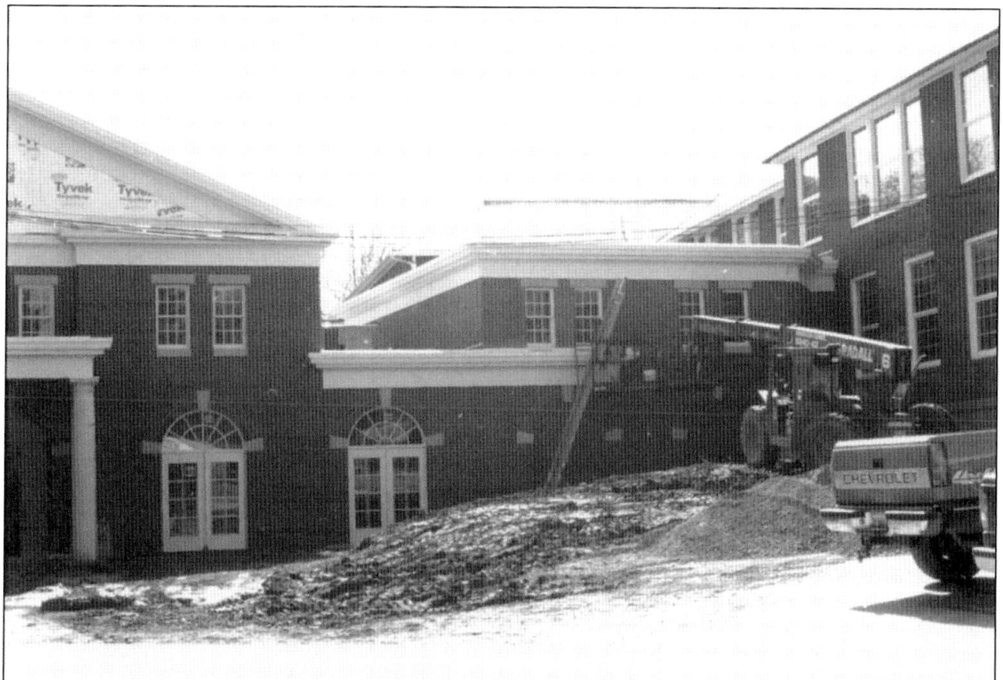

In 2004, the connector was under construction to join the middle school with McKinley Elementary to create one campus. (Courtesy of Poland schools' archives.)

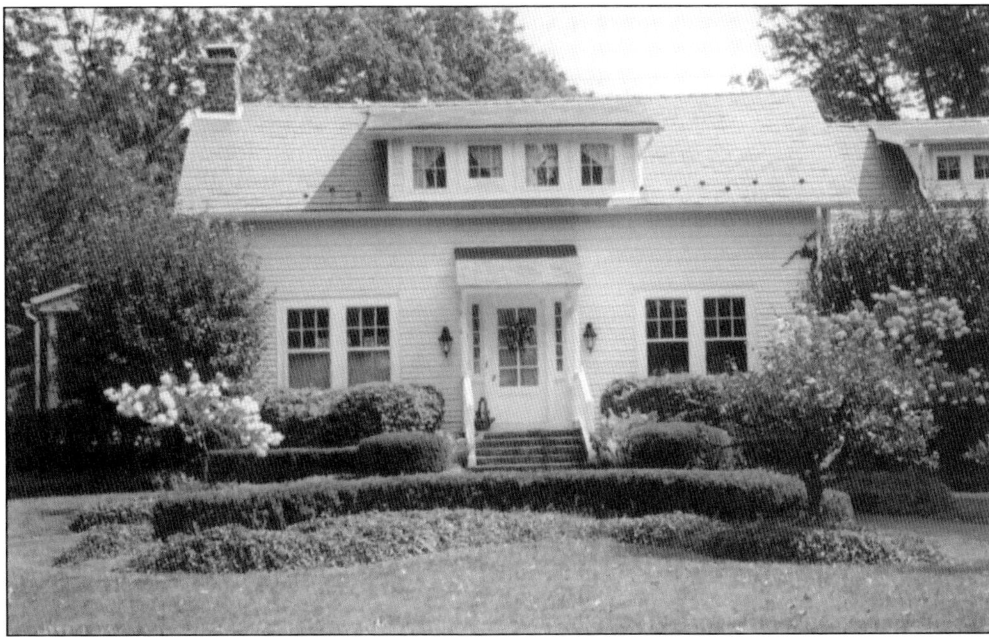

Henry Kirtland, Turhand's son, built 82 Poland Manor around 1820. It is now a restored residence. (Courtesy of Poland Historical Society.)

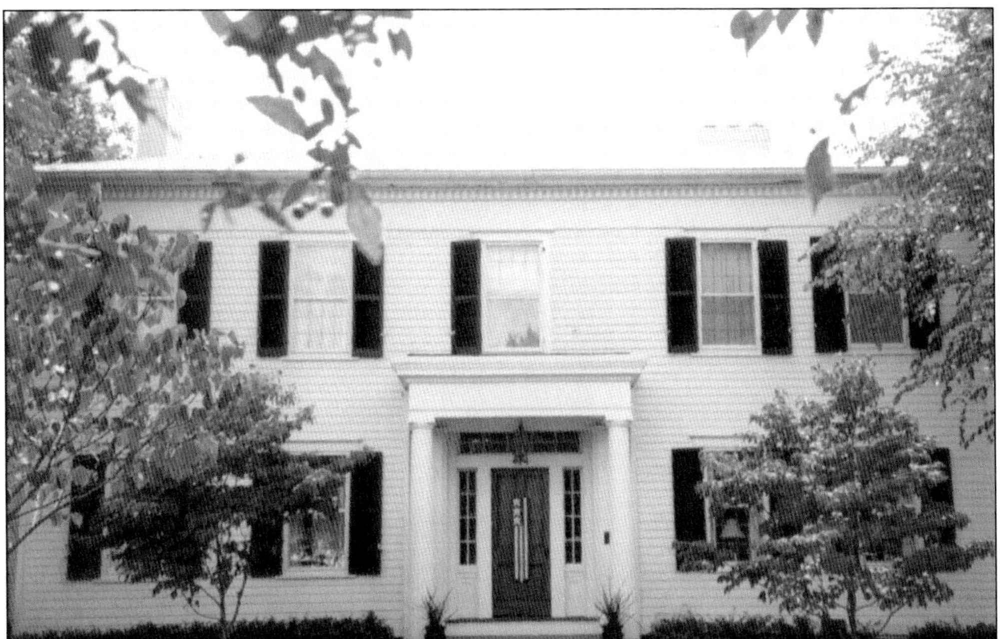

The classic, Federal-style home located at 424 South Main Street was built around 1850 by Turhand Kirtland for his grandson, Turhand Hall. Recently restored, for many years it was the Franklin B. Powers home. (Courtesy of Poland Historical Society.)

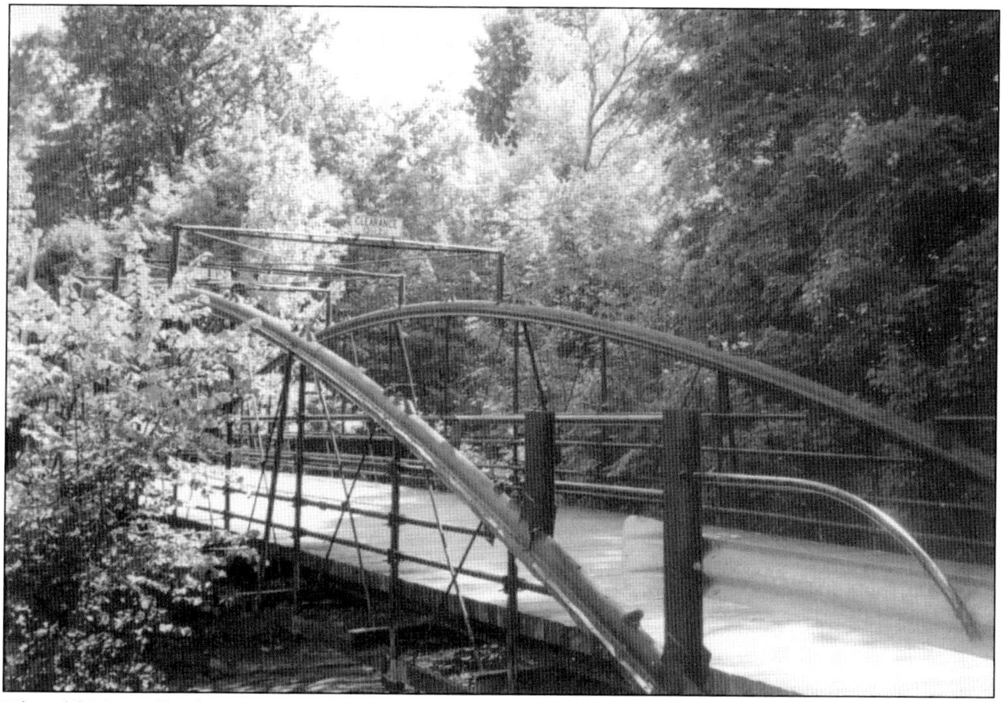

The old Morse Bridge, commonly called the cemetery bridge today, is no longer used for vehicular traffic but makes an ideal bridge over Yellow Creek for pedestrians, joggers, and bicyclers.

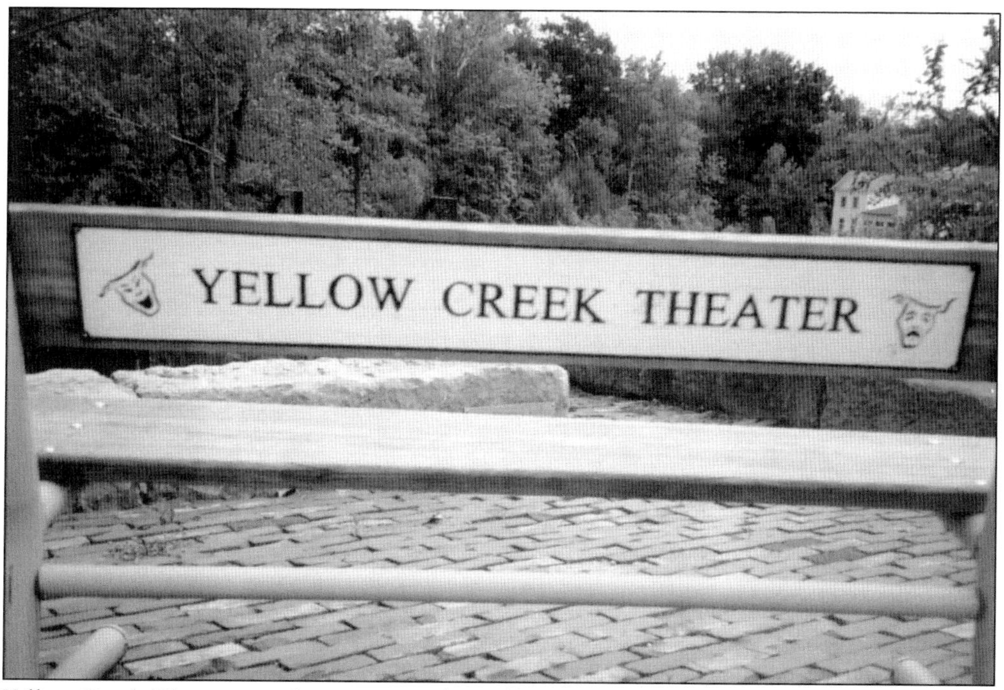

Yellow Creek Theater is a free, open-to-the-public movie theater that shows old films in the summer under the Route 224 bridge, by the creek. Snacks are available, and people bring their own folding chairs and enjoy a summer evening at the movies with friends and neighbors.

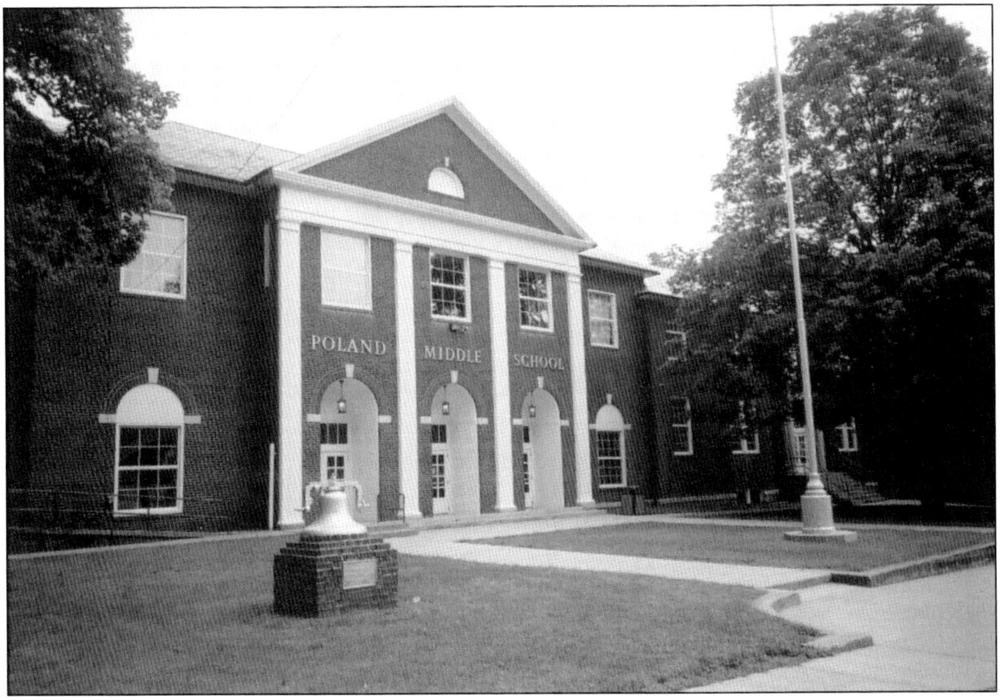

The site of the old Poland Academy and the old Poland Seminary on College Street was once Poland Seminary High School, and since 1985, it has been home to Poland Middle School. (Courtesy of Poland schools' archives.)

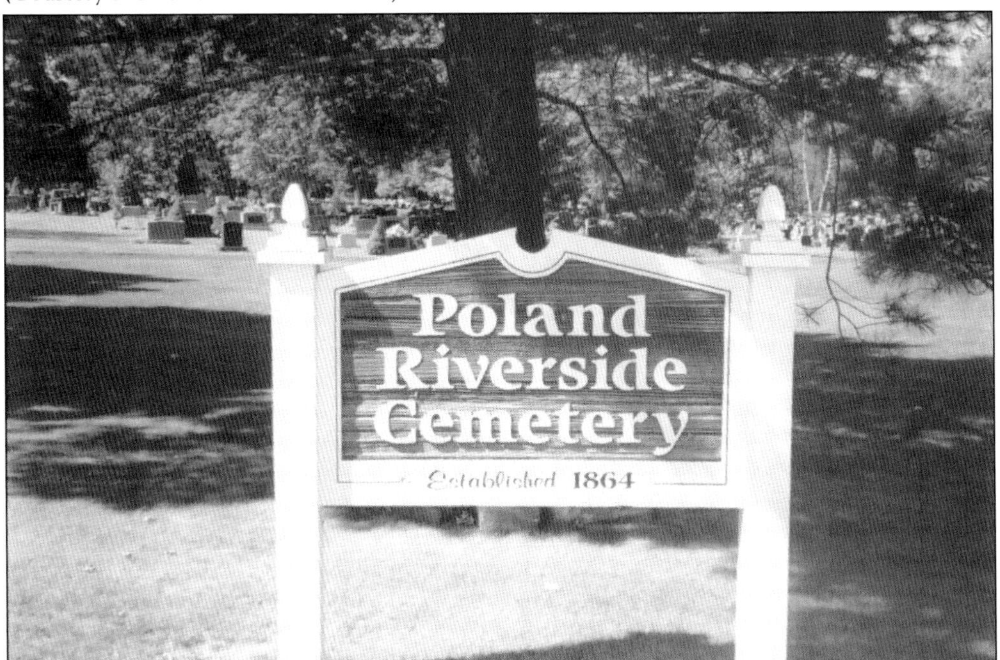

The quiet beauty of Poland cemetery is comforting to the many whose loved ones are at rest here. U.S. president William McKinley dedicated the cemetery. The cemetery was started in 1864 for Civil War burials and is now known as Poland Riverside Cemetery.

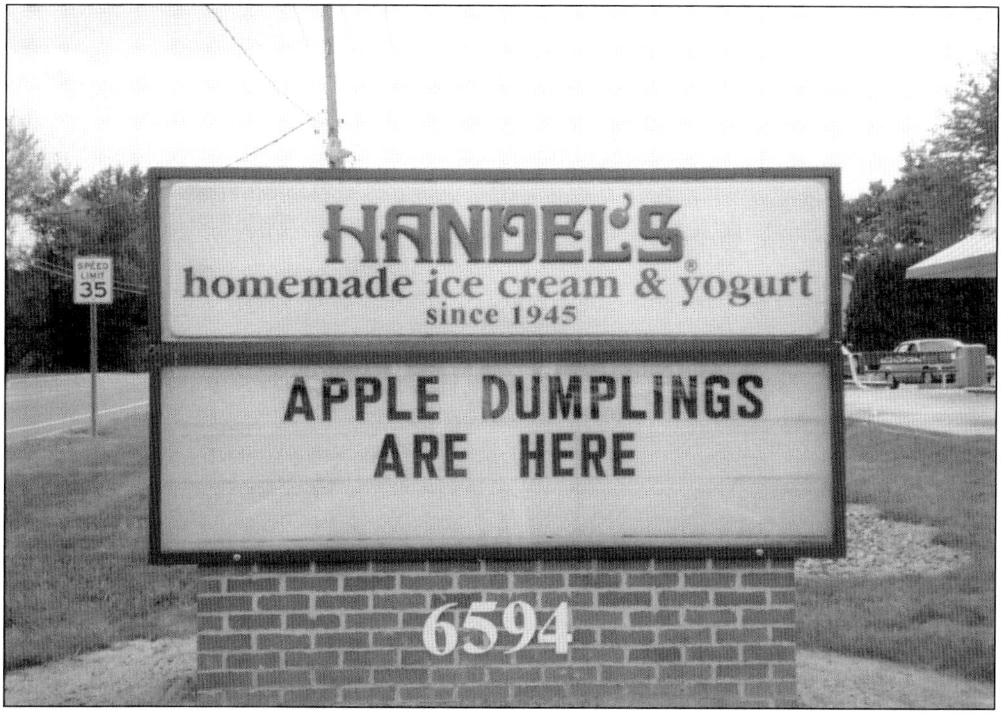

A treat for Poland residents on a summer's night is a stop at Handel's for ice cream. Nationally famous, Handel's is a favorite for its especially delicious flavors.

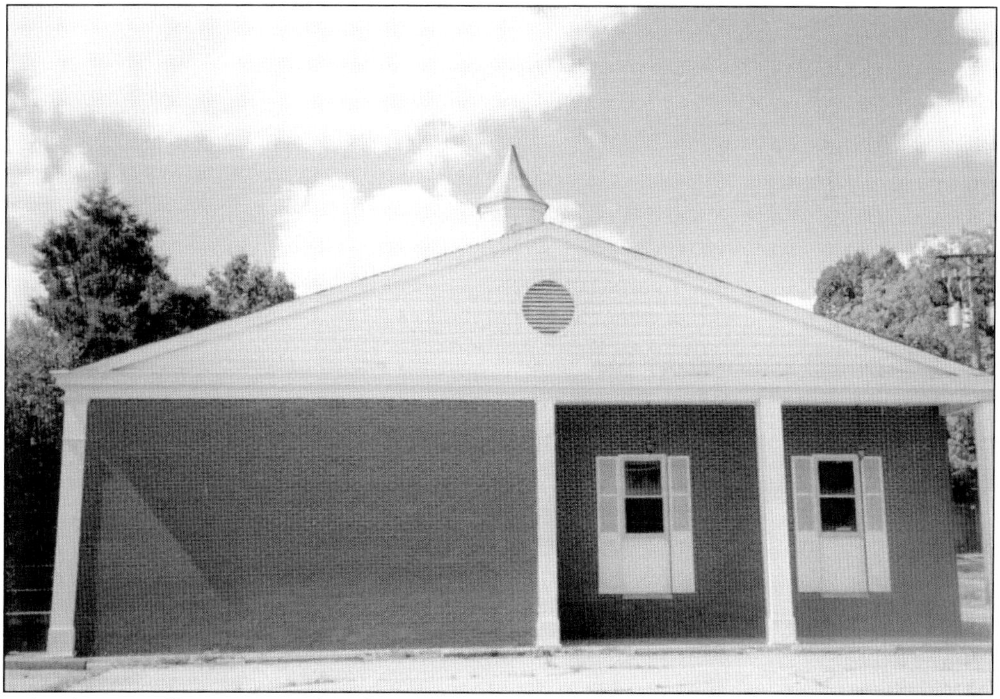
Poland's post office was on Sheridan Road from the 1950s until the new post office opened in 2001 on Route 224.

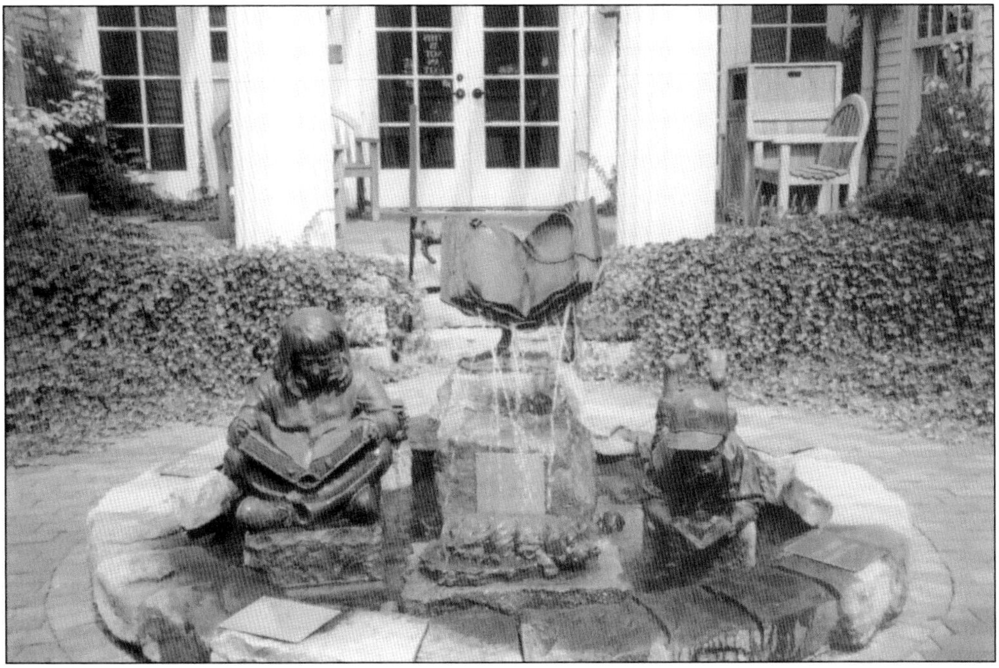

The statues in front of Poland's new public library on Main Street show a young boy and girl enjoying reading. This fountain is an attractive site, enhancing the front of the library.

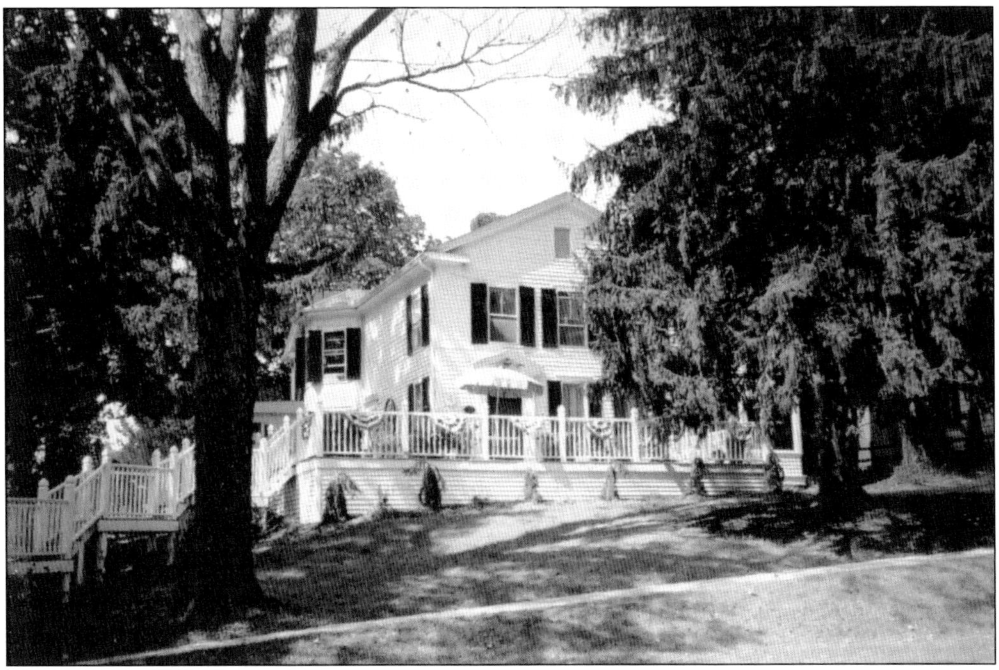

The Jacob Lee house was built in 1825 on what is now Riverside Drive. It was once the home of Dr. McMasters, later Judge James Bennett, and later the Tannehills. It is shown here in 2009 after restoration, although the new large front porch was not on the original structure.

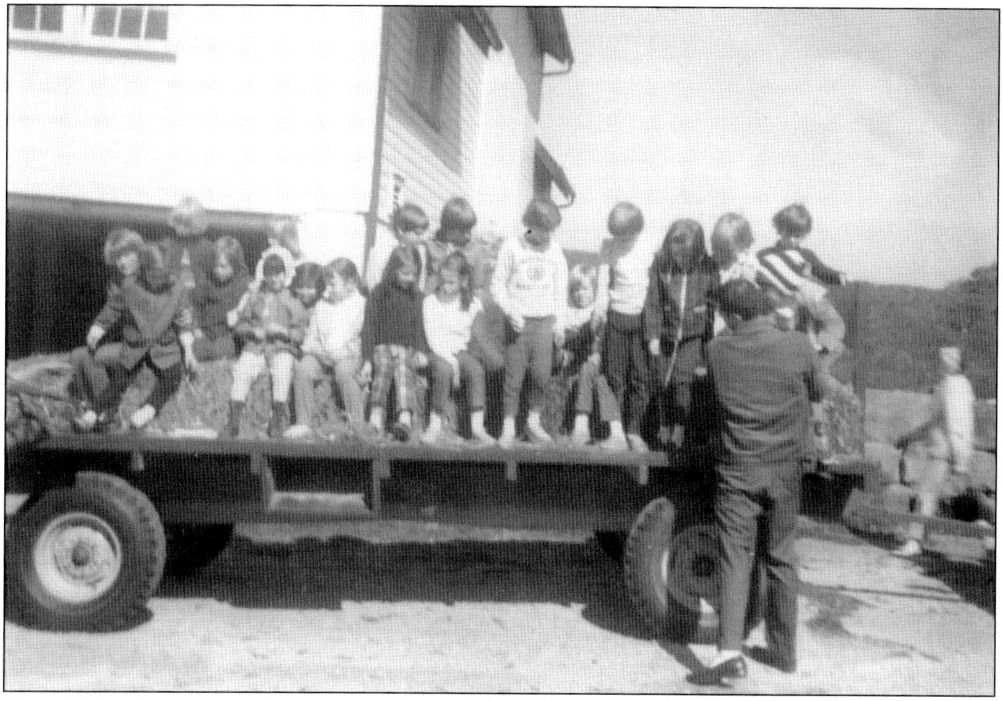

Many Poland youngsters love to go to the nearby White House fruit farm and enjoy a fall wagon ride pulled by horses.

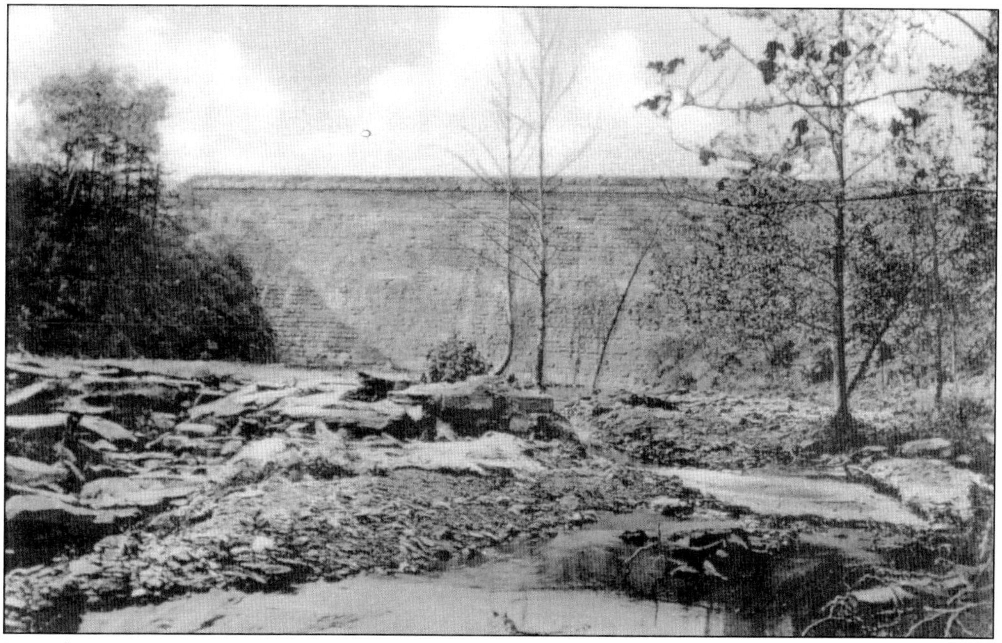

Hamilton Dam at nearby Hamilton Lake, north of the village in Poland Township, is noted as a good fishing spot. The dam is near the historic 1802 site of the Hopewell Blast Furnace.

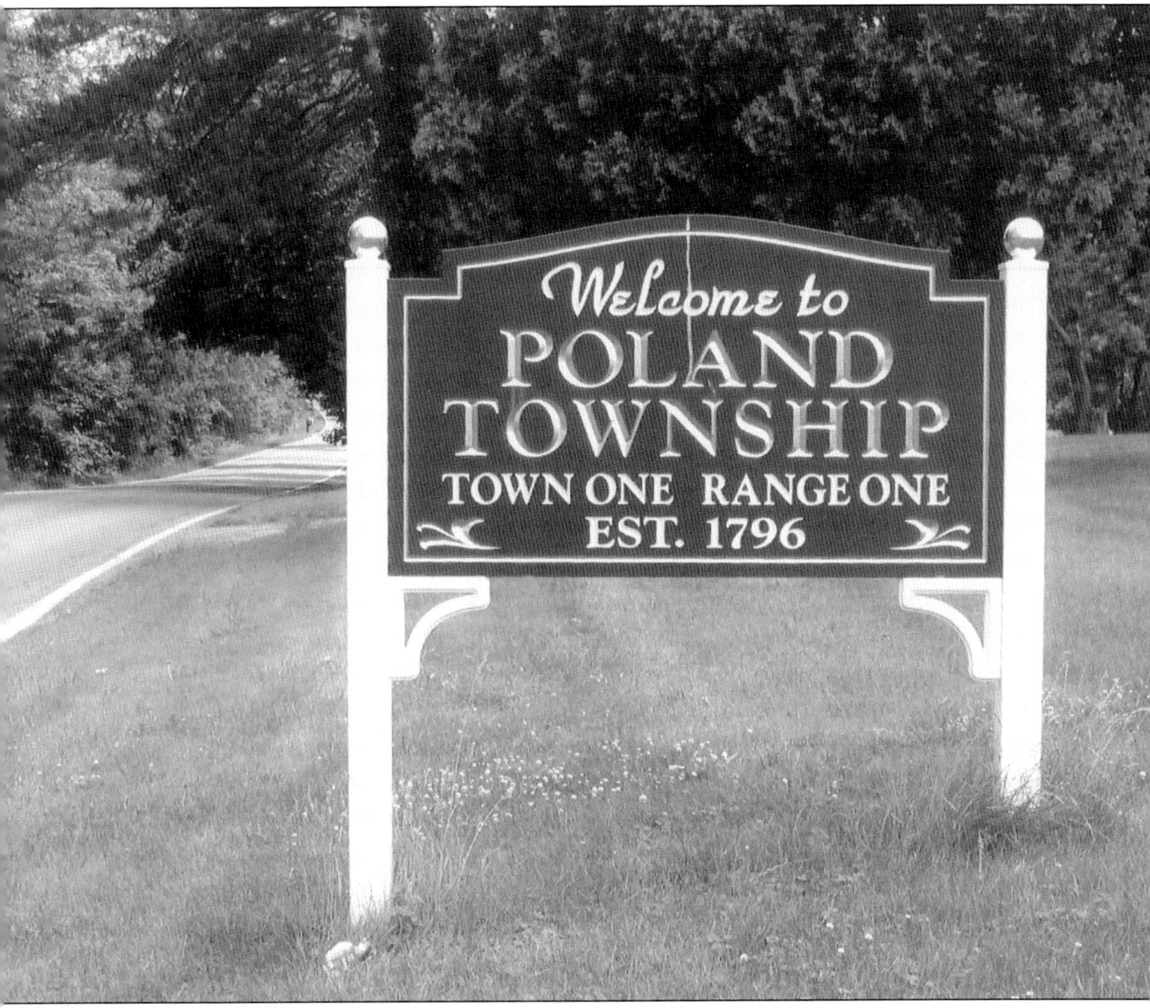

Welcome signs are on the main roadways into Poland Township, welcoming all to Town One, Range One in the Connecticut Western Reserve.

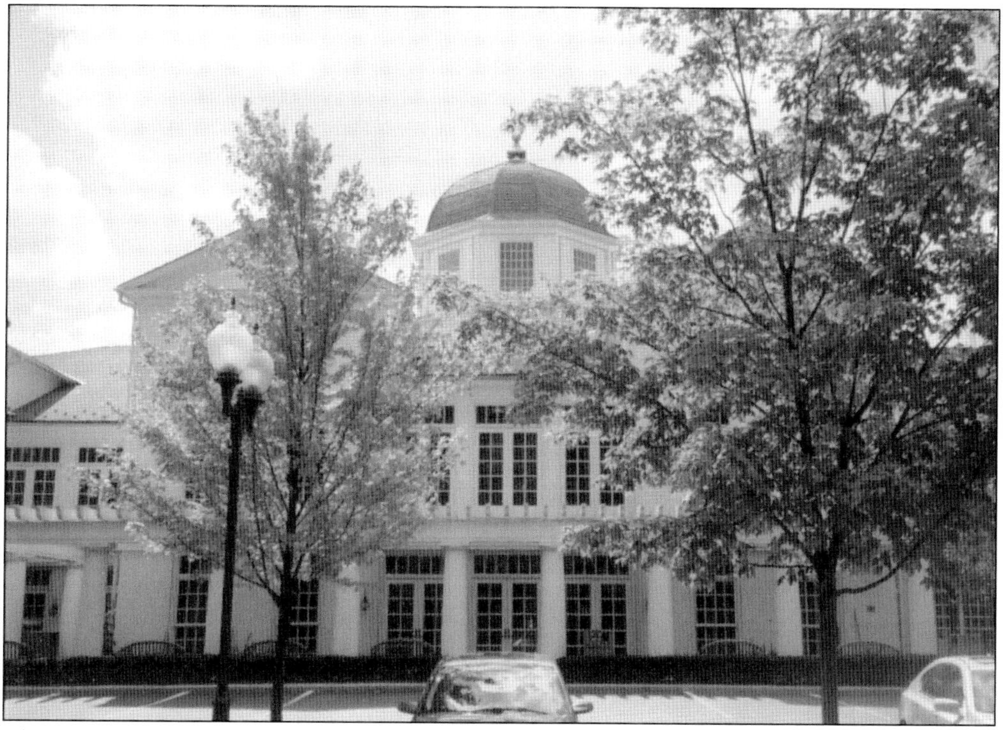

This photograph shows that the back of the new library is just as pretty as the front. A small café is located in the back of the library.

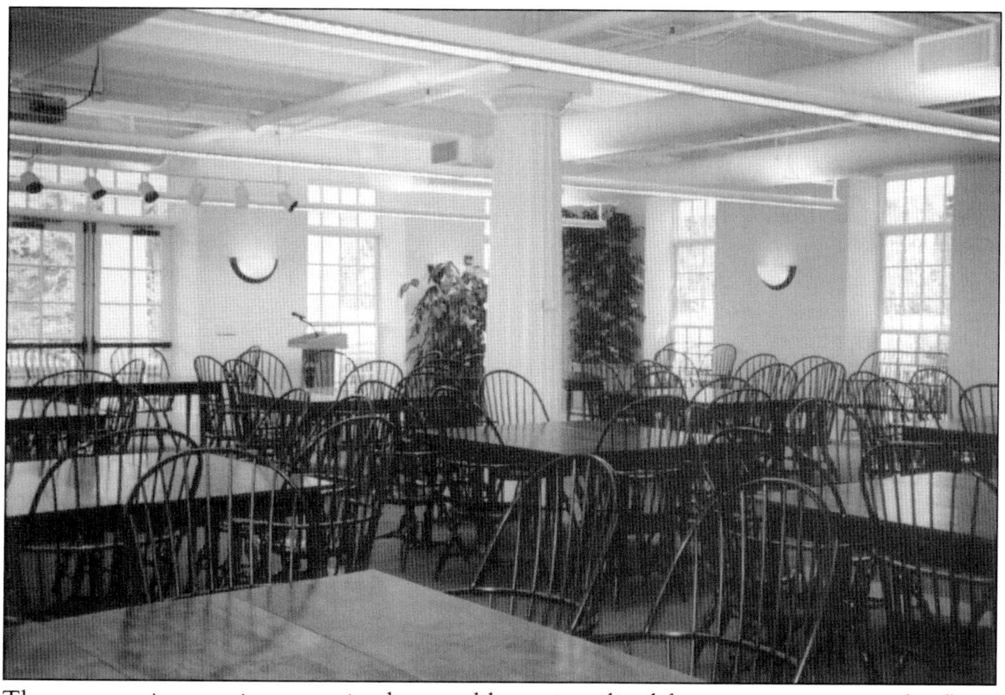

The community meeting room in the new library is utilized for many activities and reflects Poland's colonial atmosphere.

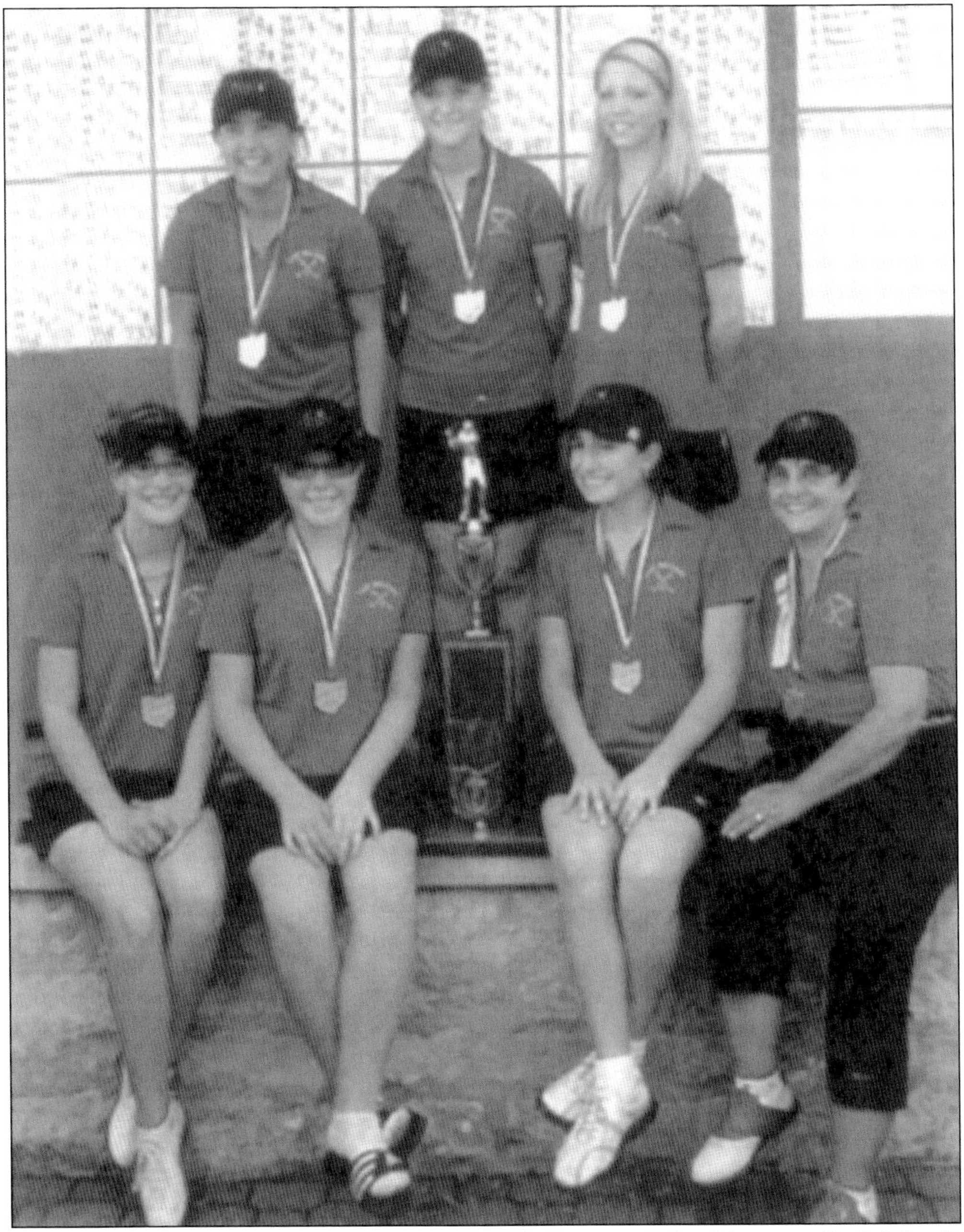

The 2008 state girls golf division II champions pose for a picture. Poland Seminary High School's girls golf team won the division II state title in 2008, shooting a final round of 333 to win the very first Ohio High School Athletic Association Division II by one stroke over Tipp City Tippecanoe High School and at the Ohio State University Gray Course. Under head coach Judy Young and assistant coach Stacy Benson, team members Samantha Cox, Mariah Groner, Lauren Erdel, Maria Mancini, Allison Mitzel, and Angela Molasky brought home the first state title in a girls' sport for Poland. (Courtesy of Poland schools' archives.)

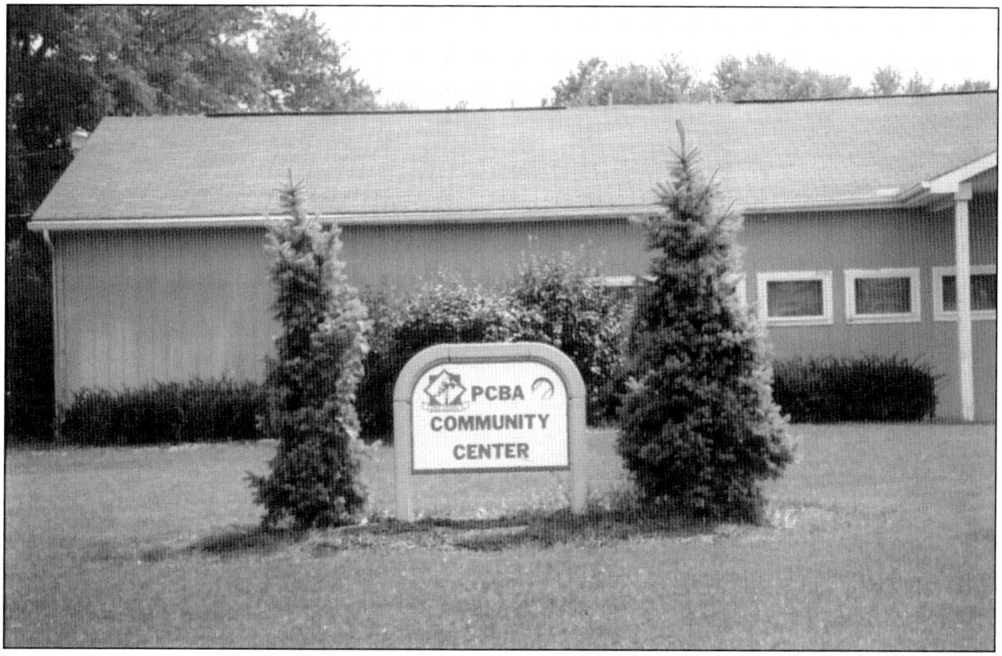

Poland Community Baseball Association's (PCBA) building on Sheridan Road opened in 1992 at the North Elementary Sports complex. This photograph was taken in 2009.

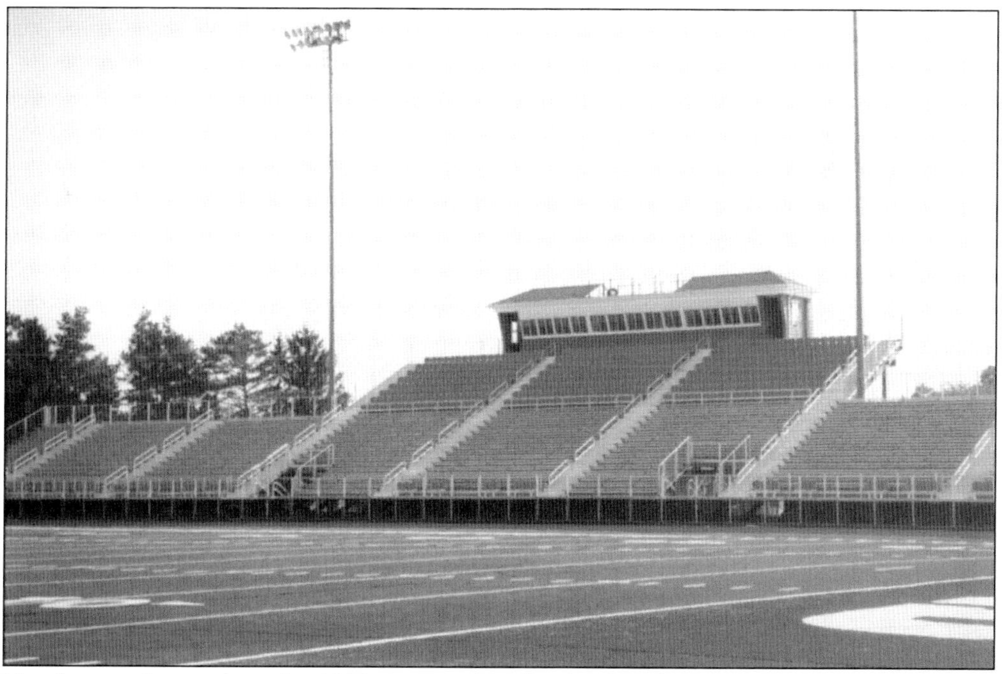
New home-side stands at the 2009 renovated high school stadium seated approximately 3,000 home fans, with 500 reserved seats with backs. (Courtesy of Poland schools' archives.)

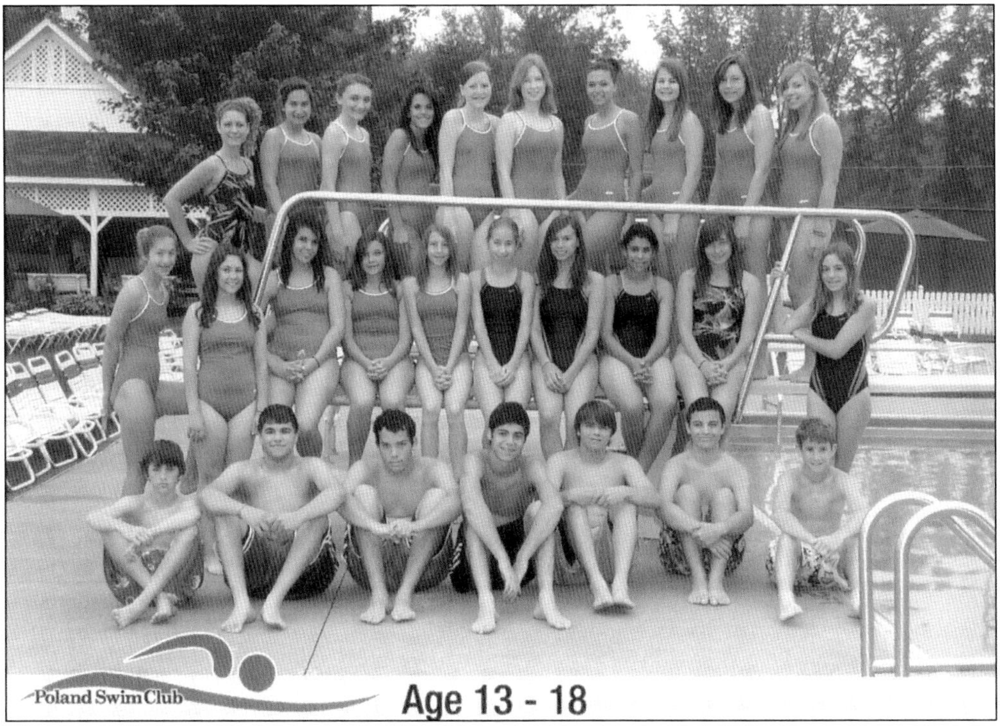

The Poland Swim Club team members are pictured here in summer 2009.

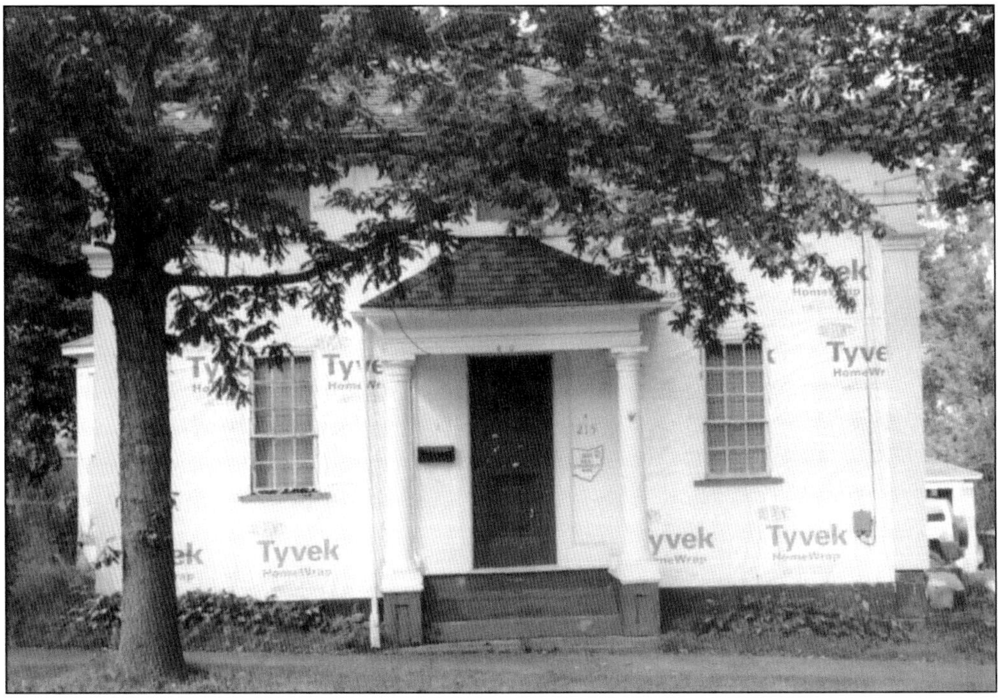

The Rice Lonergan house, now 215 South Main Street, was built in 1835. It has an unusual hip roof. It was once the home of Attorney Brooks Reed, then later housed Dr. Samuel Petraglia's medical office. This photograph was taken in 2009 as the structure was being restored to a residence.

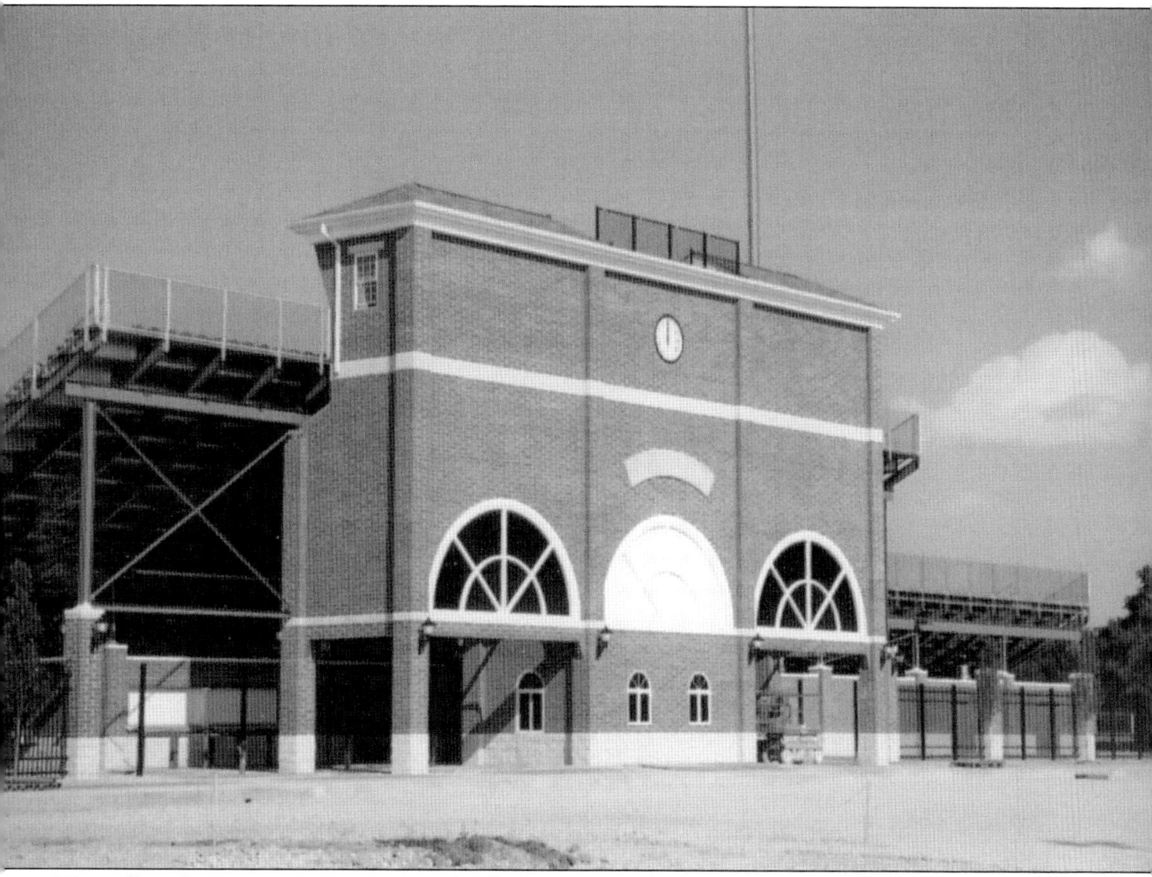

The collegial-appearing entrance to Poland Seminary High School's new stadium in 2009 was well received by the community. Built at $2.02 million, it continues Poland's colonial tradition. The Turf Club and Touchdown Club raised $700,000 for additional improvements. As one onlooker said when seeing the new stadium, the tradition of College Street has been brought to Dobbins Road. (Courtesy of Poland schools' archives.)

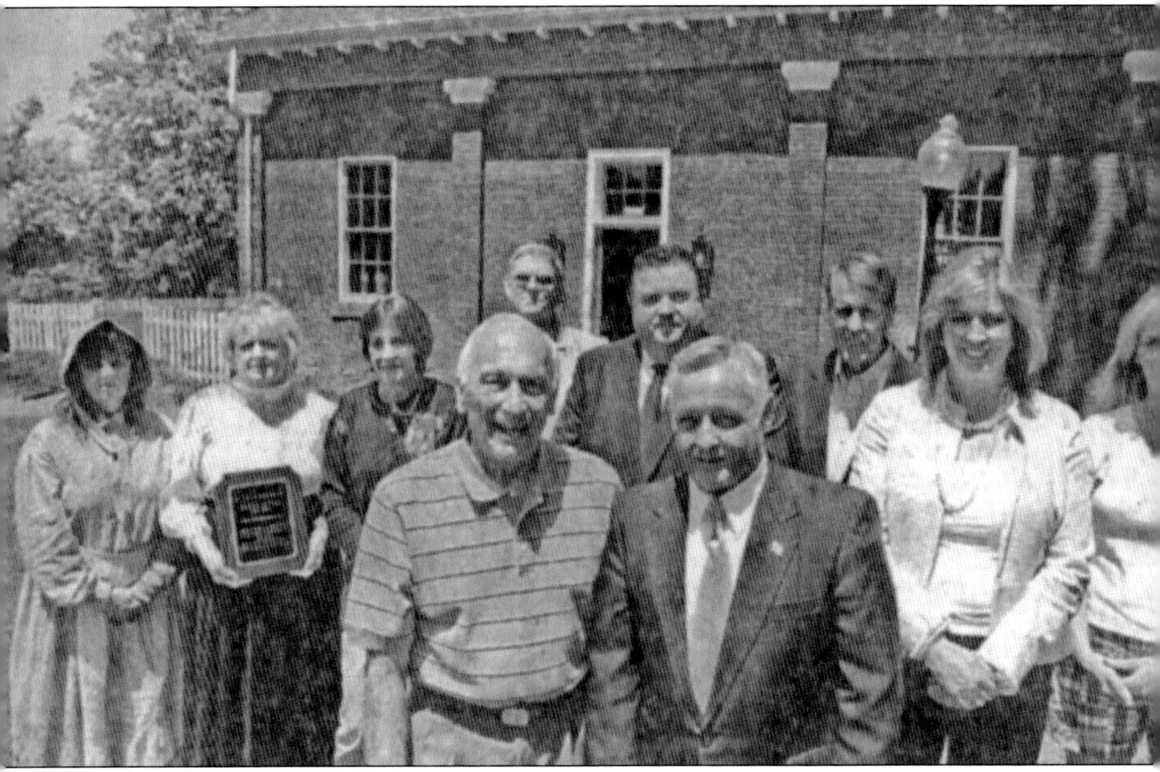

The Poland Historical Society advisory board is shown in 2009, from left to right, (first row) Andy Hamady, president of the society, and David Ludt, Mahoning County commissioner; (second row) Georgene Fry, a genealogist who works with the society; Patricia Grimm, vice president of the society; Beth Jones; Mike Heber, an officer of Allied Waste; Anthony Traficanti, Mahoning County commissioner; Dr. Robert Zorn, schools superintendent; Kelly Becker of Becker Funeral Home; and Joan Madej, recording secretary for the historical society. Also serving on the historical society advisory board but not pictured are Judge Maureen Sweeney, Poland Township trustee Mark Naples, Judge Scott Kirchbaum, Poland mayor Tim Sicafuse, attorney Susan Maruca, Poland Township administrator James Scharville, and Poland High School principal Vince Procopio.

BIBLIOGRAPHY

Aley, Howard. *A Heritage to Share: The Bicentennial History of Youngstown and Mahoning County, Ohio.* Youngstown, Ohio: Youngstown Lithographing Company, 1975.

Butler, Joseph. *History of Youngstown and the Mahoning Valley, Ohio.* Chicago: American Historical Society, 1921.

Mahoning Valley Historical Society Archival Library. Youngstown, Ohio.

Poland Centennial Committee, *Poland Historical Highlights*, 1996.

Poland, Ohio School District records and archives.

Poland Township Bicentennial Committee, Carol Klinger, ed., with Connie Coloutes. *Township One, Range One, Our Western Frontier*: Poland Township History 1796–1996, pub. 1996.

Poland Seminary High School yearbooks, 1927–present.

Poland Seminary private school records, 1861–1926.

Poland Seminary High School Alumni Directory. Chesapeake, Virginia: Harris Connect Company, 2006.

Youngstown *Vindicator. These Hundred Years: A Chronicle of the Twentieth Century*, Youngstown *Vindicator*, 2009.

Zorn, Robert L. *Triumph and Tradition: A History of Poland, Ohio Schools.* Shawnee Mission, Kansas: Intercollegiate Press, 2nd ed. 1988, third edition revised and enlarged, 1997.

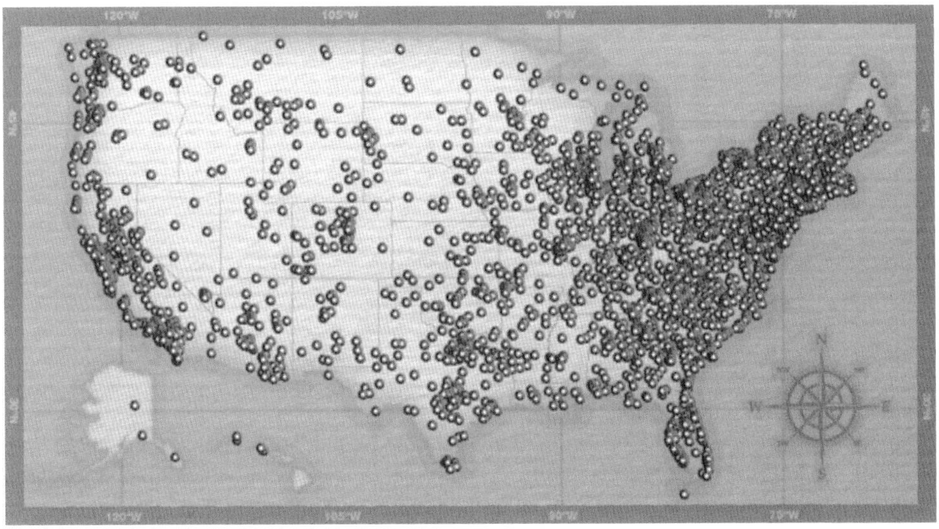

Consistent with our mission to preserve history on a local level, this book was printed in South Carolina on American-made paper and manufactured entirely in the United States. Products carrying the accredited Forest Stewardship Council (FSC) label are printed on 100 percent FSC-certified paper.

MADE IN THE USA